CONVERT
YOUR HOME TO
SOLAR
ENERGY

EVERETT M. BARBER JR. AND JOSEPH R. PROVEY

The Taunton Press

 The Taunton Press
Inspiration for hands-on living®

The Taunton Press, Inc., 63 South Main Street, PO Box 5506, Newtown, CT 06470-5506
e-mail: tp@taunton.com

Editors: Scott Gibson and Peter Chapman
Copy editor: Candace B. Levy
Indexer: Jim Curtis
Cover design: Laura Palese
Interior design and layout: Laura Palese
Illustrator: Jason Lee
Photographer: Everett M. Barber Jr. (except where noted)

The following names/manufacturers appearing in *Convert Your Home to Solar Energy* are trademarks:
Better Business Bureau®, Dowfrost™, DSIRE™, Dun & Bradstreet®, The Energy Detective™, Energy Guide℠,
Energy Star®, Energy-10™, Florida Solar Energy Center®, groSolar®, Mylar®, National Electrical Code®, PVWatts™,
Solar Pathfinder™, Solar Rating and Certification Corporation™, Solmetric Sun Eye™, Toyota® Prius, Uni-Solar®,
Window Quilt®.

Library of Congress Cataloging-in-Publication Data

Barber, Everett M.
  Convert your home to solar energy / authors, Everett M. Barber Jr. and Joseph R. Provey.
    p. cm.
  Includes index.
  ISBN 978-1-60085-252-7
  1. Solar houses. 2. Solar energy. I. Provey, Joe. II. Title.
  TH7414.B37 2010
  697'.78--dc22

                       2010036743

Printed in the United States of America
10 9 8 7 6 5 4 3 2 1

Homebuilding is inherently dangerous. From accidents with power tools to falls from ladders, scaffolds, and roofs,
builders risk serious injury and even death. We try to promote safe work habits throughout this book, but what is
safe for one person under certain circumstances may not be safe for you under different circumstances. So don't
try anything you learn about here (or elsewhere) unless you're certain that it is safe for you. If something about an
operation doesn't feel right, don't do it. Look for another way. Please keep safety foremost in your mind whenever
you're working.

TO MY BELOVED SONS:
THEODORE EVERETT BARBER (1969–)
& ALEXANDER JOSEPH BARBER (1971–2002)
—E.B.

TO MY WIFE MARY ANN,
WHO FILLS MY LIFE WITH LIGHT AND HAPPINESS
—J.P.

ACKNOWLEDGMENTS

I had to retire from teaching, sell my solar energy business, and get a call from co-author Joe Provey, who introduced me to Peter Chapman of The Taunton Press, before the stars were sufficiently aligned to get this effort under way. The task seemed daunting, but Joe, who has authored numerous articles and books, made it sound easy. And Peter had a very clear idea of the market. "This is what we believe will sell, this is the space we have for what you want to say," he told us. "We have to make it fit." For someone who tends toward the expansive side of written expression, I struggled with that constraint, but respect him greatly for that vision and determination. Scott Gibson was the editor to whom fell the daunting task of trimming the manuscript to fit the space allotted. He did a sensitive job of editing.

Major impetus for this effort came from my younger son, Alexander, who on several occasions had asked his mother, "If Dad wants to write a book about solar energy, why doesn't he stop talking about it and just do it?"

Encouragement, ideally a daily ration of it, is all-important to sustaining a year-long, mostly solitary effort, such as writing a book. My wife, Sarah, provided those daily rations.

Second only to encouragement in importance is clarity of thought. David Madigan and Paul Popinchalk critiqued the lengthy slide presentations that became the framework of this book. They also helped me sort through earlier drafts of the screed that became the chapter on active solar space heating. Tom Hopper has been a frequent source of encouragement and a critic, in the truest sense of the word, for my ideas. I am also indebted to Emaan Ammar. Among other things, she did an extensive literature search comparing evacuated-tube and flat-plate collectors, provided considerable help in putting information in a format that is clear and easy to comprehend, and was supportive when I felt discouraged along the way. Finally, Joe and I would like to thank Bob Perron for his devotion to photographing solar homes—a pursuit that now spans five decades. Thank you all.

—EVERETT M. BARBER JR.

CONTENTS

INTRODUCTION

If solar energy systems cost less to install than systems that use conventional fuels, many of us would be using solar energy now. At the moment, solar systems cost more than conventional systems. Yet they are still attractive because, once installed, the energy they provide is free, or nearly so. The challenge is to find solar applications that repay the extra cost of the installation with fuel savings in a reasonable period of time.

There have been two times in our history when solar energy was considered an attractive option. The last major surge came between about 1973 and 1985. By the end of 1985, about 1 million solar energy systems had been installed nationwide. An earlier upswing in the use of solar systems began in the late 19th century and ended shortly after 1933. During that time, thousands of solar domestic water heating systems were installed, most of them in Florida, along the Gulf Coast, in southern California, and in other warm-weather zones. The stimulus for both surges was the high operating cost of conventional systems.

In the earlier instance, solar systems provided a convenient means of reducing the cost of heating domestic water. At the time, electricity was quite expensive. Natural gas, while inexpensive, was not readily available. By the early 1930s, the cost of electricity had fallen, and natural gas had become more available. As a result, the use of solar energy faded.

This Vermont shingle-style home is heated with a ground-source heat pump powered by a grid-tied solar electric system.

During the more recent solar boom, the cost of petroleum increased rapidly after the OPEC oil boycott of 1973–1974. In 1978 and 1979, the cost of oil approximately tripled each year due mainly to the Iran–Iraq conflict. Homeowners were eager to do anything to gain some sort of buffer against the rising cost of fuel. Clearly, the pain caused by the high cost of conventional sources of energy does drive the market for renewable energy systems. Falling costs for conventional fuels nearly eliminated that same market.

Today we are once again feeling the pain caused by increases in the cost of energy, but added to that pain are worries about the effect that energy use has on our national security and on the environment. Using less energy is the most cost-effective and fastest way to reduce our energy problems as well as our security and environmental worries. But using less, for a variety of reasons, is not the first choice of many U.S. consumers. Renewable energy systems offer an attractive alternative to conservation and, unlike many conservation strategies, provide a highly visible demonstration of the owner's commitment to reducing their effect on climate change.

In this book, we give you the basis for understanding the solar resource and the various systems available. We provide guidance in determining which systems are appropriate for your needs. Because using less is always the

Architect Don Watson designed the first solar-heated house in New England, which was built in 1974. Its solar system was designed by co-author Everett Barber.

more cost-effective first step, we provide a list of conservation measures at the start of the solar application chapters to help you use less energy.

The dream of using solar energy has been with us for millennia. Endless free power, clean air, no more wars over oil. That dream is beginning to come true. Solar energy in each of its various forms can lower utility bills, shrink our carbon footprint, and contribute to a more peaceful future. And thanks to the prospect of continued high fuel costs as well as rebates and tax incentives, converting to solar energy is more affordable than ever.

But whether solar energy is used to produce electricity, heat domestic water, or keep your family warm, its successful implementation demands a knowledgeable consumer. Solar energy systems operate differently from conventional systems that use fossil fuel. Some study is strongly recommended before you can become your own energy producer.

Convert Your Home to Solar Energy will guide you from planning and installing a solar system to its operation and maintenance. With one exception, we have ordered the chapters dealing with solar energy applications by putting them in descending order of payback. That is, the application with the longest payback is presented last. The exception is solar water heating, which we put before solar pool heating. Even though solar pool heating has the fastest payback of all solar applications, everyone needs domestic hot water but not everyone has a pool.

The order of chapters is based on the assumption that there are no incentives available. In truth, however, a number of rebates and incentives are presently available, some nationwide and some local. Incentives can skew the economics of solar systems. Most incentives are put in place by political acts. There is no assurance they will always be available, particularly as administrations and the party in the majority change with elections. In addition, since incentives vary from state to state, a detailed analysis is required to determine how they affect you.

For each of the primary solar applications, we recommend conservation measures you should take before investing in solar energy. This is important because the payback on improvements, such as upgrading insulation in your home, is almost always faster than buying a large solar system.

You can expect *Convert Your Home to Solar Energy* to be a realistic assessment of the potential that solar energy holds. It discusses many issues that some solar salespeople may not fully explain or even understand. For example, who is responsible when your combination solar and conventionally fueled home heating system needs service? What do you do when the roof membrane that lies beneath your solar collectors needs to be replaced? And how do you avoid

Break time during the installation of a domestic hot water heating system on a home in Aspen, Colorado.

problems when your solar water or space heating system produces too much heat?

There have never been more reasons to install a solar system: improved equipment, higher fuel costs, attractive incentives, conservation of natural resources, reducing global warming, and an education for friends and family. But a successful installation depends on careful planning and making informed choices. *Convert Your Home to Solar Energy* was written to help with that effort.

1

SOLAR ENERGY BASICS

The energy that reaches our planet from the sun is enough to provide many times what we use. Everything from fossil fuels to wind power to the calories you burn when you jog around the block can be traced back to energy originally supplied by the sun. It's no wonder the ancients worshiped it.

The intensity of solar radiation varies with the square of the distance between the earth and the sun, a distance that changes seasonally. In the Northern Hemisphere, the distance is greatest during the summer, when the earth is about 96 million miles (154 million km) from the sun, and shortest during the winter, when the earth is about 90 million miles (145 million km) away. The difference of 6 million miles (9.65 million km) accounts for a summer–winter variation of about 7 percent in the intensity of the sun's energy.

When the earth is closest to the sun, the energy available at the outer edge of the atmosphere is about 450 Btu per hour per square foot (Btu/hr/sq. ft.) or 1,419W/m². When the earth is farthest from the sun, it's about 420 Btu/hr/sq. ft. (1,325W/m²).

FACTORS THAT AFFECT SOLAR GAIN

The numbers just given refer to the sun's energy before it enters the earth's atmosphere. What ultimately reaches the earth's surface is less than that, sometimes much less. A number of factors contribute to the losses, including atmospheric clarity, distance of travel through the atmosphere, and angle of incidence.

Atmospheric clarity

The best days for solar gain are clear and dry. Cloud cover, rain, humidity, air pollution, and dust in the atmosphere all reflect, absorb, and scatter solar radiation. Energy reflected back into space is, of course, lost to us. Absorbed radiation may heat the atmosphere and is in part responsible for winds that drive wind turbines, but it's not available for direct collection. Direct radiation, and some of that which is scattered by the atmosphere, makes up the total radiation available to solar collectors.

Distance of travel

The magnitude of solar radiation reaching the earth's surface is affected by the distance it travels through the atmosphere. That's because the energy that is not scattered is absorbed by moisture, gasses, and dust. The greater the distance traveled, the greater the atmospheric retention of the sun's energy.

The distance of travel is affected by the time of day, latitude, season, and altitude. At sunrise and sunset, for example, the sun's energy must travel through far more atmosphere than during the middle of the day. The simple fact that you can glance at the sun when it's near sunrise or sunset—but not at noon—attests to the fact that the atmosphere intercepts much of the incident radiant energy.

Latitude also affects the distance the sun's energy must travel through the atmosphere. The closer to the equator, the less atmosphere between you and the sun, thus the more solar radiation you will receive.

Regardless of where you live, you will receive more solar energy in the summer than at any other time of year. This is because the sun is highest in the sky (has the greatest solar

The solar energy that reaches the earth is more than enough to satisfy our needs, but the challenge is capturing it as heat or electricity and storing it for later use.

altitude angle) and therefore has the shortest distance to travel through the atmosphere before reaching you. For example, if you live at 40 degrees north latitude, the solar altitude is 73.5 degrees on June 21 at noon, and 26.5 degrees on December 21 at noon. With more air to pass through, the air mass is higher, 1.04 on June 21 and 2.24 on December 21. You will see the term *air mass* used in listings of solar electric collector performance. (See Tech Corner on p. 15 for more about air mass.)

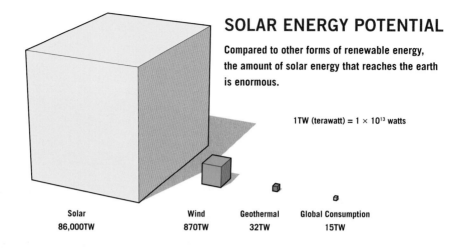

SOLAR ENERGY POTENTIAL

Compared to other forms of renewable energy, the amount of solar energy that reaches the earth is enormous.

1TW (terawatt) = 1 × 10¹³ watts

Solar	Wind	Geothermal	Global Consumption
86,000TW	870TW	32TW	15TW

MEASURING ENERGY: THE BASIC UNITS

There are several ways to measure energy, but, with a few exceptions, English units will be used throughout this book. For solar thermal measurements, we'll be using British thermal units (Btu): 1 Btu (1.05kJ) is approximately equal to the amount of heat given off when a kitchen match is completely burned. Or, for a more precise definition, it's the amount of heat needed to raise the temperature of 1 lb. (0.45 kg) of 60°F (15.5°C) water by 1°F (0.55°C) at a constant pressure of 1 atm (1 bar).

Btu per hour (Btu/hr) is a measure of the rate of heat flow. For example, if the boiler in your house produces heat at a rate of 100,000 Btu/hr (29.3kW) and runs for 15 minutes (¼ hour), then the quantity of heat delivered by the boiler is 100,000 Btu/hr × ¼ hour, or 25,000 Btu (7.9kWh). Similarly, a solar thermal collector for a domestic water heating system may be said to deliver 200 Btu/hr per square foot (0.62kW/m²) of collector area near noon on a clear day.

For solar electric energy measurements, we'll be using kilowatts (kW): 1kW is equal to 1,000W; watts per hour is a measure of electricity used. Some hair dryers draw 1,500W on the high setting. The energy drawn by the hair dryer in ¼ hour is 1,500W × ¼ hour = 375Wh; 1 kilowatt hour (kWh) is equal to 1,000 watt hours (Wh). Your electric bill shows you how many kilowatt hours you've used in the month and the amount you must pay.

HERE IS A LIST OF USEFUL ENERGY CONVERSIONS:

1W = 3.41 Btu/hr

1,000W = 1kW

1Wh = 3.41 Btu

1kWh = 3,413 Btu

100,000 Btu = 1 therm or ccf of natural gas

1 Btu = 1,055 joules (J) = 1.055 kJ

317 Btu = 1 peak sun hour

1 m² = 10.76 sq. ft.

1kWh/m² = 317.7 Btu/sq. ft. = 3.6 kJ/m²

The energy that's available to a solar collector is affected by many variables, including atmospheric clarity, distance of travel through the atmosphere, and angle of incidence.

At sunset and sunrise, there is far less solar energy available than at noon because light must travel a greater distance through the atmosphere.

The altitude of the site affects solar gain, too. If you live in Denver, at an altitude of more than 5,000 ft. (1,524 m) above sea level, the sun's radiation travels through much less air to reach you than if you lived in New York City, as much as 1.6 miles (1 km) less depending on the time of year. All other things being equal, Denver will receive up to 15 percent more solar energy than will New York. Variations in altitude of a few hundred feet, however, do not have a significant impact on available solar energy.

Solar angle of incidence and incident radiation

The angle formed by a solar ray as it strikes a surface and a line perpendicular to the surface is called the solar incidence angle. The more nearly perpendicular the solar ray is to the surface, the greater the incident radiation. An easy way to visualize incidence angle and incident radiation is to think of the sun's rays as a tightly packed bundle of pencils, with each pencil representing a ray of sunlight (see the drawing on p. 11).

COMPONENTS OF SOLAR RADIATION

There are two components to incident solar radiation that most flat-plate and evacuated-tube solar energy collectors can use. One is direct radiation and the other is diffuse radiation. Note that concentrating collectors are unable to use diffuse radiation.

Direct radiation means that the incident energy arrives as though it were a beam of parallel rays coming from one source. On clear, dry days, with no dust in the atmosphere, solar radiation is largely direct, meaning that the incident energy comes from the sun in what amounts to straight, parallel rays. Such days are the best for solar gain.

On days with cloud cover, rain, humidity, air pollution, or dust in the atmosphere, much of the solar radiation is reflected and scattered, causing the energy to come from many directions. Called *diffuse* radiation, it also contributes to available solar energy but at a lesser rate. On an overcast day, when all of the radiation is diffuse, a square foot of rooftop might receive less than 1,000 Btu (1,055kJ) for the day. That same square foot of roofing on a clear day could receive more than twice that.

DIFFUSE VS. DIRECT

Depending on the location and time of year, diffuse radiation provides between 25 percent and 50 percent of direct radiation.

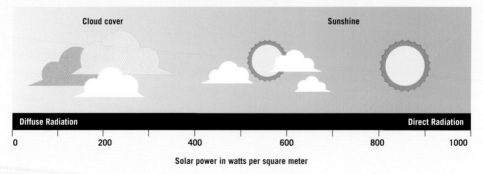

Cloud cover | Sunshine

Diffuse Radiation | Direct Radiation

0   200   400   600   800   1000

Solar power in watts per square meter

THE SUN'S ANGLE AFFECTS SOLAR POTENTIAL

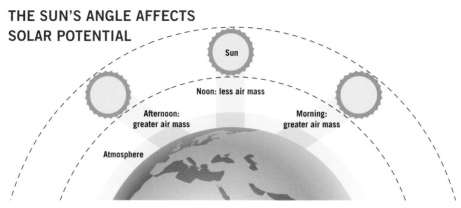

Sun

Noon: less air mass

Afternoon: greater air mass

Morning: greater air mass

Atmosphere

The amount of solar energy striking a location is greater at noon than morning or afternoon because it is passing through less air mass.

If the pencils are held perpendicular to a piece of paper and pressed down, the incidence angle is zero and the pencil marks are close together. If the same bundle of pencils is held at a 45-degree angle to the paper, and the pencils are again pressed to the paper, the pencil marks will be farther apart. In the same way, a beam of sunlight will be less intense as the incidence angle increases.

AVAILABLE SOLAR ENERGY

After all the impediments, how much solar energy actually makes it to your rooftop or yard? Quite a lot. The solar energy reaching a roof in Hart-ford, Connecticut, in 1 year, for example, is about 7 times as much energy as a typical house with average insulation in the Northeast consumes for space heating or about 24 times as much energy as is consumed to heat domestic water.

You can find out quantitatively how much solar energy is available to you at different times of the year from several sources. The Atmospheric Science Data Center distributes earth science data at NASA Langley Research Center (http://eosweb.larc.nasa.gov/sse). You can access data for your location by longitude and latitude, on maps, or in tables that include data for 1,195 ground sites. The National Renewable Energy Laboratory (NREL) is another good source; its website includes a variety of information

(continued on p. 15)

INCIDENCE AND INTENSITY

The angle at which solar energy strikes a surface (incidence angle) is another factor that affects its intensity. The lower the angle, the less the intensity and the less potential for solar energy.

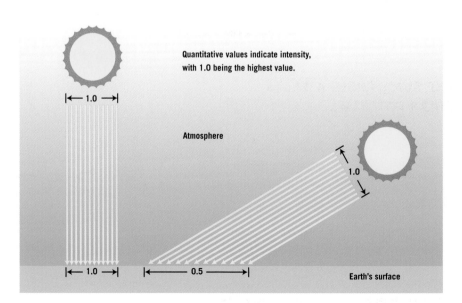

Quantitative values indicate intensity, with 1.0 being the highest value.

Atmosphere

Earth's surface

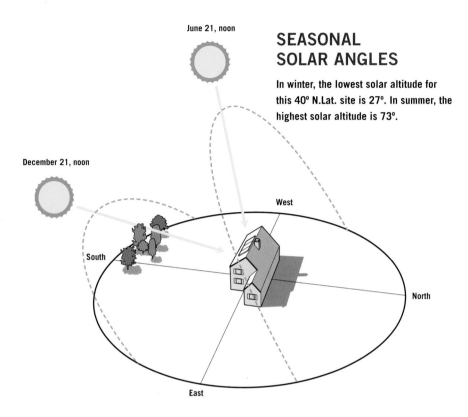

December 21, noon

June 21, noon

SEASONAL SOLAR ANGLES

In winter, the lowest solar altitude for this 40° N.Lat. site is 27°. In summer, the highest solar altitude is 73°.

West

South

North

East

COLLECTOR TILT

A fixed solar collector should be oriented and tilted to receive as much energy as possible during the period in which solar energy is needed most. Orientation and tilt are often described by the angles shown here.

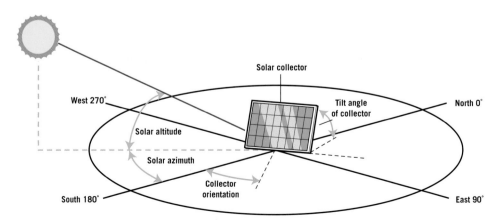

Solar collector

West 270°

Tilt angle of collector

North 0°

Solar altitude

Solar azimuth

Collector orientation

South 180°

East 90°

TECH CORNER | WHAT IS A FULL SUN HOUR?

An *equivalent full sun hour*, or, perhaps more clearly, equivalent hours of full sun, is a term developed by engineers to aid in forecasting the output of a solar electric array. The closest we come to a full sun hour in nature is at solar noon on a clear day with the sun overhead. The rest of the day, the sun is not as intense since it is not directly overhead. On overcast days, there is some solar radiation but nowhere near as much as on a clear day. By adding all of the solar radiation that arrives at the surface between sunrise and sunset for a given day, we come up with the total solar radiation for that day. By dividing that total by the amount of energy in a full sun hour, we can determine the equivalent hours of full sun for that day. Typically this is done for each day in each month, and then the average equivalent hours of full sun are put in tabular form for use by system designers.

Quantitatively, an equivalent full sun hour is defined as the amount of solar energy that strikes a horizontal surface that's 1 square meter in area, at solar noon, in 1 hour, at sea level, on a clear day, and with an air mass equal to 1.5. It is roughly equivalent to 1,000W (1kW) per square meter or, in thermal equivalent terms, 317 Btu/sq. ft. Data for equivalent full sun hours are available on daily, monthly, and yearly bases. It provides a good indication of how much solar energy is available in any given location.

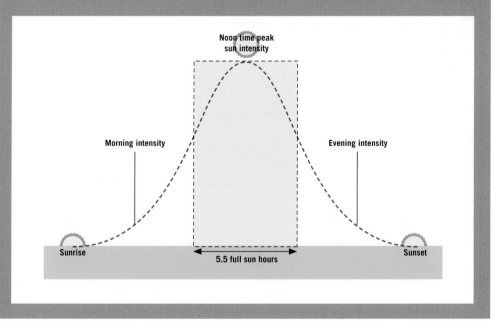

SOLAR ENERGY BASICS   13

SOLAR POTENTIAL VARIES WITH LOCATION

The amount of available solar energy depends largely on location. In the United States, for example, parts of the Southwest receive 50 percent more insolation (solar radiation) than areas in the Northwest.

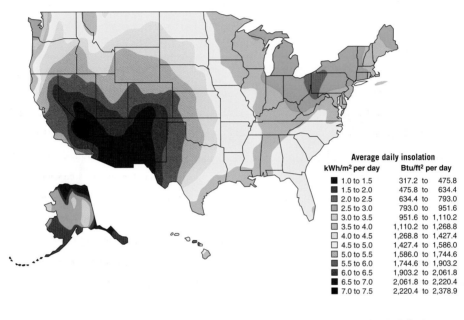

Average daily insolation

kWh/m² per day	Btu/ft² per day
1.0 to 1.5	317.2 to 475.8
1.5 to 2.0	475.8 to 634.4
2.0 to 2.5	634.4 to 793.0
2.5 to 3.0	793.0 to 951.6
3.0 to 3.5	951.6 to 1,110.2
3.5 to 4.0	1,110.2 to 1,268.8
4.0 to 4.5	1,268.8 to 1,427.4
4.5 to 5.0	1,427.4 to 1,586.0
5.0 to 5.5	1,586.0 to 1,744.6
5.5 to 6.0	1,744.6 to 1,903.2
6.0 to 6.5	1,903.2 to 2,061.8
6.5 to 7.0	2,061.8 to 2,220.4
7.0 to 7.5	2,220.4 to 2,378.9

(Adapted from the National Renewable Energy Laboratory Map.)

Just because maps show that the highest incidence of solar radiation is in the southwestern part of the United States, don't conclude that solar energy systems are feasible only there.

(continued from p. 11)

(www.nrel.gov/gis/solar.html). The PVWatts program maintained by the NREL provides a monthly listing of incident solar radiation data for the localities chosen. (See Tech Corner on p. 169 for more information.)

Measuring available solar energy

If you look up the available solar energy for your location on a chart or map, you may be surprised to find the number of sun hours indicated is far less than the number of hours the sun shines. It's quite common, for example, to have an average daily equivalent hour rating of 5 hours or 6 hours of full sun in a location where the total hours between sunrise and sunset may be 13 or 14.

The problem with using total hours of sunshine as a measure of available solar energy is the many factors that affect the incident solar radiation we've discussed so far. Consequently, a standard measure of available solar energy is used. It's called equivalent full sun hours (it may also be called peak sun hours, hours of equivalent full sun, or simply average kilowatt hours per square meter per day; see Tech Corner on p. 13 for more information).

Just because maps show that the highest incidence of solar radiation is in the southwestern part of the United States, don't conclude that solar energy systems are feasible only there. The economic feasibility of a solar system has more to do with the cost of the energy displaced by that system. For example, about 46 percent more solar energy reaches the ground each year in Albuquerque, New Mexico, than in Bridgeport, Connecticut, but the cost of electricity in Bridgeport is about three times the cost of electricity in Albuquerque (about $0.074/kwh vs. about $0.23/kwh). Hence a solar system that produces electricity or thermal energy that can be used to displace electricity (a solar water heating system for instance) is more economically viable in Connecticut than in New Mexico.

TECH CORNER | WHAT DO WE MEAN BY AIR MASS?

Air mass is one of several components used in the rating of solar electric collectors. The term is used to express the distance of the sun's travel through the atmosphere. Air mass is the ratio of the sun's actual path compared to what it would be if the sun were directly overhead. If the sun is directly overhead, the solar altitude angle is 90 degrees and the air mass is 1. If the solar altitude angle is 30 degrees, the air mass is 2, which means that the sun must travel through twice as much atmosphere as it would if the sun were overhead. Outside the atmosphere, the air mass is considered to be 0.

2 PUTTING SOLAR ENERGY TO WORK

With the exception of geothermal and nuclear energy, the sun accounts for all forms of energy on earth. Wind, waves, hydroelectric power, biofuels, and biomass all are examples of indirect forms of solar energy. Even most nonrenewable forms of energy, such as coal, petroleum, and natural gas, are really indirect forms of solar energy because they are derived from organic matter made possible by the sun.

Direct forms of solar energy, on the other hand, can be used as the energy is received. Using daylight to illuminate interior spaces (called daylighting) is a good example. In this book, we primarily focus on two direct uses of solar energy: solar thermal and solar electric, the production of heat and the production of electricity, respectively.

Direct uses of solar energy include daylighting, such as lighting a windowless bathroom with a solar tube.

PASSIVE & ACTIVE SOLAR THERMAL SYSTEMS

There are two types of solar thermal systems for capturing the sun's energy: passive and active. A passive solar system captures the sun's energy as it enters a building without relying on a motor-driven circulator or fan. Once inside the house, the heat can be stored in the mass of the building and distributed by natural means, such as conduction, convection, or radiation, or by forced means, such as with a fan.

In active solar thermal systems, collectors capture the sun's energy as heat as it enters the collector and transfer that heat to a fluid. The heated fluid is moved through the collectors by a motor-driven circulator or fan and taken to where it can be used immediately or stored for later use.

ABOVE TOP: This home combines two direct forms of solar energy conversion: thermal and electric. **ABOVE BOTTOM:** Wind power is one of many indirect forms of solar energy conversion.

With the exception of geothermal and nuclear [energy], the sun accounts for all [forms of] energy on earth.

CONSERVATION FIRST

It is much less expensive to use less energy than it is to install solar equipment. That may be difficult to accept if you're looking for a quick technological fix to rising energy costs or if you're excited about doing the right thing by installing solar equipment.

In addition to making economic sense, conservation has fewer environmental consequences than buying a renewable energy system. After all, significant amounts of materials need to be mined and energy consumed to manufacture, deliver,

It's far less expensive to improve thermal insulation than to save fuel by installing a solar system.

and install a solar panel. Don't forget all the other components required to complete a system. When you *are* ready for a solar system, conservation will have reduced the size of your investment.

There are lots of ways to conserve: upgrading insulation, installing water-saving shower heads; replacing incandescent lights with fluorescent, compact fluorescent lights (CFLs), or even light-emitting diodes (LEDs); and installing a solar blanket on a swimming pool. We'll discuss these and other ways to save energy throughout the book.

To encourage energy conservation, several utility companies in the Northeast and California have included the high and low kWhr/month consumption in monthly bills for all households in a given community. The objective is to inspire consumers to conserve more. The demonstrated result has been a gradual decrease in electricity consumption throughout that community. The national implications of this effort, if it catches on, are immense. In the average U.S. household, electricity consumption is 10,600 kWh/yr, while in the U.K. average consumption is 3,300 kWh/yr. If such a program exists in your community, try to better the low consumption level. If your utility does not offer such a program, work to have one put in place.

RESIDENTIAL SOLAR COLLECTORS

Both thermal and electric collectors can provide energy for household use. The majority of thermal collectors employed for household uses are of the flat-plate type. Evacuated-tube collectors also are used but are less common. Solar electric collectors, also known as PV collectors or PV modules, all are of the flat-plate type.

As described in more detail a little later, flat-plate solar thermal collectors are made in both glazed and unglazed versions. Unglazed collectors are usually flexible; glazed types are rigid. Flat-plate solar electric collectors are somewhat similar and available in both flexible and rigid forms, but with one major distinction. Regardless of whether they are flexible or rigid, the semiconductor material

(continued on p. 22)

ABOVE TOP: Solar electric modules do not need to be placed on the roof of your home. They can be ground mounted on a rack or pole or mounted on an outbuilding, as shown here. **ABOVE BOTTOM:** This home combines three forms of solar energy: electric (left side of main roof), thermal (right side of roof), and passive space heating (two tiers of glazing).

FOUR WAYS HEAT FLOWS

Heat always flows from an area of higher temperature to an area of lower temperature. It can't go the other way without work being done. (A refrigerator is a good example of a device that causes heat to flow from an area of lower to higher temperature. The compressor motor provides the work to force the movement of heat.)

There are four modes of heat transfer: radiation, conduction, convection, and evaporation/condensation.

RADIATION heat flow occurs between bodies that are not in contact. The objects can be separated by air or by a vacuum. Stand several feet away from a fire burning in a fireplace. The heat that reaches you from the fire arrives by radiation. Face the sun on a clear day and heat reaches you by the same means.

CONDUCTION occurs between bodies that are in contact. For example, put your hand on the hood of a dark-colored car that has been sitting in the sun. The heat flows into your hand by conduction. When you sit on a cold stadium seat, notice how heat flows away from your backside, again by conduction.

CONVECTION is the exchange of heat between bodies in a fluid. The fluid may be a gas or a liquid. Put your hand several inches above the top of a warm radiator. The warm air rising from the radiator that reaches your hand and warms it is an example of heat flow due to natural convection. (Some of the warming is due to radiation from the warm radiator.) A forced-air heating system warms the interior of a house by forced convection.

EVAPORATION/CONDENSATION heat flow occurs between bodies that are immersed in or in contact with a fluid that is present in both liquid and vapor form. To change a fluid from a liquid to a vapor (to cause evaporation), heat must be absorbed from the surroundings. To change a fluid in vapor form to liquid form (condensation), heat is released to the surroundings. For example, the water in an indoor swimming pool evaporates into the air above the pool, becoming water vapor, thereby cooling the pool. About 1,000 Btu are required to change 1 lb. (0.45 kg) of water (a pint) from a liquid to a vapor. Once the water vapor, or moisture, is in the air, it condenses on cold surfaces, such as window glass or metal window frames, giving up the same amount of heat.

All of these factors are at work in a solar heat collector. The sun's radiation strikes the black surface of the absorber and warms it. The warm absorber reradiates some of that heat to the interior of the collector where it is lost. The remaining heat in the absorber flows by conduction through the absorber sheet to fluid passages inside the absorber where heat is removed by convection. Some solar heat collectors use the evaporation/condensation mechanism to transport the sun's heat from the absorber to a heat exchanger immersed in the circulating fluid or directly to a heat exchanger in the heat storage tank.

RADIATION

The bulk of the solar energy transfer through glass is via radiation. This is the same way that solar energy passes through outer space to reach our planet.

100%

5% absorbed
in glass

8% reflected
(minimum)

87% transmitted

Heat

CONDUCTION

A masonry wall will pass heat from one side to the other via conduction.

CONVECTION

The warmed air around a radiator is less dense than the cool air in the room, so it rises toward the ceiling.

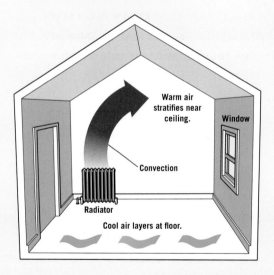

Warm air stratifies near ceiling.

Window

Convection

Radiator

Cool air layers at floor.

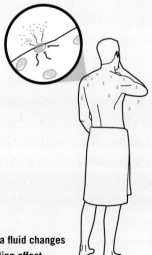

EVAPORATION

Heat is absorbed from the skin when a fluid changes from liquid to vapor, producing a cooling affect.

Solar thermal collectors come in many shapes, the most common being the glazed flat-plate collector shown here.

(continued from p. 19)

that makes up the cell must be protected from moisture. Rigid solar electric modules are encapsulated between a glass cover on the sun side and a vapor-impermeable material on the backside. While flexible solar electric collectors don't have a glass cover, they do have a highly transparent, UV-resistant cover to protect the cell from moisture.

Another class of collector concentrates the sun's rays with the use of a lens or a mirror. These, too, will be described in more detail later, but concentrating collectors are not generally used for residential applications.

Solar thermal collectors

Solar thermal collectors all have one thing in common. They convert the sun's energy directly into heat. Unglazed collectors are more efficient and cost-effective for certain low-temperature applications. Glazed collectors, while more expensive, are suitable for certain higher-temperature applications.

Put a coil of black garden hose out in the sun, run water through it, and you'll get warm water. This is how an unglazed collector functions, but with some notable advantages over the hose in terms of flow resistance and longevity.

Unglazed collectors are most widely used where the heated liquid does not need to be more than 10°F (5.5°C) to 20°F (11.1°C) above the ambient air temperature.

Glazed solar heat collectors are available in a variety of configurations. The most basic functions somewhat like the coil of black garden hose described earlier, but with the coil now placed in an insulated box that's covered with a layer of glass. Water flowing through the hose can get much hotter in a glazed enclosure than out in the air because the glass cover and insulation limit heat loss. Substitute a black copper plate with internal flow passages for the hose and you have the basic design for a solar thermal collector. The copper plate is called the absorber. Glazed collectors are used when the heated liquid needs to be 50°F (27.8°C) to 100°F (55.5°C) above ambient air temperatures.

Various strategies can further reduce heat losses from glazed collectors due to conduction, radiation, and convection. Increase the insulation level on the back and sides of the enclosure, for example, and the conduction heat losses are less. An optically selective coating on the surface of the absorber helps reduce radiation losses. The absorber with this coating still has a black surface (actually, it looks similar to the dark blue coating on a gun barrel) but also radiates very little heat outward, thereby reducing radiation losses. Add a second layer of glass to the top of the enclosure and convection losses are reduced even farther.

ABOVE TOP: Unglazed liquid-cooled thermal solar collectors are made of extruded plastic. They are used primarily for heating outdoor pool water. **ABOVE BOTTOM:** The collectors are fastened to the roof with clips and strapping.

Another way to reduce heat loss from the absorber is to coat it with an optically selective coating and isolate it with a vacuum. This is what happens in an evacuated-tube collector. The vacuum completely eliminates heat loss owing to convection. Due to the weight of the atmosphere bearing down on any evacuated space, the collectors are made in tubular form rather than as a flat plate since the former is far more capable of resisting atmospheric pressure. Typically, a number of evacuated tubes are used to make one module, which is approximately comparable in size to a flat-plate collector.

Unglazed thermal collectors

Unglazed, flat-plate, liquid-cooled collectors are designed for low-temperature applications, like heating an outdoor swimming pool. They are typically extruded from black plastic and incorporate a series of tubes through which a liquid is pumped. Almost all of them are flexible and look somewhat like a large, black mat. The hotter they are, the more flexible they become. Most have no inherent rigidity.

Unglazed, flat-plate collectors also can heat air. Most of these collectors, usually made from perforated sheets of steel, are being used to preheat ventilation air for commercial buildings. They have some inherent rigidity and thus don't require the same type or extent of support as the unglazed pool-heating collectors.

Glazed flat-plate, air-cooled collectors

Glazed flat-plate, air-cooled collectors are rectangular enclosures about the size of a sheet of

UNGLAZED POOL HEATING COLLECTOR

An unglazed thermal collector is typically extruded from black plastic. Liquid runs through the tubes and transports the heat to where it can be used, typically a swimming pool.

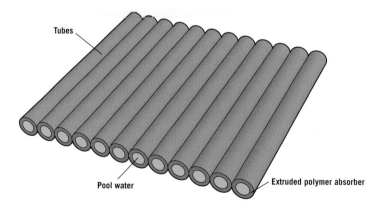

Tubes

Pool water

Extruded polymer absorber

TECH CORNER | ABSORBER COATINGS

The coating on the sun-facing side of a solar thermal collector's absorber plate can make a significant difference in performance.

The most common coatings are either a flat black or a selective black. Flat black is less expensive but less efficient. Selective coatings reduce the radiant heat loss from the absorber plates, thereby allowing more heat to be captured.

If the collector is to be used in a warm climate, such as Florida, for solar water heating, the selective coating will make little or no difference. In a colder climate, such as Connecticut or Wisconsin, however, it will make a big difference. The commonly used coating in climates where freezing seldom occurs is a sprayed-on, flat black, high-temperature paint. It absorbs energy well (about 98 percent of it) but reradiates a significant portion of that. In warm climates, with abundant sunshine, losses aren't enough to justify the added cost of a selective coating.

In cold climates, minimizing heat loss from the absorber is very much a concern, and so selective black coatings are better. Selective coatings are applied by electroplating or vacuum deposit. If electroplated, black chrome is most commonly used. If vacuum deposited, sputtered aluminum nitride is commonly used. Selective black coatings are used on the absorbers of all evacuated-tube collectors.

Here's an example of the difference the selective coating can make: In a cold climate at the end of a sunny midwinter day during which no hot water is removed from the solar tank, a solar water heating system with a flat-black coating on the absorbers of two 4-ft. by 8-ft. (1.2-m by 2.4-m) collectors will produce a maximum storage temperature of 85°F (29.4°C) to 90°F (32.2°C) in an 80-gal. (302.8L) tank. A system with the same collector area but with a good-quality selective coating on the absorbers will have a maximum tank temperature of 115°F (46.1°C) to 120°F (48.9°C).

IN 2007, **THE SQUARE FOOTAGE OF LOW-TEMPERATURE THERMAL COLLECTORS** delivered by U.S. manufacturers outpaced glazed thermal collectors by more than seven to one.

Glazed air-cooled collectors are primarily used for space heating. This house in Rhode Island, shown under construction, also features a passive greenhouse below the solar array and a ground-mounted solar domestic water heating system.

plywood, 6 in. (15.2 cm) to 8 in. (20.3 cm) thick with a glass cover. Inside is a blackened absorber sheet with integral passages through which air flows, cooling the absorber while gathering the sun's heat. The enclosure is insulated on the sides and back. Gaskets or fittings on the sides of the enclosure minimize air leakage as cooling air flows from the absorber of one collector to the absorber of the next. Collectors are connected to each other to form an array, and the array is connected to the supply and return ducting. All glazed air-cooled collectors are rigid and designed so they may be mounted parallel to the roof on standoffs or tilted up on a frame.

Homeowners who have been the happiest with their solar heating systems over the past 25 years to 30 years are those with either two or four air-cooled collectors that supply heat, via ducts, to one or two rooms during the winter days, without the complexity and cost of a heat storage system.

AIR-COOLED THERMAL COLLECTOR

The collector is called *air-cooled* because air is passed through the passages behind the blackened absorber plate to remove the sun's heat.

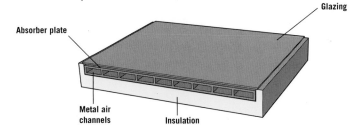

LIQUID-COOLED THERMAL COLLECTOR

The collector is called *liquid-cooled* because a liquid is passed through the tubes to remove the sun's heat from the blackened absorber plate. These collectors are the mainstay of most solar domestic water heating systems.

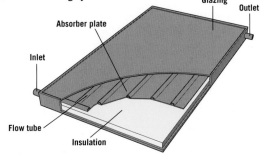

Evacuated-Tube vs. Flat-Plate Collectors: Long-Term Performance

Based on an extensive survey of the long-term performance of installed systems, flat-plate collectors outperform evacuated tube collectors for domestic water heating and space heating applications.

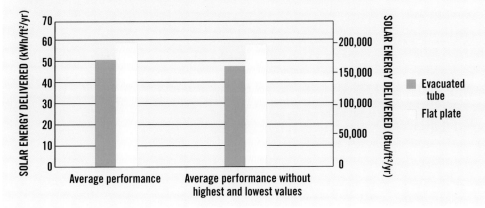

Glazed flat-plate, liquid-cooled collectors

Glazed flat-plate, liquid-cooled collectors have about the same gross area as the air-cooled type and are between 4 in. (10.2 cm) and 5 in. (12. 7 cm) thick. They look and work much the same as air-cooled collectors except that they are cooled with a liquid (usually water or antifreeze). Beneath the glass cover is a blackened absorber sheet with integral passages through which a liquid flows to cool the absorber and remove the sun's heat. The enclosure is insulated on the sides and back. Collectors are connected to each other to form an array and the array is connected to the supply and return lines. These collectors also are mounted parallel to the roof or on a frame.

Glazed liquid-cooled collectors supply domestic hot water to the owners of this Connecticut home.

Thermal Collector Sizes

COLLECTOR TYPE	STANDARD SIZES	WEIGHT RANGE	POUNDS PER SQUARE FOOT (PSF) RANGE
U.S.-made, unglazed thermal collectors	4 ft. by 8 ft. (1.2 m by 2.4 m) 4 ft. by 10 ft. (1.2 m by 3.1 m) 4 ft. by 12 ft. (1.2 m by 3.6 m)	16–25 lb. (7.2–11.3 kg) 20–30 lb. (9.1–13.6 kg) 25–45 lb. (11.3 20.4 kg)	0.5–1.5 (2.44–7.32 kg/m²)
U.S.-made, glazed flat thermal collectors	3 ft. by 7 ft. (0.91 m by 2.1 m) 3 ft. by 8 ft. (0.91 m by 2.4 m) 4 ft. by 7 ft. (1.2 m by 2.1 m) 4 ft. by 8 ft. (1.2 m by 2.4 m) 4 ft by 10 ft. (1.2 m by 3.1 m)	70–85 lb. (31.7–38.6 kg) 80–90 lb. (36.2–40.7 kg) 95–105 lb. (43.0–47.6 kg) 110–130 lb. (49.8–58.9 kg) 145–180 lb. (65.6–81.5 kg)	3.5–4.0 (17.1–19.5 kg/m²)
Imported, evacuated-tube thermal collectors	Varies with manufacturer; gross area range = 32–45 sq. ft. (2.97–4.18 m²)	150–250 lb. (67.9–113.3 kg)	3.25–5.0 (15.8–24.4 kg/m²)

Glazed liquid-cooled, flat-plate collectors are widely used for domestic water heating; they also are used for space heating, but to a lesser extent. Not only are these collectors more efficient than commercially available air-cooled collectors, but the size of the pipes that carry the heat away also are much smaller than the ducts required to carry the same amount of heat from air-cooled collectors.

While these are important advantages, provisions must be made to deal with freezing and overheating of the coolant (heat transport fluid) when there is no demand for heat. Neither is a concern with an air-cooled collector. The use of an antifreeze solution in liquid-cooled collectors solves the freezing concern, and there are various ways of dealing with overheating.

Absorbers in liquid-cooled collectors have fluid passages that are integral with or attached to the blackened absorber sheet. The fluid passages can be arranged in a grid or serpentine pattern. Grid patterns or drainable serpentine patterns are required for drain-back systems, which are discussed in Chapter 3. Grid patterns

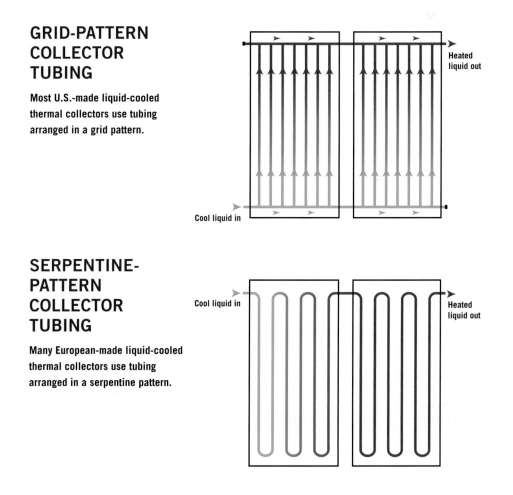

GRID-PATTERN COLLECTOR TUBING

Most U.S.-made liquid-cooled thermal collectors use tubing arranged in a grid pattern.

Heated liquid out

Cool liquid in

SERPENTINE-PATTERN COLLECTOR TUBING

Many European-made liquid-cooled thermal collectors use tubing arranged in a serpentine pattern.

Cool liquid in

Heated liquid out

also are more suitable for long arrays of collectors piped in parallel, as in a solar space heating system.

Serpentine patterns are preferred by manufacturers because they are less costly to fabricate. With few exceptions, serpentine pattern absorbers cannot be used in long parallel arrays because of losses in pressure and efficiency. In general, at this stage of the market in the United States, most collectors with grid pattern absorbers are made domestically and most collectors with serpentine pattern absorbers are imported. U.S. manufacturers have at least 20 years more experience with flat-plate technology than those in other countries.

Evacuated-tube collectors

All evacuated-tube collectors now on the market are liquid cooled. They're becoming more common, but they still represent less than 10 percent of the market. An evacuated-tube collector module typically consists of a series of individual evacuated glass tubes. Inside the tube is an absorber. The absorber design varies with the collector (two types are shown in the drawing on p. 32). A coolant (heat transport liquid) removes

heat from the absorber and delivers it to piping connected to the collector. Under clear sky conditions, flat-plate collectors are more efficient than evacuated-tube collectors for most residential applications. Under cloudy conditions, or when high fluid temperatures are required, evacuated-tube collectors are more efficient. One limitation evacuated-tube collectors have is getting rid of excess heat. Many of these collectors must use a motor-driven circulator to dump heat. When the power fails, the motor won't work and tubes can break from thermal stress. Once the vacuum is gone, the collector efficiency falls significantly and must be replaced, which is expensive.

SOLAR ELECTRIC COLLECTORS

Solar electric collectors (also called photovoltaic modules) convert solar radiation directly to electricity. When solar radiation strikes a solar cell, usually made of a semiconductor such as silicon, electrons are released. The electrons flow to a negative electrode attached to the top (sun side) surface of the cell. A positive electrode is attached to the rear of the cell and a circuit connects the two. The flow of electrons between positive and negative electrodes creates an electric current, which can power light bulbs, appliances, and motors and can charge batteries.

Because the voltage of an individual solar cell is low, a number of cells are connected together in series (in a string) to form a solar

Solar Electric vs. Solar Thermal Systems: Long-Term Performance

A survey of the long-term performance of installed solar electric and solar thermal systems shows that solar thermal systems can provide substantially more energy than solar electric systems.

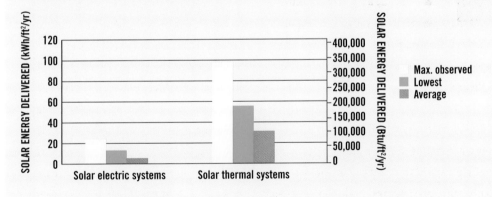

electric collector. A solar electric module is commonly made up of several strings of cells.

Most solar cells today are made with silicon, which can come in crystalline (including monocrystalline and polycrystalline) and thin-film forms. Within each general classification are numerous variations, including polycrystalline string ribbon and thin-film amorphous silicon laminates. There also are hybrids that combine amorphous and monocrystalline technologies.

EVACUATED-TUBE COLLECTORS

Evacuated-tube collectors are available in two main types. One is a single-wall glass tube, with the space inside the tube evacuated (below top). The other is a double-wall glass tube, with the space between the inner and outer tube evacuated (below bottom). In both types, an absorber is inserted into the tube to capture the sun's heat.

HEAT-PIPE ABSORBER

The absorber has a heat pipe attached to transport the sun's heat from the absorber to the array manifolds. The heat pipe passes through a glass-to-metal seal at one end of the glass tube.

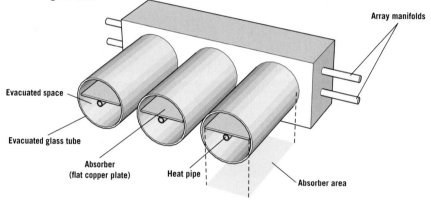

Array manifolds

Evacuated space

Evacuated glass tube

Absorber
(flat copper plate)

Heat pipe

Absorber area

CIRCULATION-TYPE ABSORBER

The absorber has a single U-shaped tube attached; the coolant runs in one end, passes down the length of the absorber, and then comes back again. Because this absorber is not in an evacuated space, the ends connect directly to the supply and return manifolds for the array.

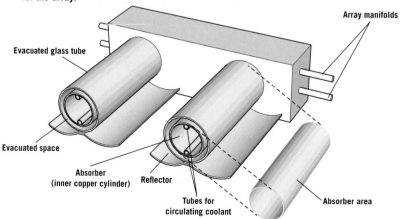

Array manifolds

Evacuated glass tube

Evacuated space

Absorber
(inner copper cylinder)

Reflector

Tubes for
circulating coolant

Absorber area

WHEN COLLECTORS ARE TO BE INSTALLED ON THE ROOF, CHECK THE ROOF'S CONDITION FIRST. If the roof membrane will need replacing within 10 years or so, it may make sense to have it done before installing the collectors. In southern New England, for example, it costs between $2,000 and $3,000 to remove and remount three solar collectors plus mounting frame for a solar domestic hot water system. The cost varies widely across the United States.

Solar electric collectors come in two general configurations: modular and laminate. In the modular type, a group of cells connected in series are sealed in a rigid, glass-topped enclosure that is weather tight. In laminate products, cells are attached to a flexible substrate and sealed from the weather with some type of flexible, UV-resistant polymer. Depending on the type of solar electric system and the voltage required, two or more modules or laminates may be connected in series.

Electrical output from the collector is in the form of direct current (d.c.). Some solar electric systems can use d.c. as is. In others, an inverter converts d.c. to alternating current (a.c.) for normal household use.

Crystalline modules

Crystalline silicon solar modules can be made from either monocrystalline or polycrystalline cells. Together they make up the vast majority of solar modules on the market. Polycrystalline modules have become the most popular type of

ABOVE TOP: A ground-mounted array of solar electric collectors, also called modules, is protected from weather by a glass-topped enclosure and EVA backing. **ABOVE BOTTOM:** Single solar cells combine to form modules. Modules combine to form arrays.

Crystalline solar modules are available in two types, monocrystalline (ABOVE RIGHT) and polycrystalline (ABOVE LEFT).

solar electric collector. They are less expensive than monocrystalline modules but also slightly less efficient.

Monocrystalline cells are made by slicing man-made silicon crystal ingots, or loaves, into wafers with laser-cutting tools. The wafers look like pieces of dark-colored glass. Polycrystalline cells are made in a similar fashion, except the ingot is formed from masses of smaller crystals. Polycrystalline wafers resemble frost crystals on a window.

Polycrystalline cells also can be made by drawing crystals from molten silicon on wires, a technique known as *string ribbon technology.*

Thin-film modules and laminates

Thin-film collectors are made by depositing semiconductor materials in very thin layers on various substrates, including glass and flexible backings. Materials include copper indium diselenide, cadmium telluride, and amorphous crystalline silicon.

Efficiencies are lower than for crystalline wafer cells, ranging from 5 percent to 6 percent for amorphous silicon to 7 percent to 8.5 percent for cadmium telluride and 9 percent to 11 percent for copper indium diselenide. Amorphous silicon is by far the most widely used, even with its rather low efficiency.

When the semiconductor material is protected by glass and is not flexible, the collector is called a module. When the semiconductor is protected by a flexible cover, the collector is usually called a laminate.

Although thin-film modules and laminates are significantly less efficient than crystalline modules, their cost per watt of electricity produced is lower. Laminates have another advantage. They weigh much less than a layer of roofing and as much as one tenth the weight of a crystalline module. The difference can be significant when it comes to installing a solar electric array on an existing roof that would otherwise need reinforcement.

SOLAR ELECTRIC MODULE

A solar electric collector, or photovoltaic module, is typically made up of solar cells sandwiched between a layer of EVA on the rear and a sheet of glass on the sun side to protect it from the weather.

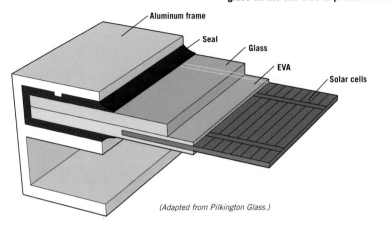

(Adapted from Pilkington Glass.)

Nevertheless, thin-film modules and laminates presently account for a small fraction of total solar electric sales, partly because they require three to four times more roof space to produce the same output and partly because some installers are not convinced these products are as durable. The best use for them is on commercial buildings with large flat roofs where their light weight allows them to be used without roof reinforcement.

Building-Integrated Solar Electric Arrays

When solar cells are designed to be an integral part of the building roof, wall, or glazing, they are called building integrated photovoltaic (BIPV) arrays and serve the dual role of keeping the weather out and generating electricity. They look much like traditional building components. Some homeowners and many architects prefer their appearance to that of modular solar electric collectors that are typically attached to the roof of a building and are located outside the weather membrane.

Presently, there are two approaches to BIPV arrays: solar laminates and small solar modules. The former are available in rolls for application on standing-seam metal roofs. Until recently, they were also available in shingle form. The latter are available as either solar slates or solar tiles.

There are a number of factors to consider when selecting a BIPV array:

Efficiency

Efficiency is important when selecting solar electric collectors because the south-facing roof area of most homes in the U.S. is less than is needed to provide all of the electricity consumed in the average U.S. home when modular collectors are used. The efficiency of laminates is between 25 percent and 33 percent of that of modular solar collectors. The efficiency of thin-film products, however, is generally not affected as severely by partial shade or heat as are the higher efficiency modules. The efficiency of solar slates and tiles is about the same as that of modular solar electric collectors, 16 percent to 18 percent.

Weather membrane integrity/ electrical connections

For perhaps obvious reasons, it is desirable to keep to a minimum the number of holes made in the weather membrane of any house. The roll laminates are designed so the electrical connections can be made outside the roof membrane. Solar slates and solar tiles are interconnected one to the next above the roof membrane. The solar shingles that were marketed until recently required that two wires from each shingle pass through the roof membrane. These wires were then connected to those from other shingles on the underside of the roof. The result was multiple holes in the weather membrane and myriad wires on the underside of the roof. This design usually precludes the use of insulation or wallboard on the underside of the roof.

Availability

The roll laminates, as well as solar slates and solar tiles, are readily available. At present, solar shingles are not offered by any manufacturer. The company that used to make them has taken them off the market. CertainTeed, a building products manufacturer, plans to offer their BIPV roofing system, EnerGen, at some time in the near future. While it is not a true solar shingle, it supposedly can be integrated with conventional shingle roofs, and, most important, the design allows electrical connections to be made above the roof membrane. Dow Chemical has announced that it will introduce a solar shingle, called the Dow™ PowerHouse™ Solar Shingle.

LEFT: Thin-film solar electric collectors are available in self-adhering rolls for application to metal roofing. **ABOVE:** Thin-film technology has also been used to fabricate solar shingles. **FACING PAGE:** On this Florida home, the laminate was applied to a metal roof of a zero-energy home. The 3.3kW system supplies all the electricity the homeowner needs, including enough to power the air-conditioning system.

TECH CORNER | INNOVATIONS IN SOLAR CELLS

A great deal of innovation and development is going on in both crystalline and thin-film technology. It will be interesting to see how the two competing technologies play out. For now, where maximum electrical output per square foot is a priority, high-efficiency crystalline cells are the choice. Where the roof structure cannot accept any significant added load and roof reinforcement is not practical, then thin-film technology has the edge.

Hybrid solar cells are getting a lot of attention. They are a cross between crystalline and thin-film technologies. The result is multicrystalline wafers that are produced in thin sheets without the need to slice the material. While not currently available commercially, this process may soon enable mass-production of wafers and should result in less-expensive solar panels.

Concentrating collectors

Not all solar collectors are flat or tubular. Some focus the sun's energy on a small area, using mirrors or lenses to produce higher efficiencies and much higher temperatures than can be achieved with flat-plate or evacuated-tube collectors. As a group, these are called concentrating collectors. Concentrating collectors are grouped into those that focus the sun's energy on a linear target and those that focus on a point.

Point-focus concentrators generate the highest temperatures but require more expensive equipment to track the sun. Linear-focus concentrators are more common, but neither is practical for residential applications. Tracking equipment and maintenance are too expensive. Concentrating collectors are most suitable for commercial applications where on-site maintenance is available.

CONCENTRATING COLLECTORS

Concentrating solar thermal collectors can produce much higher temperatures than flat plates, but they use only the direct component of solar radiation. They cannot use the diffuse component. The mirror, or lens, of a concentrating collector focuses direct radiation onto an absorber. It is by cooling the absorber with a fluid that the sun's energy can be removed for use. In parts of the country where direct radiation is a high percentage of the total incident solar radiation, concentrating-type collectors are practical. In parts of the country where diffuse radiation is a high percentage of the total, concentrating collectors are less practical. There, flat-plate or evacuated-tube collectors, which use both direct and diffuse solar radiation, are better. Neither flat-plate nor evacuated-tube collectors can achieve the high temperatures that the concentrating collectors are capable of producing.

Solar Collector Efficiency

How efficiently solar collectors turn sunlight into useful energy varies dramatically.

COLLECTOR TYPE	PEAK EFFICIENCY (PERCENT)
Flat plate, nonevacuated	
Unglazed collectors (outdoor pool heating)	85–90
Glazed collectors (domestic water or space heating)	70–77
Flat plate, evacuated	
Evacuated tube (domestic water or space heating)	28–60
Concentrating	
Point focus	80–87
Linear focus	58–80
Electric collectors (flat plate)	
Module	11–19
Building integrated PV (BIPV)	4.4–6.3

LEFT: Point-focus (dish) concentrating collectors, such as this solar cooker, achieve high temperatures and efficiencies. BELOW: Linear-focus solar electric concentrators are generally used for commercial applications.

MOUNTING SOLAR COLLECTORS

Solar collectors (either thermal or electric) can be mounted on the roof or on the ground. They are usually installed on the roof, parallel to the surface. This tends to lower installation costs, as long as the roof is strong enough to support the weight of the collectors. Roof installations also preserve yard space and lessen the risk of winter shade when the sun is lower in the sky and shadows cast by buildings or trees are longer.

At least two types of parallel-to-roof mounts are available. One uses four brackets that are secured to the corner of each collector. The brackets are usually fastened through the roof membrane to the structure below with lag screws. A sealant is used at each penetration. If there are three collectors in an array, then 12 holes would have to be drilled through the roof membrane.

An alternate mounting scheme is to secure the collectors to rails that, in turn, are secured to the roof with their own sets of mounting feet. This sort of mounting scheme, while somewhat more costly than the four-bracket approach, can reduce the number of roof penetrations by as much as 50 percent on smaller arrays and more on larger arrays. And fewer roof penetrations mean less chance of roof leaks in the future.

Tilt-correction frames

To improve efficiency, tilt-correction frames are often used where the roof pitch is either horizontal or nearly so. They are also used on pitched roofs that face well away from south.

Solar collectors are typically mounted parallel to and slightly above the roof (ABOVE TOP), although some are mounted on racks that are anchored to a roof, a deck, a wall, or the ground (ABOVE BOTTOM).

COLLECTOR MOUNTING

Collectors can be mounted parallel to the roof. Usually they are secured to rails, and the rails are fastened to L-foot brackets or standoffs that themselves are secured through the roof membrane to the roof structure below.

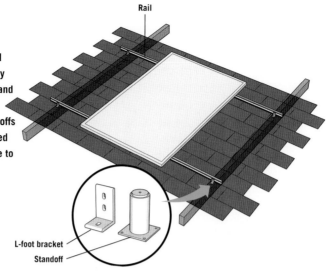

Rail

L-foot bracket

Standoff

Tilt-correction frames also are used for sidewall mounting and for ground-mounted arrays.

There are a variety of tilt-correction frames available. The choices are similar to those for parallel-to-roof mounts. When a solar array is tilted up from the roof, local code officials may require a structural engineer to check the roof and frame to make sure they can handle wind loads.

Ground-mounted collectors

Solar collectors also can be attached to frames or poles on the ground. This is a common route when the roof isn't big enough or strong enough for an array. If the array is to be frame mounted, the feet of the frame are usually secured to individual concrete footings or to concrete grade beams. If the array is to be pole mounted, the pole usually extends well into the ground and is connected to a large buried concrete slab.

Both solar electric and solar thermal collectors are commonly connected to ground-mounted

Tilt-correcting ground mounts allow for optimal collector tilt and orientation. Note the footings required for ground-mount installations.

ABOVE TOP: Ground-mounted evacuated-tube collectors. The lower end of the collector array should be high enough to remain above expected snowfall, and trees should be cleared about 100 ft. (30.5m) south of the array. **ABOVE BOTTOM:** A pole-mounted solar electric array.

frames. However, only solar electric collectors have been installed on pole-mounted frames. In either case, the collector support must be capable of withstanding design wind loads for the area. The frame mount is the less expensive of the two, but the pole mounting can be more visually attractive.

POSITIONING SOLAR COLLECTORS

A variety of site factors can affect the performance of solar collectors, including shade, collector orientation, and tilt. All are important factors for both thermal and electrical collectors.

Shade

Shade drastically reduces the output of solar collectors. Even when deciduous trees shed their leaves, their bare branches can obstruct between 30 percent and 60 percent of the incident sunlight.

Many solar contractors will perform a site survey, usually for a fee, to determine the suitability of your home for a solar system. An experienced solar contractor can, with a compass and tilt meter, tell which trees or surrounding objects will cast shade on the array and at what time of year. If a rebate for the system is possible, then some record of the shade analysis is usually required for approval. An analysis also is useful when talking to a tree service about which trees need to be cut or topped and if system performance issues develop later.

Several tools are available for performing the shade analysis. One is the Solar Pathfinder™. It's simple to use, affordable, and has been in

COLLECTOR TILT

The ideal tilt of any solar collecting surface is perpendicular to the sun's rays. But because the sun's altitude and azimuth vary throughout the day and with the seasons—and because sun-tracking equipment is expensive—fixed mounts are generally used.

The best year-round tilt for a solar hot water collector is equal to the local latitude, measured from horizontal. For example, if you live in Philadelphia, at 40 degrees north latitude, the collector tilt should be set at 40 degrees. For a winter application, usually for space heating, you would add 15 degrees to the latitude, making the tilt 55 degrees. This maximizes solar gain during the winter. For an outdoor pool heating system that's used in the summer, on the other hand, you would subtract 15 degrees and use a tilt angle of 25 degrees. Although these are optimum values of tilt, a surprising amount of variation can be used without much loss of performance.

Optimum Tilt Angle and Orientation

This table shows the effects of tilt and orientation (azimuth) on a solar hot water system at 40 degrees north latitude. The collectors operate at 100 percent of their potential when pointed due south (0 degrees azimuth) at a tilt angle of between 35 degrees and 45 degrees. Percentages are lower for different azimuth and tilt settings. The array measures 100 sq. ft.

(Adapted from a chart by Emaan Ammar.)

	AZIMUTH	0	5	10	15	20	25	30	35	40	45	50	55	60	65	70	75	80	85	90
													TILT							
South	0	78	83	87	91	94	97	99	100	100	100	99	97	95	92	88	83	77	70	63
	20	78	83	87	90	94	96	97	98	98	98	97	96	93	90	86	82	76	70	63
	40	78	82	85	88	91	93	94	95	95	94	93	91	89	86	82	78	73	68	61
	60	78	80	83	85	86	87	88	88	88	87	85	84	81	78	75	71	67	62	56
	80	78	78	79	80	80	80	80	80	80	77	75	73	71	68	64	61	56	52	48
East/West	90	78	78	78	77	77	76	76	74	73	71	69	67	64	61	58	55	51	47	43

	100–90	89–80	79–70	69–60	59–50	49–40	
HIGH							LOW

Table values above are percentages.

ABOVE: Shade, even from bare branches, will compromise the performance of any solar collector. It has a more negative effect on solar electric collectors than on solar thermal collectors. RIGHT: This instrument, the Solar Pathfinder, is one of several that enable solar contractors to map the hourly shade falling on a given location for an entire year.

use since the late 1970s. Two other options, both more precise and with more options, are the ASSET by Wiley Electronics and the SunEye™, made by Solmetric. They're newer to the market and more expensive.

Year-round access to the sun without shade is important! In many instances, it is not worth the expense to install a solar electric or thermal system unless you have unshaded solar access. Some states have laws that allow homeowners to create binding solar easements to protect access to sunlight. They may specify northern property line setbacks (the minimum distance from the border of a property to a building) and limit the height of buildings and of vegetation that would otherwise shade your roof. Easements must be executed in writing. In addition, some states have passed laws that prohibit homeowner associations from prohibiting the installation of solar panels; see the Database for State Incentives for Renewables & Efficiencies (DSIRE™) website for details (www.dsireusa.org).

Collector orientation

Solar collectors should face the sun for as much of the day as possible. Given that the sun travels across the southern sky (for those living in the Northern Hemisphere), the ideal orientation for collectors is true south. (It is the opposite in the Southern Hemisphere.)

Keep in mind, however, that in most parts of the country true south is not the same as the magnetic south you read on a compass. The local magnetic variation determines how true south relates to magnetic south. Just within the United States, magnetic south can be as much as 20 degrees east or west of true south. The local variation can be determined from local nautical charts, aeronautical charts, or a local surveyor.

For a variety of reasons, all site related, it is not always feasible to face collectors exactly true south. Fortunately, there is some leeway here; an

SOLAR AESTHETICS

Appearance is an important issue for most homeowners. This is especially true for solar systems that require large collector arrays. Although a solar domestic water heating system may require only two or three collectors (of 64 sq. ft. to 96 sq. ft., or 5.9 m² to 8.9 m², each), a solar space-heating array can be as large as 25 percent of the heated floor area of the house. The array for a solar electric system also can be large, in some cases larger than the array of a solar space-heating system.

In most instances, solar arrays are mounted on the roof simply because it is less costly. Solar arrays can be mounted on the ground to minimize their visual impact, provided there's a large enough unshaded area. Ground-mounted arrays offer greater flexibility. But mainly due to the need for some type of support structure and footing, ground mounting costs more (assuming the roof doesn't need any structural reinforcement). In addition to the cost of the mounting frame and footings, underground piping or conduit must be run from the array to the house. If it enters the house below grade, the foundation penetration will have to be sealed carefully to keep out ground water.

Before dismissing a roof array for the sake of appearance, it is worth considering alternative means of mounting the collectors. Perhaps, with an acceptable compromise in performance, the roof array can be mounted on an east- or west-facing roof or mounted parallel to the roof rather than tilted up on a mounting frame. (See p. 43 for array performance at off-optimum tilts and orientation.)

BELOW TOP: An energy-efficient home in coastal Maine seamlessly combines arrays of glazed thermal and electric collectors. BELOW BOTTOM: Low-profile building-integrated collectors are less obtrusive for some homeowners.

This label shows typical rating data for a flat-plate thermal collector as it appears on SRCC-rated collectors.

array can face 15 degrees to 20 degrees off south without much loss in performance. In fact, facing off true south by as much as 40 degrees can result in as little as a 5 percent reduction in the energy collected, depending on the array tilt.

COLLECTOR EFFICIENCY AND PERFORMANCE

The efficiency of a given thermal collector depends on the collector design, ambient air temperature, the temperature of the heat-transfer fluid, and solar availability. As the ambient temperature increases for a given operating temperature, the efficiency of a given collector increases. Efficiency is typically expressed as an equation and depicted in graph form. The horizontal axis of the graph shows the temperature differential between the fluid inside the collector (T_i), and the ambient air (T_a), divided by the solar radiation at the time of the test. The vertical axis shows efficiency.

The efficiency of any solar thermal collector decreases as the temperature difference between the fluid passing through the collector and the ambient air goes up. This is a very important

concept. Put another way, the bigger the difference between the outside air temperature and the fluid passing through the collector, the more heat is lost from the collector to the environment.

To compare the performance of solar thermal collectors, visit the Solar Rating and Certification Corporation™ (SRCC) website (www.solar-rating. org). The SRCC provides an extremely valuable service to consumers, helping them separate

NOT ALL TYPES OF SOLAR COLLECTORS ARE EQUAL WHEN IT COMES TO EFFICIENCY. A solar electric module, for example, is much less efficient at peak output than is a solar thermal collector. At noon on a clear day, the peak efficiency range of a photovoltaic module using crystalline silicon cells is between 11 percent and 19 percent. Less than one fifth of the sun's energy is being converted into useful energy. By contrast, a nonevacuated-tube solar thermal collector has a peak efficiency ranging from 70 percent to more than 77 percent. The peak efficiency of an evacuated-tube collector is between 40 percent and 50 percent.

fact from the sometimes wild claims of performance. It is an independent, third-party testing organization that certifies the performance of solar thermal collectors and gives the Btu output of more than 250 collectors under various conditions. The SRCC also certifies and rates solar domestic water heating systems.

Solar electric collector output is a function of the ambient temperature and incident solar radiation. As incident solar radiation drops off, the output of the collector drops as well. Typically, as the incident solar radiation drops off, the output voltage remains nearly constant and the amperage from the collector declines. Also, as the collector temperature increases, the collector output also drops off. In this case, the amperage remains about the same and the voltage falls. The performance of solar electric collectors is determined by the California Energy Commission (CEC), an independent, third-party testing organization. CEC ratings are accepted by rebate-issuing organizations nationwide.

You may see the wattage ratings for many solar electric collectors on its website (www.gosolar california.ca.gov).

There are two sets of test conditions under which solar electric modules are tested: standard test conditions (STC), and PVUSA (for photovoltaics for utility scale applications) test conditions (PTC). The results of the former are stamped or printed on the module nameplate. PTC results listed by the CEC are more conservative. They're often used as the basis for computing rebates. For example, a monocrystalline silicone module with a nameplate rating of 175W might have a PTC rating of 155W. It would deliver 155W at PTC conditions, 1,000W/m² of solar radiation at an ambient temperature of 68°F (20°C).

Neither rating, however, accounts for all real-world losses, according to the CEC. The commission further states that actual solar systems will produce lower outputs due to soiling, snow cover, shading, wire and inverter losses, and a variety of other conditions.

ADDED VALUE WITH A SOLAR HOUSE

Some homeowners are hesitant to invest in energy-saving strategies, insulation, efficient windows, a solar water heating system, or a solar electric system, fearing they may not stay in the house long enough to recover their investments in avoided fuel costs. Further, they question whether they'd recover those investments when they sold the house.

Two studies from the 1990s reported in the *Appraisal Journal* indicate that the market value of a home increases immediately by about $20 for every $1 reduction in annual operating costs due to energy-saving investments. Historically, mortgage rates have an after-tax effective interest rate of about 5 percent. If a dollar of reduced operating cost is put toward debt service at 5 percent, it can support an additional $20 of debt. To the borrower, that total monthly cost of ownership is identical. The studies on which this finding was based were done nationwide and were sponsored by the Department of Housing and Urban Development. In short, there is no reason to wait to install an energy-saving improvement to your home.

3 SOLAR DOMESTIC HOT WATER

In the average U.S. home, and depending on where you live, heating domestic water accounts for between 15 percent and 30 percent of total household energy use, based on the average consumption of about 20 gal. (75.7 L) of hot water per person per day. (Thirty-minute showers can change those numbers in a hurry.) In many other developed countries, the average per-capita consumption is less than one quarter of that.

Solar domestic hot water (SDHW) has a long track record. Thousands of systems were installed in the United States in the late 19th and early 20th centuries. And approximately 1 million were installed during the last large surge of interest in solar energy that began in the early 1970s and ended in 1986. Perhaps half of the systems installed during the most recent surge continue to function today. A lot has been learned from solar hot water system successes and failures. Rather than becoming outdated, the technology continues to be refined.

SO THERE'S NO CONFUSION, domestic hot water is the water used for bathing, dishwashing, and doing the laundry. It is not the same as water used for hydronic space heating or in a heated swimming pool.

Solar domestic water heating systems were popular at the turn of the 20th century, especially in Florida and southern California.

A solar domestic water heating system, such as the one in this Colorado home, can supply most of the household's hot water needs.

HOW SDHW SYSTEMS WORK

Solar water heating starts with the collector, typically of the flat-plate, liquid-cooled type (for more, see p. 24). Fluid (typically water or a nontoxic antifreeze) circulates through the collector and then heats domestic hot water in one of two ways: directly or indirectly.

Direct and indirect

Direct systems, also known as open-loop systems, circulate potable water directly through the collector. Heated water is stored in a tank until needed. Indirect systems, also known as closed-loop systems, circulate a nonpotable liquid, often a nontoxic antifreeze, between the collector and a heat exchanger, which heats the domestic water. In indirect systems, potable water and the circulating fluid in the collector do not mix.

IN 1920, MORE THAN 1,000 SOLAR WATER HEATERS were sold by the Day and Night Solar Heater Company, one of many manufacturers at that time. The industry would have continued to thrive were it not for the growing availability of cheap natural gas and oil.

Climate is one factor that determines whether you can use a direct or indirect system. If freezing weather is not a concern, the more efficient and simpler direct-type system can be used. If freezing is a concern, then the somewhat less efficient and more complex indirect system must be used.

CONSERVATION FIRST

Before installing a SDHW system, it's important to reduce hot water use. Doing so may enable you to purchase a smaller system than you would otherwise need or allow you to meet a greater proportion of your hot water needs (called the solar fraction). Here are some suggestions.

SAVING IN THE SHOWER In most households, the largest portion of hot water is used for showering, so an obvious first step is to take shorter and fewer showers. Aim for a shower time of between 3 minutes and 5 minutes, and consider a showerhead with a shutoff valve so you can turn off the water while you lather up. Install a low-flow showerhead that draws 1.5 gal./minute (0.096 L/second).

LAUNDRY New or old, a washing machine can be one of the larger energy-consuming appliances when hot water cycles are used. Reduce hot water use by washing clothes with cold or warm water whenever possible and always use a cold rinse. Launder full loads if you can. For a partial load, adjust the water level to match the size of the load.

WATER HEATERS Set the thermostat on your domestic water heater to 120°F (48.9ºC) or, if there's no temperature scale, to the lowest setting that still adequately provides hot water. If you plan to be away from home for at least 3 days, turn the thermostat to its lowest setting or turn off the water heater.

If you have a storage-type water heater, add insulation around the tank so total insulation equals R-24, and insulate hot water supply lines within 10 ft. (3.05 m) of the tank to R-7. When you replace your water heater, buy an energy-efficient model.

DISHWASHING If you wash dishes by hand, don't run hot water while scrubbing. If you use a dishwasher, turn off the electric heater for the dry cycle; while this does not save hot water, it does save electricity. Run the dishwasher with full loads only, and if it offers cycle selections, choose a shorter one. Don't rinse dishes before putting them in the dishwasher; wipe dishes with an abrasive pad or use a scraper instead. If you're in the market for a new dishwasher, invest in an energy-efficient model.

OTHER WAYS TO CONSERVE Don't use hot water recirculation systems that constantly circulate hot water through supply lines. They dramatically increase energy use. If you have a long wait (45 seconds or more) for hot water at a shower or sink, install a small storage-type water heater close to the fixture, or consider an on-demand water heater.

Use aerators at faucets. Aerators mix air into the water stream, maintaining the pressure but using considerably less water, and they're inexpensive.

Don't run the hot water at the sink while you shave or wash. Put some water in the basin and use it instead.

Wherever the building architecture, roof structure, climate, and visual concerns permit, passive solar water heating systems are better than active systems. Until someone repeals the law of gravity, they will work for many years and require very little attention.

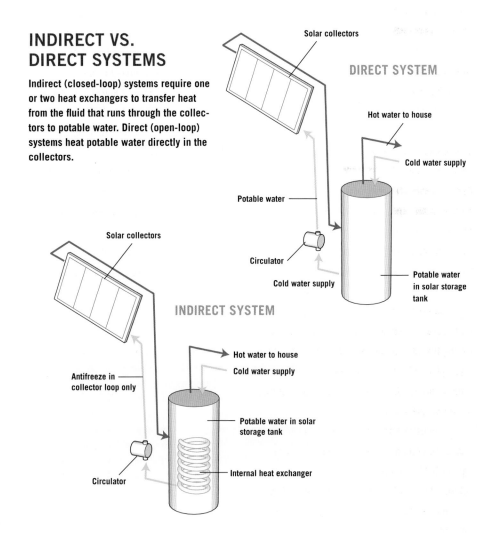

INDIRECT VS. DIRECT SYSTEMS

Indirect (closed-loop) systems require one or two heat exchangers to transfer heat from the fluid that runs through the collectors to potable water. Direct (open-loop) systems heat potable water directly in the collectors.

DIRECT SYSTEM

Solar collectors

Hot water to house

Cold water supply

Potable water

Circulator

Cold water supply

Potable water in solar storage tank

INDIRECT SYSTEM

Solar collectors

Antifreeze in collector loop only

Hot water to house

Cold water supply

Potable water in solar storage tank

Circulator

Internal heat exchanger

Comparing Conventional Residential Domestic Water Heaters

This table provides a summary of the most common types of conventionally fueled residential domestic water heaters in use in the U.S. Homeowners with efficient water heaters should lean toward small solar fraction systems; those with inefficient water heaters are better off with large fraction systems.

(Analysis by Everett M. Barber Jr.)

STORAGE	Efficiency (Percent)	Typical Tank Capacity (Gallons)	First Hour Rating	Extent of Use in United States
Electric resistance elements in a tank	80–95	40–120	Low	Second most widely used
Electric heat pump supplement	*		Lowest	Infrequent use
Gas-fired tank *(natural gas or propane)*	52–65	40–60	Moderate	Most widely used
Fuel oil–fired tank	55–65	30–50	Highest	Northern states
Indirect-fired tank *(tank heated by a boiler)*		40–50	Moderate	Northern states
Summer	15–25			
Winter	75–80			
* Measured by coefficient of performance, not efficiency				
INSTANTANEOUS			Max. gpm	
Electric resistance heater	99	No tank	0.2–1.0	Rare
Gas-fired tank *(natural gas or propane)*	70–85	No tank	2.0–4.5	Small but growing use
Heat exchange coil in oil- or gas-fired boiler *(tankless coil)*		No tank	2.0–3.5	Most common type in Northeast, rare elsewhere
Summer	15–25			
Winter	75–80			

This house incorporates a large solar water heating system, a solar electric system, passive solar heating, and super insulated construction.

Active and passive systems

A further distinction among system types is whether the system is active or passive. Active systems use a circulator to move water or anti-freeze through the collector. Most SDHW systems installed in North America are of this type.

Passive systems rely on natural convection rather than on motorized circulators. Movement of fluid through the system is due to differences in density: Heated water is less dense than cool water and therefore rises. Consequently, the hot water storage tank for a passive solar water heating system must be located above the collector. Outside of North America, passive systems predominate.

COMMON TYPES OF SDHW SYSTEMS

Five types of solar water heating systems together make up more than 90 percent of all the systems installed in North America. In the sections that follow, they are presented in order of most common type first. No matter what a salesperson may tell you, no one type of system is the most appropriate for all parts of the country. Consumers should sort through the choices and make an informed decision based on their needs and climate.

Active-indirect systems

There are two types of active-indirect systems. In the first, a collection loop is completely filled and pressurized with coolant, usually nontoxic antifreeze. In the second type, the collection loop is partially filled with a similar type of liquid, or in some cases with water, under atmospheric

HEATING DOMESTIC WATER WITH THE SUN provides between 2 and 18 times as much energy per square foot of collector as does a solar electric system.

In this partially filled, active-indirect SDHW system, collector coolant drains back to a reservoir (A) at the end of the day or when the storage tank (B) has reached the maximum temperature.

ACTIVE-INDIRECT FILLED SYSTEM

Indirect systems, such as this one, are used primarily in northern climates. An antifreeze solution in the collectors prevents freeze damage.

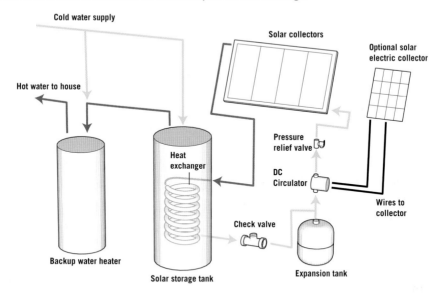

Cold water supply

Solar collectors

Optional solar electric collector

Hot water to house

Pressure relief valve

Heat exchanger

DC Circulator

Wires to collector

Check valve

Backup water heater

Expansion tank

Solar storage tank

ACTIVE-INDIRECT DRAIN-BACK SYSTEM

A drain-back system is not pressurized. It includes a reservoir to which collectors drain the heat-transfer liquid when the circulator shuts off (which happens when the storage tank is warmer than the collectors or the tank is too hot).

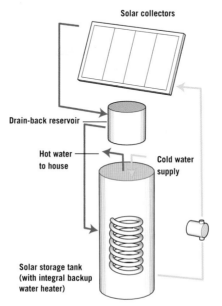

Solar collectors

Drain-back reservoir

Hot water to house

Cold water supply

Solar storage tank (with integral backup water heater)

pressure. Air fills the rest of the system. The antifreeze used in both types of systems is typically a solution of inhibited propylene glycol and water. Propylene glycol is considered nontoxic (and is commonly used as a moisturizer in many baked goods, in some soft drinks, and in many cosmetics).

WHERE THEY'RE USED Both types of solar collection loops are well suited to climates where freezing temperatures can be expected or where the potable water quality is not suitable for use in the collectors. The partially filled systems, equally well suited to climates where freezing occurs, are superior to the filled systems when the demand for hot water is irregular. Together, these two types constitute about two thirds of all systems now in use in North America.

HOW THEY WORK In both the filled and partially filled systems, heat is transferred from the collector to the coolant and then from the coolant to potable water via a heat exchanger, which may be inside or outside a storage tank. The tank also may have an integral supplemental heater, or any one of a variety of supplemental heaters downstream from the solar tank may be used.

Indirect systems that are completely filled with coolant are usually pressurized to between 35 psi (2.4 bar) and 75 psi (5.1 bar) to help suppress boiling at higher operating temperatures. Under normal conditions when the collectors are warmer than the storage tank, a control turns the collection loop circulator on and circulates the coolant through the collectors. At the end of the solar heat collection period, or when the storage tank has reached its maximum set

WAYS TO AVOID SYSTEM OVERHEATING

There are a variety of strategies that can prevent overheating in indirect, filled, pressurized systems. For example, during the summer when the house will be vacant for more than 2 days, you could simply open a hot water tap a small amount and let it run until you return. Not very economical, and an egregious waste of water, but it works.

Here are some other, more sensible options:

- Run the collection loop circulator 24/7, thereby dumping heat from the solar tank through the collectors at night. This is perhaps the most sensible low-cost way of dealing with the problem.

- Install a heat waster to dump the heat. Heat wasters may be several lengths of fin-tube baseboard in the basement, a small air-handling unit, or a coil of tubing buried outside in the ground.

- Use a heat transport oil with a high boiling point in the collection loop. (This works for flat-plate collectors but not for evacuated-tube collectors.)

- Drain enough antifreeze to empty the collectors before going away and recharge the collector loop with antifreeze when you get home. This works as long as you have a convenient means of recharging the system.

- Cover the collectors (obviously easier to do when they're ground-mounted).

ACTIVE-DIRECT SYSTEM

The most common form of an active-direct (open loop) system uses a circulator to move potable water through the collector and into a storage tank.

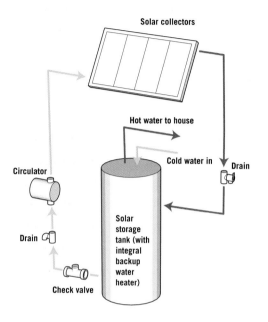

Solar collectors

Hot water to house

Cold water in

Drain

Circulator

Drain

Solar storage tank (with integral backup water heater)

Check valve

Solar domestic hot water systems can replace some, but usually not all, conventional sources of energy used to heat water. Nonetheless, compared to other types of solar systems, they will pay for themselves in avoided fuel costs in a relatively short time.

temperature, the control shuts the circulator off. When there is no demand for hot water for extended periods of summer weather, this type of system requires some provision for coping with excess solar heat. The solar collectors for these systems can use an absorber with either a grid or a serpentine flow pattern (see p. 29). Completely filled indirect systems are the most widely used system in regions of North America where freezing weather occurs.

Indirect systems that are partially filled with coolant or water are sealed but operate at or near atmospheric pressure. Under normal conditions when the collectors are warmer than the storage

tank, a control turns the circulator on and lifts the coolant to the collectors and continues circulation until the collectors cool. At the end of the solar heat collection period, or when the storage tank has reached its maximum set temperature, the control shuts the circulator off and the coolant drains out of the collectors and back to a reservoir. Air that was forced to the lower part of the system when the circulator was running moves back into the collector. Coolant remains in the reservoir until the solar tank cools or until the next sunny day.

Because it cannot overheat, this type of system (which is also called a drain-back system)

Discreet handling of exposed plumbing on this home preserves the clean lines of the house.

partially filled systems (drain-back systems) don't overheat and have fewer components to malfunction.

Active-direct systems

In an active-direct system, potable water is heated directly in the collector. A circulator moves the potable water between the collector and the storage tank.

WHERE THEY'RE USED Active-direct systems are best suited to warm climates where freezing conditions occur for no more than a few weeks a year. In the United States, they're used in Florida, Hawaii, southern California, and along the Gulf Coast. They can also be used for summer-only operation, as on vacation homes in cold climates.

HOW THEY WORK As with active-indirect systems, a control turns on a circulator to move water between the collectors and storage. The control functions in response to the temperature difference between collectors and storage. When collectors are warmer than the storage tank, the circulator runs; when the collectors cool to near storage temperature, the circulator is shut off. Storage tanks may have an integral heater or there may be a separate supplemental water heater downstream.

PROS AND CONS Active-direct systems are simpler, less costly, and easier to install than active-indirect systems and are more efficient because no heat exchanger is needed. But they're

is more reliable than the filled-pressurized system described earlier, particularly when the coolant used in the collection loop is a nontoxic antifreeze and not water. It also has fewer components. Solar collectors used with this type of system require an absorber with a grid flow pattern or serpentine flow pattern that permits drain back.

PROS AND CONS As long as the antifreeze is properly maintained, neither of these systems will freeze in cold weather, and the indirect nature of the system protects the collectors from hard or low-pH domestic water. Due to the use of a circulator, the collectors and storage can be separated by 100 ft. or more of piping. This is a distinct advantage over the passive systems described later, which require the collectors and storage to be close to one another. In addition,

ACTIVE-DIRECT WITH DRAIN-DOWN SYSTEMS

In a drain-down system, a differential thermostat turns the collection loop circulator on and off in relation to the temperature between collectors and storage, just like other active systems. The thermostat also operates motor-operated valves. The valves open to allow water to fill the collection loop when the collector temperature is safely above freezing. The valves also move to drain the collectors when a sensor at the collectors approaches the freezing temperature, or when the solar tank reaches a high limit setting. This type of system was once used in climates where freezing conditions occur.

Unfortunately, the collectors often did not drain when they were supposed to, and many collectors were damaged by freezing. Drain-down systems are not recommended in freezing climates. However, in warm climates, where freezing conditions are not a concern, the drain-down systems work well, particularly because they can drain when the storage tank gets up to the desired high limit. In this way they avoid overheating the water in the tank.

Drain-down and drain-back systems are often confused. A drain-back system uses a nonpotable coolant. When the system is off, the collectors and adjacent piping are empty. The control turns on the circulator, and the circulator lifts the coolant from the drain-back reservoir to the array and circulates it. The heated antifreeze returns to the heat exchanger in or near the solar tank. The circulator remains on until either the collector cools to near storage tank temperature or the tank reaches its high limit setting. Once the circulator shuts off, the coolant drains from the array back into the reservoir, where it remains until the solar tank cools. A drain-back system with glycol is not as efficient as a drain-down since it must transfer heat across a heat exchanger and use a transport liquid that does not transport heat as well as water, but it's much more reliable.

ACTIVE-DIRECT SYSTEM WITH DRAIN-DOWN FEATURE

In response to the outside air temperature and the solar tank temperature, a series of motor-controlled solenoid valves must change position to drain or fill the collectors.

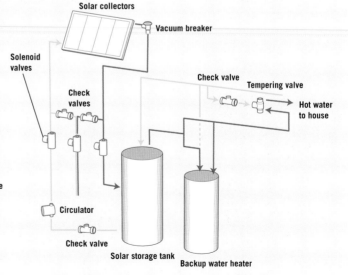

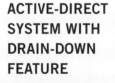

susceptible to freezing, a concern for much of North America. Limited freeze protection is typically provided by one of two methods: circulating water from the solar tank to the collectors when the temperature of the collector falls below about 45°F (7.2°C) or draining the collectors in freezing temperatures. Circulating warm water through the collectors is a reliable means of freeze protection, as long as the circulator and control work properly. But the longer that freezing conditions persist, the greater the likelihood that collectors will freeze, splitting tubing and forcing expensive repairs. Collectors and storage can be separated by 100 ft. or more of piping.

The most basic type of active-direct system is also prone to overheating. When that happens, hot water vents from a pressure and temperature relief valve, usually located at the collector outlet on the roof. Make-up water comes from the well or city main.

With a passive direct, or thermosyphon, domestic water heating system, the solar storage tank is located above the collector. Potable water fills the collectors and storage tank.

Another potential drawback is hard water. In the presence of heat, calcium carbonate precipitates out of the water and builds up as lime on the interior walls of the absorber tubing. Eventually, the lime deposits will completely obstruct the tubing, and the absorber must be replaced. One solution is to flush the collector loop every few years with a mild solution of muriatic acid.

The drain-down system, a variation on the active-direct system, is one way of preventing overheating (see the sidebar on the facing page). There also are other options.

Passive-direct systems

In a passive-direct system, potable water is heated directly in the collector and circulates between collector and storage by natural convection rather than by a circulator.

WHERE THEY'RE USED Sometimes called thermosyphon systems, passive direct is the most widely used solar water heating system type in the world. In the United States, they are used mostly in warm climates: Florida, Hawaii, southern California, and along the Gulf Coast.

HOW THEY WORK As with any passive solar water heating system, the solar storage tank must be located above the collector. When potable water in the collector is warmed by the sun, it becomes less dense and rises through piping to the storage tank. There may be an auxiliary heater in the storage tank or farther downstream.

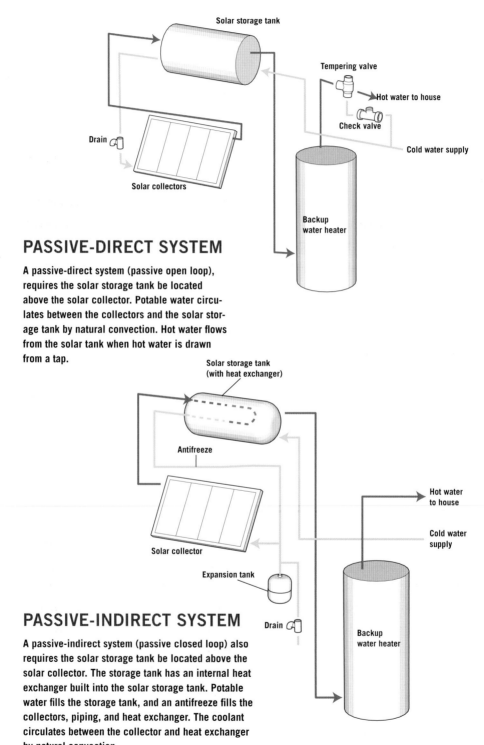

Solar storage tank

Tempering valve

Hot water to house

Check valve

Cold water supply

Drain

Solar collectors

Backup
water heater

PASSIVE-DIRECT SYSTEM

A passive-direct system (passive open loop),
requires the solar storage tank be located
above the solar collector. Potable water circulates between the collectors and the solar storage tank by natural convection. Hot water flows
from the solar tank when hot water is drawn
from a tap.

Solar storage tank
(with heat exchanger)

Antifreeze

Hot water
to house

Cold water
supply

Solar collector

Expansion tank

Drain

Backup
water heater

PASSIVE-INDIRECT SYSTEM

A passive-indirect system (passive closed loop) also
requires the solar storage tank be located above the
solar collector. The storage tank has an internal heat
exchanger built into the solar storage tank. Potable
water fills the storage tank, and an antifreeze fills the
collectors, piping, and heat exchanger. The coolant
circulates between the collector and heat exchanger
by natural convection.

PROS AND CONS Passive solar hot water systems are simpler and more efficient than active systems. There are fewer mechanical or electrical parts to worry about, and the systems are less expensive. One of the potential problems is appearance: adding an 80-gal. (302.8-L) to 120-gal. (454.2-L) storage tank to collectors already on the roof can be an aesthetic concern for many homeowners. Another concern is the potential for leaks if the storage tank is installed in an attic. A drip pan placed beneath the storage tank and plumbed to the house waste line can catch some water, but not if the tank ruptures. Experience has shown that if a water tank must be inside the building envelope, it should be as low as possible in the house, thereby making a good case for active systems. Ignore anyone who says otherwise.

Rooftop tanks also raise structural concerns. An 80-gal. (302.8-L) steel tank filled with water weighs close to 900 lb. (409 kg), and that doesn't include the weight of the collectors themselves. Since few residential roofs are designed to resist such a concentrated load, structural reinforcement is often required. Passive systems work best if the collectors and storage are separated by relatively short piping runs.

Passive-indirect systems

Similar to passive-direct systems, passive-indirect systems use a nontoxic antifreeze or a refrigerant as a collector coolant instead of water, and a heat exchanger in or near the solar storage tank.

WHERE THEY ARE USED Passive-indirect systems are used in cold weather zones where a passive-direct system might freeze.

HOW THEY WORK When an antifreeze is used as the collector coolant, the systems operate like the active-indirect filled systems, except that no circulator control or circulator is required. Circulation between collectors and storage is by natural convection, similar to the passive-direct systems already described. The storage tank must be above the solar collectors.

Another variation uses a refrigerant to transfer the sun's heat from the collectors to a heat exchanger in a nearby storage tank. At night, the refrigerant is in liquid form and nearly fills the collectors but not the piping between the collector and the storage tank. When the sun hits the collectors, the refrigerant boils and evaporates. The warmed vapor fills the piping loop between the collector and the heat exchanger, usually located inside the storage tank. There, the refrigerant vapor condenses, giving up heat to the potable water. The condensate then returns to the lower end of the collectors. The storage tank can be above or even at the same height as the collector, increasing options for tank placement.

PROS AND CONS Like other passive systems, neither of the two types requires a circulator or control. Since these systems have few parts, they are quite reliable. They are not susceptible to freezing, but the antifreeze or refrigerant charge can be lost if there is no hot water demand for prolonged periods of time. Also, most solar installers are not skilled at working with refrigerants. This type of system works best when the collectors and storage are separated by short piping runs.

Batch heaters

Batch heaters, also called integral collector storage (ICS) units, combine the collector with the storage tank in the same glazed enclosure. This feature distinguishes them from all the above types of systems, which have the collectors and storage separated.

WHERE THEY'RE USED Batch heaters are another warm climate option, best suited to Florida, Hawaii, southern California, and the Gulf Coast.

HOW THEY WORK One or more tanks, which are painted black, are placed inside a glazed, insulated box and connected to the potable water supply. When hot water is drawn, heated water from the ICS flows to the supplemental heater and then to the taps. In the words of one advocate, "Put it on the roof, add water, and it's ready to use."

PROS AND CONS Batch heaters are the simplest of all solar hot water systems and for this reason alone deserve consideration if your climate permits. While they are capable of operating in climates where freezing conditions occur, due to their design, the heat loss from them is greater than that from active systems that permit the storage tank to be placed inside a heated building. If used in freezing climates, particular care must be taken to protect the water supply and return piping where it connects to the collector and passes through the roof. Since the weight of the batch heater is much greater than that of a flat-plate collector, structural reinforcement of the roof may be needed.

Batch heaters combine the collector and storage in a single unit.

BATCH HEATER

Batch heaters combine hot water storage and the solar collector in one unit. When a hot water tap is opened, cold water flows into the batch heater and warm water from the batch heater flows into the backup heater and from there to the open tap.

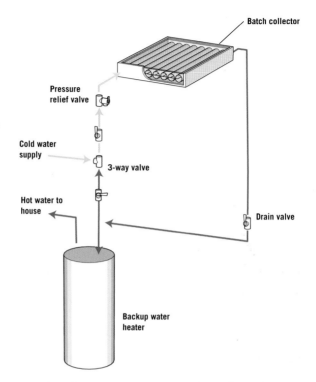

Batch collector

Pressure relief valve

Cold water supply

3-way valve

Hot water to house

Drain valve

Backup water heater

KEEP THE POOL SEPARATE

Although you may be tempted, it's not a good idea to use the same collectors for both domestic water heating and pool heating. The collector area needed to make any noticeable contribution to heating an outdoor pool is typically 50 percent to 80 percent of the pool's surface area, depending on the length of the desired swimming season. If the pool is shaded, even more collection area is needed.

For example, in the Northeast an 18-ft. (5.5-m) by 36-ft. (10.9-m) pool would require at least 324 sq. ft. (30 m²) of collector area to make a noticeable difference in the water temperature, assuming there's no shade on the pool between 9 A.M. and 3 P.M. The solar collector area for domestic water heating would typically be between 64 sq. ft. (5.9 m²) and 96 sq. ft. (8.9 m²). So heat delivered to the pool by an array used to heat domestic water would hardly be noticeable. Moreover, using solar hot water for the pool diverts it from the domestic supply, where it is needed year-round.

Some homeowners have run pool water directly through the copper absorbers of domestic water heating collectors, but unless the pH of the pool water is carefully maintained above 7.0, the pool water will turn green and the pool sidewalls will be stained green as well.

A better idea for pool heating is to use a collector specifically designed for the job (for more information, see Chapter 4).

SYSTEM COMPONENTS

At the heart of any solar system is the collector, discussed in detail in Chapter 2. Most solar hot water systems are mounted on the roof, and because skylights have become an accepted part of our roof vocabulary, many homeowners prefer their solar collectors to resemble skylights.

This means the preferred way of mounting collectors is parallel to the roof rather than tilted up from the roof, even if the tilt or orientation isn't ideal (see Optimum Tilt Angle and Orientation table on p. 43). If the reduction in collector output is too large due to a low-tilt roof, collectors can be tilted up for optimum exposure or an additional collector can be added to the parallel mounted array.

To truly look like a skylight, of course, the collectors would have to be mounted flush, or integral, to the roof. However, 35 years of experience have shown that roof leaks will often develop around such arrays, and that these are far more costly to repair than leaks in the roof around collectors that are not installed flush with the roof. Instead, parallel-to-roof mounts should hold the backside of the collector 3 in. (7.62 cm)

 THE LONGEVITY OF SDHW COMPONENTS VARIES but most well-made flat-plate collectors installed in the mid-1970s are in excellent condition after more than 35 years of service and should last at least another 20 years. Storage tanks don't do as well. Their average life is between 10 years and 15 years.

to 4 in. (10.2 cm) above the roof surface with a conventional roof membrane under the collectors.

In climates where freezing conditions occur for more than a few weeks a year, liquid-cooled flat-plate or evacuated-tube collectors can be used for domestic water heating, although the use of flat-plate collectors far outweighs that of the evacuated-tube type. In warm climates, flat-plate collectors are used almost exclusively for solar hot water.

Generally, collectors used in climates where little or no freezing occurs require no more than a flat black coating on the collector absorber. In temperate and cold climates, it makes sense to use flat-plate collectors with a selective coating on the absorber plate. Although they are more expensive than those with a flat black coating, they are also a lot more efficient during cold weather.

To a limited degree, evacuated-tube collectors also are used for domestic water heating. The evacuated-tube collector is claimed to have a higher efficiency than flat-plate collectors because the absorber is surrounded by a vacuum, thus minimizing heat losses. The evacuated-tube collector is presently about twice the cost of a flat-plate collector of the same area.

In addition to its higher cost, an extensive literature search of long-term, third-party test results indicates that, for domestic water heating, evacuated-tube collectors are slightly less efficient than flat-plate collectors (see p. 27 for a chart comparing evacuated-tube collectors with flat-plate collectors). In part, the explanation for this is the tendency of evacuated-tube collectors, due to their excellent insulation, to retain frost and snow cover for longer periods than flat-plate collectors. Tilting evacuated-tube collectors at a

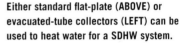
Either standard flat-plate (ABOVE) or evacuated-tube collectors (LEFT) can be used to heat water for a SDHW system.

higher tilt than is normally used for flat-plate collectors has shown some benefit in shedding snow. A minimum tilt of 55 degrees from the horizontal is recommended.

For extended periods of overcast or partially overcast skies during the winter months, the evacuated-tube collector, when it is not snow-covered, does have an edge over the flat plate. All of this is to say that, contrary to popular belief, evacuated-tube collectors are neither more efficient nor more cost-effective for domestic water heating applications. They do, however, have their place where extended periods of overcast weather occur and, when installed at higher tilts, where higher temperatures are required, such as for industrial processes.

Solar hot water systems have a number of other key components as well, although not all of those listed here are needed in every type of system.

Solar hot water storage tanks

There are two ways to store heat from a solar hot water system. The more common approach is to use a pressurized tank containing potable water that's heated by the solar array. This type of tank is used in all direct systems and in most indirect systems as well. The second approach is to use an unpressurized tank containing nonpotable water heated by the solar array. Potable water passes through a heat exchanger either inside or outside the tank. In North America, unpressurized tanks are used only with indirect systems.

Most SDHW systems include both a solar storage tank (A) and a supplemental water heater (B).

coolant to the potable water in the tank. Alternatively, a less costly tank with no internal heat exchanger can be used, in which case an external heat exchanger with a second circulator may be used. Both configurations are widely used.

Pressurized tanks are usually designed so that cold water from the well or city main enters at the bottom. Solar heated potable water leaves at the top. The hot outlet of the solar tank is usually piped to the cold water inlet of a supplemental heater. Two-tank systems are the norm for SDHW system retrofits.

Pressurized solar tanks are also available with internal supplemental heating coils. The supplemental heating coil may be a simple electric element or a coil filled with water heated in a boiler. These tanks are sometimes used in new construction for single-tank systems where they serve two functions: storing solar heated water and boosting the water temperature as needed. They also can be used for retrofits where there isn't room for two tanks. Single-tank systems are somewhat less efficient than two-tank systems.

If the solar array is large enough, the supplemental heater can be shut off and bypassed during the summer. This can represent a considerable savings, particularly when the supplemental heater is inefficient.

PRESSURIZED TANKS Pressurized solar tanks are available with or without internal heat-exchange coils. A storage-type electric water heater is a good example of the former, and an indirect water heater, such as that used to heat water with a fuel-fired boiler, is an example of the latter. In direct-type solar water heating systems, storage-type electric water heaters are commonly used to store the solar-heated water because a tank without an internal heat exchanger is required. The electric element, which adds little to the tank cost, may or may not be connected to a circuit.

Where indirect solar water heating systems are used, a tank with an internal heat exchanger can be used to transfer heat from the collector

UNPRESSURIZED TANKS The appeal of an unpressurized tank is lower cost. Practically any type of insulated, watertight container can work: lined fiberglass, stainless steel, even concrete with an epoxy or rubber lining.

The tank is filled with water that simply sits there for the life of the tank. That water is heated by the solar array and cooled by the circulation of domestic water. In one configuration, water in the tank is heated by the solar array, either directly or indirectly. A heat-exchange coil filled with potable water is immersed in the water in the upper part of the unpressurized tank. When there's a demand for hot water, the potable water flows through the coil, to a supplemental heater and from there to the hot water taps. With this type of storage, it's rare that a supplemental heater can be bypassed.

Homeowners frequently ask, "We don't use much hot water, so can't we use a much smaller tank than the standard tanks you offer?" What most folks don't understand is that for efficient operation, the collector area and the tank size are related. Typically, the tank volume in gallons should be 1.5 times to 2 times the collector area in square feet. A tank that's too small for the collector area makes the system less efficient, and both the collector coolant and the domestic water will run very hot.

Supplemental water heaters

Virtually all types of SDHW systems used year-round must have a supplemental source of heat. Supplemental water heaters (sometimes called backup water heaters) are used to boost the temperature of water from the solar tank. Backup heaters can be direct-fired gas, oil, or electric tanks, or instantaneous (on-demand) type.

Piping

In virtually all solar hot water systems, supply and return piping runs between the collector array and storage tank, and the best piping has proved to be smooth copper tubing.

In a direct system, type-L copper tube is usually required by code because its thicker walls are more resistant to corrosion, particularly from acidic water. For indirect systems, piping carrying the antifreeze can be the thinner type-M tubing, but for the potable water side of these systems, type-L tubing should be used.

Neither corrugated flexible copper tubing nor plastic tubing has performed as well in the solar collection loop. Corrugated copper tubing shows a tendency to develop leaks over time. Manufacturers of plastic tubing say their products will not withstand the few, brief surges that may send 300°F (149°C) and 100 psi (6.8 bar) coolant through the piping. Steel piping is suitable, but it's more labor intensive to install and is rarely found in residential systems. Plastic piping or tubing is safe to use on the water side of these systems.

Collector coolants

In direct systems, potable water is the coolant used to transport heat from the collectors to the storage tank. In indirect systems, some type of nonpotable liquid is used to transport heat from the collectors to the storage tank. A variety of liquids have been used, including glycols, deionized water, silicone, and petroleum-based oils. The most common is a mixture of inhibited propylene glycol and water, a nontoxic antifreeze. In systems with vented double-wall heat exchangers, ethylene glycol (a toxic antifreeze) has been used successfully.

Deionized water has been used in some drain-back systems. Water transports heat better than does antifreeze, but of course it can points, but neither is as good at transporting heat as a glycol and water solution, and both are more expensive.

Expansion tanks

Coolant expansion tanks are required in indirect filled closed systems to cope with the expansion and contraction of the collector fluid and to maintain near constant pressure in the system. Expansion tanks are not required in direct systems or in drain-back systems, where the large volume of air in the piping allows plenty of room for expansion and contraction. A different type of expansion tank is also required on the potable water side of many solar domestic hot water systems to allow for the thermal expansion of heated potable water in the solar tanks.

Heat exchanger

Heat exchangers are essential components of indirect systems. They transfer heat from the collector coolant to potable water. As noted above, a solar tank can be purchased with or without an internal heat exchanger. Tanks with internal exchangers cost more, but a single collection loop circulator can be used, which offsets some of the cost.

Expansion tanks are commonly used to help maintain a constant pressure in filled indirect SDHW systems.

freeze. Propylene glycol is a better choice than water in drain-back systems because it eliminates any risk of freeze damage in the event of a control malfunction. Silicone oil and another oil called Bray oil were used in the 1970s and 1980s due to their high boiling

Throughout my 35 years of experience with SDHW systems, the only piping material that has consistently served well in the collection loop is rigid or soft smooth copper. —E.B.

Inside a copper-brazed heat exchanger, heat carried by the collector coolant is transferred to potable water. Shown here is the CB range of brazed-plate heat exchangers from Alfa Laval.

If the tank does not have an internal heat exchanger, an external heat exchanger can be installed. This type of tank is less expensive but a second circulator is usually required between the tank and the heat exchanger to circulate potable water between the tank and the heat exchanger. A few system designs use natural convection to move potable water through the heat exchanger. Also, several tank manufacturers make a tank with a heat-exchange coil wrapped around the exterior of the tank. These tanks have a relatively small heat-exchange surface area compared to tanks with internal heat exchangers.

Circulator

Circulators (also called pumps) are required in active systems, both direct and indirect, to circulate water or antifreeze between the collectors and storage tank. Circulators may use alternating current (a.c.) or direct current (d.c.). The a.c.-powered circulators are by far the more common. The d.c. circulators are usually powered by small solar electric collectors.

Circulators that move potable water usually have impeller housings made from bronze or stainless steel. Cast-iron housings tend to rust in the presence of potable water. When the circulator moves nontoxic antifreeze, the housing can be cast iron, meaning lower cost.

PREASSEMBLED CIRCULATOR MODULES

Most imported preassembled SDHW systems sold in the United States have a circulator module (also called a pump module) that serves a number of functions. It includes the circulator, differential thermostat, temperature indicators, ports for charging the system, check valve, pressure gauge, relief valve, and drain valves.

Most of these individual components are needed in active-indirect filled systems, and having them all in one place simplifies installation (and permits the use of less experienced installers). The downsides to using the modules are higher cost and more difficult service. In addition, components are often not in U.S. pipe sizes, so finding replacement parts may not be easy.

Any *experienced* domestic SDHW integrator can provide the same system with U.S.-made components for less money, and it will be easier to service.

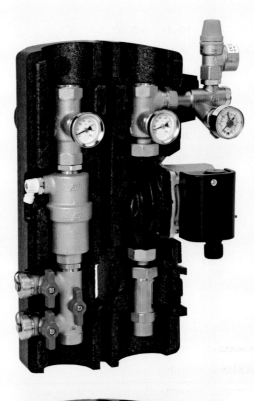

Preassembled circulator modules neatly package various components, including differential control, circulator, gauges, and valves, in a single unit. The unit is shown with the cover off and on.

Backflow preventer

Indirect systems require a backflow preventer so nonpotable liquid can't be drawn into the city water main when there's a loss of main pressure and a leak in the heat exchanger. If a vented double-wall heat exchanger is used, some municipalities do not require a backflow preventer. Before having a system installed, check with a local code official or the water department.

Thermostatic mixing valves

All SDHW systems require thermostatic mixing valves. The temperature in a solar tank during the summer can easily reach 160°F (71.1°C) to 180°F (82.2°C), well above the minimum temperature needed to scald. Most plumbing codes require a thermostatic mixing valve in the hot outlet of the solar tank to limit the maximum temperature of the water flowing from the solar tank to an open hot water tap. The valve automatically blends cold water with hot until the outgoing water reaches the desired temperature.

Supplemental heater bypass

Having some means of bypassing the supplemental heater is a requirement for all SDHW systems that are designed to provide 100 percent of domestic hot water for more than 1 month a year. Bypassing the supplemental heater and shutting it off is better than simply shutting it off because standby losses in the tank will be avoided. A quarter-turn manual, three-way valve is the best option. It allows one to divert the flow of solar heated water around the supplemental heater and is less confusing to the homeowner than having a number of two-way valves.

TOP: A backflow preventer is usually required on indirect SDHW systems because they use nonpotable coolants as heat-transfer liquids. MIDDLE: A mixing valve is required on all solar water heating systems because it prevents scalding water from reaching the tap by adding cold water to the hot water leaving the tank. BOTTOM: Three-way valves allow homeowners to manually bypass their supplemental water heater during the period of the year when it is not needed.

Isolation valves

Two-way valves for isolating key components make repairs or replacement possible without draining the entire system. Isolation valves with a bypass around the solar tank and isolation valves with a bypass around the supplemental heater may seem an unnecessary expense at the time the system is installed. But when the solar tank or supplemental heater leaks (and all tanks leak, some just sooner than others, and they always seem to leak at 2 A.M.), they will quickly seem like a very good idea.

An AC collection loop control

Active systems using AC-powered circulators, the most common configuration, require some means of controlling the circulator in the solar heat collection loop. The typical differential control activates the circulator when the collector is about 20°F (11.1°C) hotter than the storage tank. It shuts the circulator off when the collector cools to within 4°F (2.2°C) to 5°F (2.7°C) above the storage tank. The control also has a high limit feature, which stops circulation when the solar tank has reached a predetermined limit, typically 160°F (71.1°C).

A DC collection loop control

An alternative to the AC circulator and control is a DC circulator powered by a solar electric module. The main advantage is a savings of AC electricity, which can be anywhere between 3 percent and 15 percent of the energy collected. The disadvantages are higher equipment costs and the absence of any high limit temperature control. The circulator runs when there's enough sunlight hitting the module to operate it. When

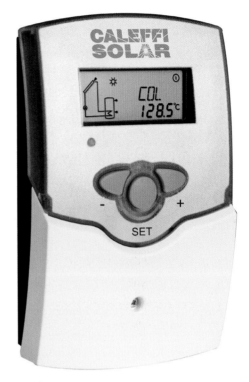

In all active SDHW systems, a differential thermostat automatically starts and stops circulation of coolant between the collectors and storage.

there is no hot water demand, the solar electric module continues to power the circulator, moving heat from the solar array to the storage tank. In the absence of a demand for hot water over several days or more, the tank temperature ratchets upward until the relief valve on the tank opens, venting very hot water from the tank onto the floor. Pressure also can build up in the collection loop to the point that collection fluid is lost through the relief valve. One manufacturer offers an AC adapter for its DC circulator. The adapter can be plugged into an AC outlet to run the circulator 24/7, dumping excess heat from the storage tank at night through the collector, until the period of low hot water demand or high incident solar radiation has passed.

THE ECONOMICS
OF SOLAR HOT WATER

Many variables affect potential savings in a SDHW system. One is the price of conventional fuels that would otherwise be used to heat domestic water. Electricity varies in price across the United States from about 7¢ to 25¢ per kilowatt hour. Natural gas varies from about 70¢ to $2 per hundred cubic feet (2.83 m³).

Future energy costs are difficult to project but have much to do with the economics of these systems. Before 2000, the 30-year rate of fuel cost increases in the United States was between 5 percent and 7 percent per year, depending on the fuel. Since 2000, the rate has been much higher. For instance, between 2000 and 2008,

fuel oil increased at nearly 15 percent per year. That's a doubling time of 5 years (see "Calculating Payback," below).

A variety of other factors affect potential savings, including how much hot water is consumed, the size of the system, the climate, and the efficiency of the supplemental water heater. As a result, the installed cost of a solar system varies by region: $2,500 to $4,000 in Florida but between $10,000 and $12,000 in the Northeast. (These figures are before incentives.)

To determine the extent to which a solar domestic hot water system will reduce your energy use, check the tables for a scenario that reflects your locale and hot water use.

Calculating Payback

Just how long it takes to recoup the cost of installing a solar domestic water heating system depends on a number of factors, including the installed cost of the system and the annual rate of increase in the cost of fuel the system displaces. These estimates for a household in Hartford, Connecticut, assume hot water usage of 20 gal. (75.7 L) per person per day with collectors measuring 64 sq. ft. *(Analysis by: Everett M. Barber Jr.)*

YEARS TO PAYBACK

	ANNUAL RATE OF FUEL COST INCREASE		
Installed cost	5%*	10%	15%
$100/sq. ft.	7	6	6
$120/sq. ft.	9	8	7
$140/sq. ft.	11	9	8
$160/sq. ft.	12	10	8
Estimated annual savings (year 1)	$522	$522	$522
Estimated annual savings (year 10)	$810	$1,231	$1,837

* 1970 to 2000 rate for CT 5.1% (EIA data); 2000-2008: 7.4% CL&P. Assumes homeowners paid cash for system, includes 30% federal tax credit.

SIZING A SYSTEM
FOR YOUR NEEDS

A solar water heating system delivers energy in relation to its size, efficiency, water demand, and local climate. Generally speaking, if a solar water heating system is sized on the small side, so that it never meets more than 99 percent of the monthly hot water load, you're assured the collectors are fully used year-round. Thus you're getting the maximum work out of the system (but not necessarily the maximum savings).

If, on the other hand, a solar water heating system provides 100 percent of the hot water demand for several months of the year or more, there are many hours when the collectors are not fully used because there's no practical way to store all of the heat that is collected. The more months of the year the system provides 100 percent of the hot water load, the greater the percentage of time the collectors are being underused.

However, the larger system may yield greater savings. A key factor is the efficiency of the system's supplemental water heater. If it's very efficient—an electric resistance-type instantaneous heater (99 percent), for example—a solar system large enough to supply all the hot water for several months a year (or more) doesn't make economic sense. However, if the supplemental heater is very inefficient—a tank-less coil in an oil- or gas-fired boiler (15 percent to 25 percent efficient), for example—then the larger system makes good economic sense.

The tables we've included on p. 76 will help you determine the collector area and tank size you will need for two common scenarios: In the first, the system provides no more than 100 percent of hot water needs for 1 month of the year. In the second scenario, the system provides 100 percent of hot water needs for 4 months or more per year. The tables allow you to make your selection based on the climatic region in which you live and the number of hot water users in your home.

If the solar system is to go into an existing home, the installer usually has to work with the water heater that's already there. Between 40 percent and 45 percent of the space heating systems in the northern tier of the country use dual-function boilers (meaning the appliance heats the house and the domestic water). In these cases, a larger solar system makes sense because it saves the owner the expense of operating an inefficient boiler during the summer just for hot water. For the months the boiler is used for space heating and domestic hot water, the efficiency of domestic water heating is reasonably high, 75 percent to 80 percent.

Aside from those in the northern-tier states, most houses in the United States have natural gas or electric tank-type water heaters. Low-efficiency (50 percent to 60 percent) gas-fired, storage-type water heaters are candidates for larger solar water heating systems but not quite so compelling a candidate as when the water heating efficiency is 15 percent to 25 percent. Local natural gas prices have a lot to do with the exact economics. Since storage-type, electric water heaters are relatively efficient (82 percent to 95 percent), the smaller solar water heating system is the better choice when used with them.

To find out the efficiency of a new water heater, see the Gas Appliance Manufacturers Association Directory (GAMA) of water heaters.

Because GAMA has merged with the Air-Conditioning, Heating, and Refrigeration Institute (AHRI), you'll need to access it at www.ahrinet.org. The GAMA directory lists only the latest products that are on the market. Older appliances will almost undoubtedly have a lower efficiency than those listed in the directory.

SYSTEM MAINTENANCE

Most solar hot water systems require little maintenance, but there are a few things to check from time to time.

All systems

🏠 Perhaps once a year, if you have easy access to the collectors, use the touch test. On a sunny day, between about 11 A.M. and 2 P.M., put your hand on the cover glass; the cover should be cool to the touch if the system is collecting heat. If the glass is hot, the system is probably not working properly and should be serviced. However, many circulator controls have a high limit setting, thus the circulator may have been shut off automatically if the solar tank is quite hot. In that case, the glass cover will feel hot and there may not be a problem. If you don't have easy access to the collectors, use the first technique listed below for active systems.

🏠 If you live in a dry climate or a place where wildfires are common, such as southern California, it is worth the trouble to hose off the collector covers once or twice a year. In most parts of the country where rainfall is more common, Nature will do it for you.

🏠 As you should with any water tank, occasionally look for signs of dampness on the floor, or even water at the base of the tank, which usually indicates a tank leak. A leaky tank must be replaced, since, after a time, a small leak can turn into a tank rupture.

🏠 Nearly all manufacturers of storage-type domestic water heaters recommend that tanks be flushed once a year. It's a good idea. If you don't know how, ask a plumber to show you.

Active systems

🏠 Once a year, confirm that the collection loop is heating the tank. This can be done by putting your hand on the brass tank

SHOULD YOU REPLACE YOUR EXISTING WATER HEATER?

If you have an old or inefficient water heater, you should consider replacing it when your solar hot water system is installed. Most homeowners tend not to replace water heaters unless they leak ("If it ain't broke, don't fix it"). Once you have a plumber on the premises, however, and assuming it's within your budget, it makes sense to replace a water heater that's 10 years to 12 years old. If access to your existing water heater will be blocked by the new solar tank, there's another good reason for a new conventional water heater.

Sizing a Solar Hot Water System

These two tables provide array and tank sizing guidelines for solar domestic water heating (SDWH) systems for four cities in the U.S. Use the "Small Solar Fraction" chart if your supplemental heater is efficient, such as an electric storage-type or gas tankless heater. Use the "Large Solar Fraction" chart if your supplemental heater is relatively inefficient, such as a storage-type, direct-fired, oil or gas water heater; an instantaneous (tankless coil) heater in an oil- or gas-fired boiler; or an indirect-fired water heater heated by an oil- or gas-fired boiler. *(Adapted from F-Chart by Emaan Ammar.)*

SMALL SOLAR FRACTION
INDIRECT SYSTEMS (sized to provide no more than 1 month of 100% of hot water requirement)

CLIMATE (data for given city)	NUMBER OF HOT WATER USERS IN HOUSEHOLD collector area sq. ft./gal. storage (max. solar fraction)					
	2	3	4	5	6	7
Northeast (Hartford, CT)	40/80 (0.82)	64/80 (0.89)	80/120 (0.90)	80/120 (0.83)	96/120 (0.83)	120/160 (0.87)
Southeast (Atlanta, GA)	40/80 (0.90)	64/80 (0.96)	64/80 (0.91)	80/120 (0.94)	80/120 (0.89)	80/120 (0.84)
Southwest (Albuquerque, NM)	42/80 (0.99)	40/80 (0.92)	64/80 (0.99)	64/80 (0.92)	64/80 (0.85)	80/120 (0.90)
Northwest (Eugene, OR)	40/80 (0.93)	64/80 (0.98)	80/120 (0.95)	80/120 (0.93)	80/120 (0.87)	120/160 (0.97)

LARGE SOLAR FRACTION
INDIRECT SYSTEMS (sized to provide 4 or more months of 100% of hot water requirement)

CLIMATE (data for given city)	NUMBER OF HOT WATER USERS IN HOUSEHOLD collector area sq. ft./gallon storage (months @ 100%)					
	2	3	4	5	6	7
Northeast (Hartford, CT)	80/120 (5)	96/120 (4)	128/240 (4)	160/240 (4)	160/240 (4)	200/320 (4)
Southeast (Atlanta, GA)	64/80 (5)	80/120 (5)	120/160 (5)	120/160 (5)	120/160 (5)	160/240 (4)
Southwest (Albuquerque, NM)	40/80 (4)	64/80 (4)	80/120 (5)	80/120 (4)	96/120 (4)	120/160 (5)
Northwest (Eugene, OR)	80/120 (4)	120/160 (5)	128/240 (4)	128/240 (4)	160/240 (4)	200/320 (5)

COLLECTOR AREA: Table based on most common U.S. collector module sizes: 3 ft. x 7 ft., 4 ft. x 8 ft., 4ft. x 10 ft.

SOLAR TANK SIZE: Most common solar tank size increments are 80 and 120 gal. The smallest storage to collector area ratio to use is 1.25:1 (as 80 gal./64 sq. ft.). As a rule, try to use no less than 1.5 gal./sq. ft. of collector, and no more than 2.0 gal./.sq. ft.

CAVEAT: The above collector areas and tank volumes are based on the computer model F-Chart. From years of experience with SDHW systems, we believe these figures to be conservative.

METRIC EQUIVALENTS

COLLECTOR SIZES								
sq. ft.	40	64	80	96	120	128	160	200
m²	3.7	5.9	7.4	8.9	11	12	15	19
TANK SIZES								
gal	80	120	160	240	320			
L	303	454	606	908	1211			

relief valve near the end of a clear day during which little or no hot water was used. Be careful, the valve may be quite hot! Use a lot of hot water at the start of the day so the tank starts the test period cool or cold. If the tank has a separate internal heater, such as an electric element, be sure that it is turned off for 12 hours before making the test. If the brass relief valve is warm or hot, then the system is collecting heat.

- Once a year, check the collection loop circulator at night, several hours after dark. The circulator should not be running. However, on a warm summer night when someone used hot water earlier in the evening, incoming cold water may have chilled the bottom of the solar tank and the control may turn the circulator on for 5 minutes to 10 minutes.

- If your house has experienced a power surge, such that the computer modem, garage door operator, or DVD player has been damaged, then the solar system circulator may have been damaged as well. Check the collection loop circulator at night; if the circulator is running, the control may have been damaged. Check the control on a sunny day in the late morning; if the circulator is not running, the control may have been damaged.

- If there is heavy snow cover, and the collectors can be accessed from the ground with a snow rake, use the rake to pull the snow cover off the collectors. If the snow cover is no more than 5 in. (12.7 cm) to 6 in. (15.2 cm), the sun will do the work for you in a day or two. Don't use a snow rake on evacuated-tube collectors. They may break.

Other systems

- **ACTIVE-INDIRECT (PRESSURIZED) SYSTEMS:** Every 6 months or so, check the pressure gauge on the collection loop some time after dark or early in the morning before the sun starts to heat the collectors. If the gauge pressure reads below about 10 psi (0.68 bar), service is probably needed to boost the coolant pressure and look for a leak.

- **ALL DIRECT SYSTEMS:** If there has been a particularly cold spell with below-freezing temperatures, listen for the sound of running water in the piping. It is possible the collectors or exposed piping on the roof have frozen. If that is the case, the sound of water running in the piping will be evident once the ice thaws.

- **ALL SYSTEMS:** If at the end of a clear, summer day, the hot water coming from the hot tap is too hot, run hot water from a tub faucet for 15 minutes to cool off the solar tank somewhat. Request service to have the temperature mixing valve checked.

4 SOLAR POOL HEATING

For most homeowners, installing a swimming pool is a big investment. Consequently, anything they can do to extend their enjoyment of the pool is an attractive proposition. That's why so many pools are heated. The only problem with heating a pool is the expense. In most parts of the country, the cost of heating a pool with a conventional heater can be several times the cost of heating the house.

There are far more cost-effective ways to maintain comfortable pool water temperatures than by using conventional pool heaters. Three solar options discussed in this chapter are:

🏠 a solar pool cover

🏠 a solar thermal pool heating system

🏠 a solar electric–assisted heat pump pool heater

Regardless of the pool type, conservation should be your first step because it will reduce the size of the solar system required to keep the pool comfortable (see the sidebar on p. 82).

An active solar pool heating system will extend the swimming season and save you thousands of dollars over the life of the system when compared to a conventional pool heater.

LEFT: A pool cover warms the water only if you use it. A reel, either manually or automatic, greatly increases the likelihood that the cover will be used.

BELOW: In warm climates such as southern Florida, a solar pool heating system can heat the pool during the cooler months and cool the pool during the hotter months.

ABOVE: For above-ground pools, collector arrays can be mounted beside the south-facing wall of the pool. RIGHT: Solar pool covers are a heavier weight version of plastic bubble wrap used for shipping. The material can be cut to fit the shape of the pool.

A PASSIVE APPROACH: SOLAR POOL COVERS

The simplest way to heat a pool with the sun is by direct gain. Let the sun shine on the pool's surface, and the water will heat up. Unfortunately, the heat is continually lost to the surroundings and once the sun goes down, the water temperature can drop by several degrees overnight. One remedy is a solar pool cover, also called a pool blanket or solar cover.

A pool blanket helps retain heat that would otherwise be lost to radiation, convection, and evaporation. Even in cool climates, a cover will extend the swimming season by 4 weeks to 6 weeks. And because they reduce evaporation, pool blankets also reduce the need for make-up water by 30 percent to 50 percent and cut consumption of pool chemicals by 35 percent to 60 percent, according to the U.S. Department of Energy (DOE). To be most effective, the blanket

should fit tightly at the pool's perimeter. And, of course, the pool blanket should be in use, rather than left sitting on the grass beside the pool.

Pool blankets are available in several types, including bubble, vinyl, and insulated vinyl. The bubble type can be fitted to any type, size, or shape pool. Made of UV-stabilized polyethylene or polypropylene plastic, these blankets look somewhat like bubble wrap used for packing but they are not as thick and are made of a much heavier gauge material. They increase the average pool water temperature (over an uncovered pool) by between 4°F (2.2°C) and 5°F (2.7°C) and possibly more.

Bubble covers range in thickness from 8 mils to 16 mils. Buy a heavy, 16-mil product for better durability and a longer warranty. Colors include blue, blue-silver, clear, and translucent black. Clear covers do the best job because they allow more radiation to reach the water. Bubbles can

THREE TYPES OF POOL COVERS

Bubble-type covers allow more solar radiation to reach the pool water and cost less, but they don't last as long as vinyl covers.

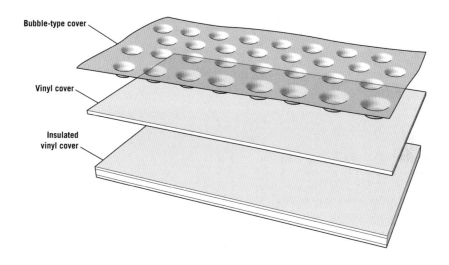

Bubble-type cover

Vinyl cover

Insulated vinyl cover

be round or diamond-shaped, with the latter purportedly insulating slightly more effectively. Prices range from about 15¢ to 30¢ per square foot ($1.61 to $3.22 per square meter). Manually operated cover reels are available for bubble covers (discussed on pp. 84–85).

Vinyl covers

Vinyl covers are stronger and made of a heavier-gauge material than bubble covers, but they are considerably more expensive—about $1 per square foot ($10.76 per square meter). They reduce evaporation but are opaque, so they don't absorb as much solar radiation as a bubble cover. Whereas a bubble cover reduces transmitted radiation by only 5 percent to 15 percent, an

BUBBLE-TYPE COVERS are not intended for use as winter pool covers. In winter, a vinyl cover must be used to keep your pool clean and reduce evaporation.

opaque vinyl cover will reduce it by 20 percent to 40 percent, according to the DOE.

Vinyl covers, however, offer several benefits. First, they can be used year-round. Second, they can be deployed and retracted automatically. In cases in which you want to prevent a pool from becoming too warm, a definite problem in the southern parts of the United States, vinyl covers can limit solar gain. Finally, they offer a greater measure of safety. When secured by tracks along the sides of the pool or to the pool decking, a

(continued on p. 84)

CONSERVATION FIRST

It comes as a surprise to many first-time pool owners that heating an in-ground pool often uses more heat than heating a house in a cold climate, so being conservation-minded can have a big impact on the size of the solar system you must buy. Here are some tips.

FOR OUTDOOR POOLS

🏠 Site your pool where it will receive as many hours of direct sun as possible. The entire surface should get full sun from at least 9 A.M. to 3 P.M., and preferably from 8 A.M. to 4 P.M.

🏠 If necessary, remove tree limbs or trees that shade the pool. Any amount of shade on the pool water surface will diminish the pool water temperature. If shade from a neighbor's trees will affect your pool, see if it's possible to negotiate a solution before you have the pool installed. Offering to let them swim in your pool might be an inducement, for example.

🏠 Plant shrubs around the pool to minimize wind across the surface, thereby reducing evaporation, the primary way that pools lose heat.

🏠 If possible, avoid the use of infinity or horizon pools or pools with waterfall hot tubs. Both act as evaporative coolers for the pool water, greatly increasing the energy required to heat the pool.

FOR INDOOR POOLS

🏠 Allow humidity levels in the pool room to go as high as possible without causing condensation. That will reduce heat loss from the pool. However, be mindful that if condensation occurs it is very likely to cause damage to the structure.

🏠 Don't try to heat the pool room with the pool water. That will not result in any savings and will greatly increase the rate of evaporation from the pool.

FOR BOTH INDOOR AND OUTDOOR POOLS

🏠 Use a solar pool cover. For indoor pools, keep the cover on the pool at all times when the pool is not in use.

🏠 Use a high-efficiency motor to power the filter pump.

🏠 Buy a new filter pump that requires less energy. In recent years, the major pool equipment manufacturers have begun to offer pumps and other equipment that can significantly reduce the electricity needed to keep the pool water clear.

HOW INDOOR POOLS LOSE ENERGY

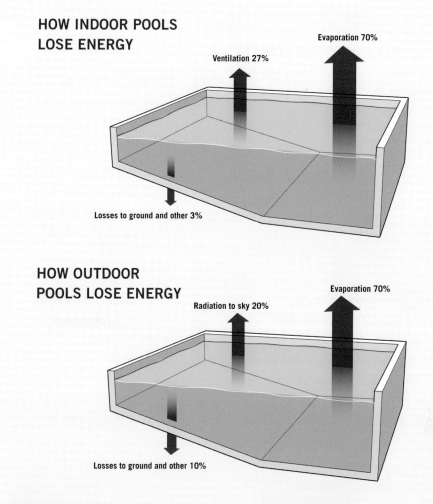

Evaporation 70%

Ventilation 27%

Losses to ground and other 3%

HOW OUTDOOR POOLS LOSE ENERGY

Evaporation 70%

Radiation to sky 20%

Losses to ground and other 10%

A solar pool heating system used in combination with a pool blanket will help bring pool water to the desired temperature faster than without the blanket.

(continued from p. 81)

vinyl cover can easily support the weight of a person.

Insulated vinyl covers have a thin layer of flexible insulation sandwiched between two layers of vinyl. This, of course, slightly improves the R-value of the cover. Otherwise, they are similar to the plain vinyl covers. Insulated covers cost $2 to $3 per square foot ($21.50 to $32.25 per square meter).

Solar pool cover reels

Most prospective pool owners dream of being able to walk out the door and jump into their pool any time of day or night. Having to remove a pool cover first does not jibe well with that dream. In fact, a surprising number of pool owners will pay many thousands of dollars for a pool heater and many more thousands a year to heat the pool just to avoid having to use the cover.

A solar pool cover is much more likely to be used if it is mounted on a reel, and even more likely to be used if the reel is motorized. Without a reel, the cover is awkward to retract or deploy, takes up space around the pool, picks up grass clippings and leaves, and will kill grass if left on the lawn too long.

Reels for above-ground pools are operated by a hand crank or wheel. They are typically portable, with brackets that have wheels or casters, and range in price from $150 to $600. Reels for in-ground or indoor pools may be portable or permanently mounted. They can be manually operated by a crank or motor-operated with the

ABOVE TOP: Irregularly shaped pools can be covered with a rectangular vinyl cover that runs in tracks set into the deck. ABOVE BOTTOM: An added benefit to vinyl covers is that because they can support the weight of an adult, they help lessen the risk of accidental drownings.

push of a button. Semiautomatic covers have motor-driven reels that roll up the cover automatically but usually require operator assistance when unrolling the cover. A fully automatic cover has a motor-driven reel that both covers and uncovers the pool automatically. The latter is the easiest to use but also the most expensive option. Automatic covers begin at $5,000.

SOLAR THERMAL POOL HEATING

Available since at least the early 1970s, solar thermal pool heating systems are well proven and widely used. Over a 25-year period, they are the least costly way to heat a pool. Like solar domestic water heating systems, pool-heating systems use liquid-cooled collectors to heat water or glycol. But instead of storing the captured heat in a tank, the swimming pool itself is the heat storage.

Pool-heating collectors for outdoor pools are usually unglazed and made of a lightweight, durable polymer. Pool water can be circulated directly through the collector. No antifreeze or heat exchanger is needed. When heating an indoor pool, the need for heat is usually year-round so collectors for indoor pools are often glazed. They're basically identical to the collectors used for domestic water heating.

Glazed flat-plate collectors also are used to heat the pool when the house has a liquid-cooled solar space heating system. By using the same array to heat the house during the winter months and the pool during the summer, the solar system economics improve significantly.

Whether heating indoor pools or outdoor pools with a solar space heating system, an antifreeze is typically used in the collector loop and a heat exchanger is required to transfer heat from antifreeze to the pool water. A drain-back, indirect type collection loop should be used for this type of system so it can cope with many hours of no demand for heat.

SOLAR ELECTRIC– ASSISTED HEAT PUMPS

A relatively new approach to pool heating, solar electric–assisted heat pump systems use an array of solar electric collectors to power a heat pump pool heater, either air source or ground source, which in turn heats the pool water.

Although more costly than a solar thermal system, this approach is gradually increasing in use. Homeowners and architects who don't like the look of big solar thermal arrays may find the appearance of solar electric collectors more appealing. Yet another benefit is that the solar electric array can be sized large enough to power the pool filter pump as well, something that a thermal array cannot do.

How Much Will It Cost to Keep the Pool Warm?

To estimate how much you would spend heating a pool with a conventional gas or heat pump heater, select your city, or one with a similar climate. Then select the energy rate that most closely matches what you pay. The costs shown are for heating a 1,000-sq.-ft. pool to 80°F. For the heat pump, a coefficient of performance of 3.0 is assumed. Adjust the table value given for your locality to the size of pool that you have. (Different rates are given since energy prices vary significantly across the U.S.)

For example, to determine the cost of heating an 18-ft. x 36-ft. pool in Miami with gas at $1.00/therm, determine the ratio of the pool's area to 1,000 sq. ft. (648 sq. ft. ÷1,000 sq .ft. = 0.648), and multiply this ratio by $5,696 to get the adjusted heating cost of $3,691.

(Adapted from www.energysavers.gov by Emaan Ammar.)

NATURAL GAS

City	Number of Months of Heating	Annual Cost of Heating Pool at:				Energy Consumed (therms/yr)
		$0.50/therm	$1.00/therm	$1.50/therm	$2.00/therm	
Miami	12	$2,848	$5,696	$8,544	$11,392	5,696
Phoenix	8.5	$1,776	$3,552	$5,328	$7,104	3,552
Dallas	7	$1,920	$3,840	$5,760	$7,680	3,840
Los Angeles	7	$2,376	$4,752	$7,128	$9,504	4,752
Atlanta	5	$2,248	$4,496	$6,744	$8,992	4,496
Kansas City	5	$1,872	$3,744	$5,616	$7,488	3,744
New York	4.5	$1,904	$3,808	$5,712	$7,616	3,808
Chicago	4	$2,072	$4,144	$6,216	$8,288	4,144
Denver	4	$2,120	$4,240	$6,360	$8,480	4,240
Boston	3.5	$2,096	$4,192	$6,288	$8,384	4,192
Minneapolis	3	$1,776	$3,552	$5,328	$7,104	3,552
San Francisco	3	$1,856	$3,712	$5,568	$7,424	3,712
Seattle	2.5	$1,784	$3,568	$5,352	$7,136	3,568

HEAT PUMP

City	Number of Months of Heating	Annual Cost of Heating Pool at:				Energy Consumed (kWh/yr)
		7¢/kWh	15¢/kWh	25¢/kWh	30¢/kWh	
Miami	12	$3,115	$6,675	$11,125	$13,350	44,500
Phoenix	8.5	$1,943	$4,163	$6,938	$8,325	27,750
Dallas	7	$2,100	$4,500	$7,500	$9,000	30,000
Los Angeles	7	$2,599	$5,570	$9,283	$11,139	37,130
Atlanta	5	$2,459	$5,270	$8,783	$10,539	35,130
Kansas City	5	$2,048	$4,388	$7,313	$8,775	29,250
New York	4.5	$2,083	$4,463	$7,438	$8,925	29,750
Chicago	4	$2,267	$4,857	$8,095	$9,714	32,380
Denver	4	$2,319	$4,970	$8,283	$9,939	33,130
Boston	3.5	$2,293	$4,913	$8,188	$9,825	32,750
Minneapolis	3	$1,943	$4,163	$6,938	$8,325	27,750
San Francisco	3	$2,030	$4,350	$7,250	$8,700	29,000
Seattle	2.5	$1,952	$4,182	$6,970	$8,364	27,880

HEAT PUMP PLUS SOLAR-ELECTRIC SYSTEM

This air-source heat pump warms the pool water. Electricity for the heat pump
and filter pump come from the main electrical distribution panel for the house.
Electricity for the panel is supplied by the power grid and by a solar electric array.

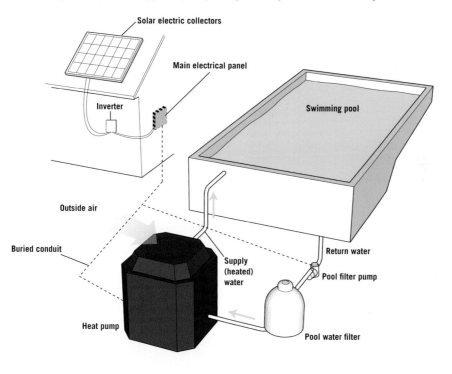

Solar electric collectors

Main electrical panel

Inverter

Swimming pool

Outside air

Buried conduit

Supply (heated) water

Return water

Pool filter pump

Heat pump

Pool water filter

INSULATING THE POOL SHELL will somewhat help reduce the heat loss from the pool water to the ground if the pool is an in-ground type or to the air if it is an above-ground type. However, the benefit derived from the use of the insulation is small in relation to the cost.

The heat pump, assisted by a solar electric system, is installed in exactly the same way that a conventional heat pump pool heater is installed, right down to the connection of the heat pump to the circuit breaker box. The only difference is that now the power source is both the utility company and the solar electric array.

The pool filter pump draws water from the pool; it then forces it through the filter, through the heat exchanger of the heat pump pool heater, and finally back to the pool. The compressor motor and fan motors of the heat pump are connected to a dedicated electrical circuit in the house. An array of solar electric modules is installed on the house roof or on a mounting frame near the house. The direct current from the array flows to an inverter where it is

An inexpensive, unglazed collector can lie on the ground beside the pool. At the end of the season, roll it up and put it away.

the electricity required to power the heat pump and filter pump during the swimming season. At present installation costs and ignoring incentives, such a solar electric system would cost between $26,000 and $30,000 installed.

Outdoor above-ground pools

Solar thermal pool heating systems for above-ground pools are generally quite simple, relatively inexpensive, and often designed for do-it-yourself installation. A typical system for an 18-ft.- (5.5-m-) to 24-ft.- (7.3-m-) diameter above-ground pool consists of two or three flexible 4-ft. (1.2-m) by 20-ft. (6.1-m) unglazed solar panels that connect to the filter pump discharge with flexible hoses and hose clamps. The panels typically rest directly on the ground beside the pool. Before the first frost, the panels must be drained or blown out with compressed air, rolled up, and stored in the basement or the garage.

To reduce installation costs, many designs for these collectors allow them to be connected in series. A drawback to this approach is that the water gets warmer and warmer as it moves from one collector to the next, thereby lowering the

converted to alternating current and fed into household electrical circuits. Solar-generated electricity then flows to all of the loads in the house, including the heat pump. Any solar-generated electricity not used in the house goes back to the utility company. An important benefit of this type of system is that it continues to supply electricity to the house even when the pool has been closed for the season.

For an 18-ft. (5.9-m) by 36-ft. (11.8-m) pool located in a relatively sheltered site, for a 12-week swimming season in the Northeast, with a pool cover that is used nightly and with water maintained at 80°F (26.7°C), the pool would require about a 4kW solar electric system. Over the period of a year, that system would supply all of

SOLAR POOL COVERS SHOULD BE USED AT NIGHT TO CONSERVE POOL HEAT and be removed during the day to allow the sun to heat the water. To save even more energy, cover the pool whenever it's not in use. An exception is during sunny, warm, and humid weather. At such times, evaporation rates decrease, and it may be better to remove the cover during the day even when you're not using the pool.

SOLAR HEATING SYSTEM FOR ABOVE-GROUND POOLS

One or more unglazed collectors are rolled out on the ground on the south side of the pool. Water from the filter pump discharge is forced through the collector, where it is heated and then returned to the pool.

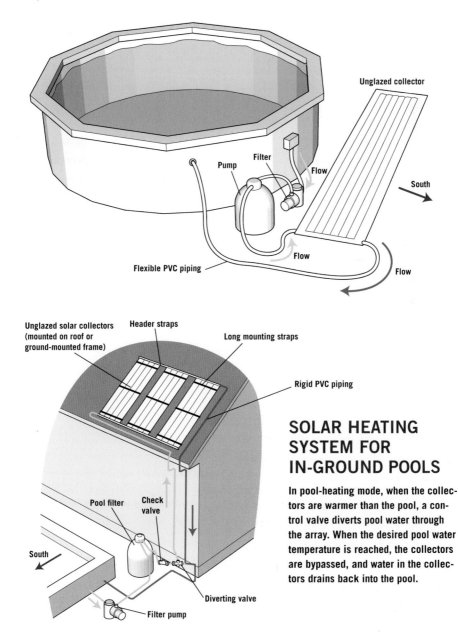

Unglazed collector

Filter

Pump

Flow

South

Flow

Flexible PVC piping

Flow

Unglazed solar collectors (mounted on roof or ground-mounted frame)

Header straps

Long mounting straps

Rigid PVC piping

SOLAR HEATING SYSTEM FOR IN-GROUND POOLS

In pool-heating mode, when the collectors are warmer than the pool, a control valve diverts pool water through the array. When the desired pool water temperature is reached, the collectors are bypassed, and water in the collectors drains back into the pool.

Pool filter

Check valve

South

Diverting valve

Filter pump

The size of the swimming pool collector array is based on the size of the pool. The large pool at this house requires arrays on three roof sections.

efficiency of heat collection in the downstream collectors and increasing the resistance to flow. No more than two or three should be connected in series; otherwise the flow rate through the filter will be reduced and adversely affect the effectiveness of the filter.

The pool's existing filter pump is typically sufficient for circulating water between two or three collectors and the pool. A manual bypass (diverting) valve allows the homeowner to bypass the solar array when the pool water is too warm. In general, pool water should pass through the collectors when the array is in the sun. If the filter pump is running at night, when it is raining, or when the pool water is too warm, then the pool water should bypass the solar collectors. Passing pool water through the collectors at night will cool the pool.

POOLS WILL LOSE HEAT IF THE POOL WATER IS ALLOWED TO CIRCULATE THROUGH THE COLLECTORS AT NIGHT. If the filter pump is shut off or bypassed, heat loss will not occur. If you run the filter pump at night, a diverting valve must be used to bypass the collectors. The only time that pool water should intentionally be circulated through the collectors at night is to cool the water if it gets too warm during the day.

Outdoor in-ground pools

Solar thermal systems for in-ground pools are more elaborate but similar in concept to those for above-ground pools. The pool filter pump draws water from the pool, usually from the skimmers, forces it through the filter, and then through an array of unglazed liquid-cooled solar collectors. From the collectors, the sun-heated

Pool covers are recommended for all types of pools, especially for indoor pools where they not only help maintain water temperatures but also minimize moisture damage to the structure from high humidity.

Perhaps no other building feature has greater potential for serious damage to the structure than an indoor swimming pool. The damage is due primarily to condensed moisture from the pool, so controlling humidity in the pool room is critical. In addition to a pool cover, a venting system with an air-to-air heat recovery unit is essential.

water returns to the pool water return pipe and from there flows to the pool supply jets.

When compared to collectors for outdoor above-ground solar pool heating, collectors for outdoor in-ground systems tend to be more substantial, larger in area, and are permanently mounted to a roof- or ground-mounted frame. Collectors are designed so they can be connected in parallel flow arrangement rather than in series. When the piping runs above grade, rigid plastic piping is used to connect the filter outlet to the array. When piping runs on or below grade, flexible polyethylene tubing, similar to that used for well water lines, is used.

Plumbing for an in-ground solar pool heating system also is more involved than for an above-ground pool. Because the collectors and piping may be subject to freezing temperatures, the array and piping must be pitched so they can be easily drained at the end of the season.

Although a separate collector loop pump is not required for the solar heating of outdoor in-ground pools, the filter pump must have sufficient capacity to lift the water from the pool to the top of the solar array. In retrofit situations, if the array is only one story above the pool water, the existing filter pump is usually able to handle that lift. If the solar array is higher than one story, the existing pump may need to be replaced with one that has a higher lift.

Solar collectors can be used in conjunction with an existing pool heater. The solar system should be plumbed as a preheater to the existing heater. In most cases in which solar pool heating systems have been added, homeowners soon stop using the conventional heater and eventually have it removed. Thus, when a solar system is installed in an existing pool, it is a good idea to include a bypass for the conventional heater.

Indoor pools

Indoor pools receive little or no direct heat gain from the sun. Consequently, they must be heated year-round or they will be too cold for swimming. Maintaining a constant pool temperature with a heater using conventional fuels can cost between $2,000 and $5,000, depending on the size of pool, room humidity, water temperature, and fuel costs. Solar pool heating is therefore as good a solution for indoor pools as it is for outdoor pools. If the collector area is approximately equal to the pool water surface area, the need for the conventional heater can be minimized or eliminated.

There are several solar options for heating an indoor pool. One is to use unglazed thermal collectors when outside temperatures are above

ABOVE TOP: For year-round swimming, an indoor pool is the only solution for much of North America. Heating indoor pools requires glazed collectors, antifreeze solution, and a heat exchanger.

ABOVE BOTTOM: Indoor pools also benefit from the use of a pool cover and ventilation. They help prevent humidity and condensation inside the pool house, which can cause structural damage.

freezing and a conventional pool heater the rest of the year. The advantage is that these collectors are much less expensive than the type that can heat the pool year-round. On the downside with this setup, in cold weather the pool still must be heated with a conventional heater.

Another possibility is to heat the pool year-round with a glazed collector array, similar to the type of collector used for heating domestic water. Any supplemental heat would be provided by a conventional heater.

In these indoor pool heating systems, pool water must be heated indirectly to avoid the risk of freezing in the collectors. Usually, a separate piping loop and pump are used to circulate an antifreeze solution between the array and one side of a heat exchanger in the pool equipment room. Pool water is circulated through the other side of the heat exchanger by the filter pump. A drain-back, indirect solar heat collection loop will be almost essential for this type of system to deal with those times of the year when there's little demand for the large amount of heat from the array.

Glazed collectors are also preferred for higher-temperature applications, such as spas and hot tubs. As is the case with outdoor in-

ground pools, solar collectors can be used in conjunction with an existing spa or hot tub heater.

SOLAR THERMAL POOL HEATING COMPONENTS

In this section you'll find a list of the key components commonly found in outdoor solar pool heating systems and an explanation of what each one does. Many of the components necessary for solar heating an indoor pool are not included here but may be found in Chapter 3. Not every component is needed in all systems.

Collectors

Unglazed liquid-cooled solar collectors are typically used for outdoor pool heating. They can't heat a liquid to as high a temperature as a glazed collector, but outdoor pool heating is a low-temperature application that requires water to be heated only slightly above the ambient air temperature. Unglazed collectors also are much less expensive than glazed collectors and are actually more efficient for this application.

Glazed collectors can also be used for pool heating, typically when the pool is indoors where heat is required year-round or for supply-

TILTING AND ORIENTING SOLAR POOL HEATING COLLECTORS

While the ideal array orientation is true south, pool heating collectors can face from southeast to southwest with little penalty in performance. The preferred solar collector tilt will vary with location and period of use. For outdoor pools, the collector tilt (measured from the horizontal) should be approximately 15 degrees less than the local latitude (e.g. at 40°N. Lat the collectors should be at 25 degrees tilt from the horizontal).

ABOVE: Indoor pools are often heated with flat-plate, glazed collectors, similar to those used for an active solar domestic hot water system. RIGHT: Unglazed collectors lack rigidity and must be mounted directly on a roof or on a platform.

ing heat to outdoor pools during the summer and then for supplying heat to the house during the heating season.

Pool filter pump

Filter pumps are an important part of any pool installation since they draw water from the skimmers or the bottom of the pool and force it through the filter and pool heater and then back to the pool. Residential pool filter pumps typically vary in horsepower from ½ hp to 1½ hp. The larger the volume of water pumped and the higher the pump must lift the water, the more horsepower is required. Filter pump motors are usually controlled by a timer, but a solar control is used when the pump may be run 24/7 or when the collector array is used as a heat dump for the pool during the night.

Pump controls, valves, and sensors

When a timer is not used to control the filter pump, a pump control is required. Sensors allow the control to determine the temperature difference between the pool water and the collector array. When the collectors are warmer, the controller can turn on the pump and open a motorized valve that diverts pool water to the collector.

When the pump is turned off and water drains from the collectors, a check valve prevents water from going back into the pool through the filter. Were it not for the check valve, the water draining from the array would flush debris and filter media into the pool.

A vacuum relief valve installed in the piping at the top of the collector array or in its supply–return piping allows air to enter the collectors

BYPASSING THE ARRAY

In hot, humid parts of the country, such as south Florida, the swimming pool won't need a solar boost during the middle of the swimming season. In fact, pool water may become too warm if the array is not bypassed. Not only is very warm pool water no longer invigorating, the high water temperature causes more rapid chemical loss and promotes the growth of algae. Instead, make sure the array can be bypassed and used to make swimming comfortable primarily on the shoulders of the season.

The surface area of the pool is the basis for sizing the solar array. The larger the pool, the larger the solar array needed to heat it.

and piping so water can be quickly drained from the collectors.

A bypass or diverter valve allows pool water to circulate through the filter but to bypass the solar collectors or a conventional heater.

An isolation valve separates the solar collectors from the filter and is used when it's necessary to backwash the filter.

Estimating Collector Size

This table gives the minimum collector area needed to heat the most common pool sizes. Estimates assume water is kept at about 80°F (27°C).

(Analysis by Everett M. Barber Jr.)

	POOL SIZE		
	16 ft. × 32 ft. (4.9 m × 9.8 m)	18 ft. × 36 ft. (5.5 m × 11 m)	20 ft. × 40 ft. (6.1 m × 12 m)
Minimum collector area (sq. ft.)	256 (23.8 m²)	324 (30.1 m²)	400 (37.2 m²)

This above-ground pool is heated by two arrays on the dormer and gable roof sections.

THE ECONOMICS OF SOLAR POOL HEATING SYSTEMS

When compared to a conventional means of heating a pool, such as a gas-fired heater, a solar pool heating system will pay for itself in 18 months to 7 years, according to the Department of Energy. For a quick region-by-region approximation of payback for a solar heating system installed for an in-ground pool, refer to Appendix 3: "Cumulative Costs of Heating a Swimming Pool."

Pool heaters using conventional fuels are sized to heat the water quickly, in 12 hours to 24 hours, so the volume of water in the pool is a key factor in choosing a fuel-fired heater. Solar heating systems, however, are sized mainly to offset heat losses during the normal swimming season (for most folks, that's when the outdoor air temperature is about 65°F [18.3°C] or higher). In this case, the surface area of the pool is the basis for sizing the solar array. The larger the pool, the larger the solar array needed to heat it.

Many homeowners believe solar collectors can be located on the roof of a pool cabana, but that's seldom possible, unless the cabana is large. For example, if the pool is 16 ft. by 32 ft. (4.9 m by 9.8 m), a minimum collector area of about 256 sq. ft. (23.8 m²) is desirable. Not many cabanas have roofs that large.

In general, for outdoor in-ground pools, the collector area should be between 50 percent and 80 percent of the pool water surface area. Provided the entire pool surface is fully exposed to the sun from 9 A.M. to 3 P.M., and the pool is well protected from wind, the lower end of the range (50 percent) will provide 80°F (26.7°C) water for most of the swimming season. For example, in the Northeast, collectors with half the surface area of the pool might extend the normal 6-week unheated season to as much as 12 weeks. Using an insulated cover would increase water temperatures early and late in the season and could extend the comfortable swimming season by an additional 4 weeks. A cover would be essential if the pool site is exposed to the winds.

A larger collector area, as much as 80 percent of the pool surface area, will, in most of the Northeast, provide comfortable water temperatures (80°F [26.7°C]) for 15 to 16 weeks, as long as there's no shade on the pool or the array. An insulated pool blanket used with the larger area will extend the comfortable water temperatures about 2 weeks on either end of the season.

When the pool doesn't get full sun, an even larger collector area is required. If the pool is in complete shade, the collector area may need to be 100 percent of the pool water surface area, and even then the swimming season may be abbreviated. In these cases, an insulated pool cover is essential.

In warm, humid climates, such as in south Florida, solar thermal heating systems allow homeowners to use their pools year-round. Because direct solar gain to the pool water is so great, collectors aren't needed during the summer. In fact, pool water often is cooled by running it through the array at night during the summer season.

Sizing an array for an indoor pool

Typical indoor pool water temperatures are usually 81°F (27.2°C) to 82°F (27.7°C), with the recommended air temperature in the pool room about 2°F (1.1°C) above that. For maximum solar heating, the surface area of glazed collectors should equal the surface area of the pool. Even then, a small amount of supplemental heat will be required in very cold weather in the northern part of the country. In the southern part of the country, for the same-size system, little or no

WHERE TO PUT THE COLLECTORS

A large collector area relative to the pool surface area means a longer swimming season, but when collectors are going to be roof-mounted, the available roof area can become a limiting factor. If the roof is too small, either the length of the swimming season must be reduced or a ground-mounted array should be considered. Ground arrays are typically more than twice the cost of roof-mounted arrays, but they may be the only way to provide sufficient collector area to heat the pool effectively.

supplemental heat will be required. In either case, the solar heat collection system should be the indirect drain-back type, so the system does not overheat during the summer when there is a considerable surplus of heat.

Estimating costs

If unglazed solar collectors can be roof-mounted, the approximate cost of an installed system is $7 to $15 per square foot ($75.2 to $161.30 per square meter) of solar collector. If the collectors are ground-mounted, the price can be $20 to $30 per square foot ($215 to $322 per square meter) of collector, depending on the cost of support frames and footings for the collectors and the cost of trenching between the array and the pool filter.

For example, a 400-sq.-ft. (37.2-m²) roof-mounted array and system could cost between $2,800 and $6,000 to install. If the pool is heated by a conventional heater and fuel costs are $1,500 per year, the payback period would be between 1.8 years and 4 years.

A conventional pool heater using natural gas or propane could cost somewhat less to install, between $3,500 and $4,000, but you can count on paying for fuel every year for as long as you use the heater. Further, expect to replace the heater every 5 years to 7 years. With a solar system, there are no recurring fuel costs. In addition, solar pool heating collectors can be expected to last 25 years, three or four times as long as a gas heater.

Federal and state incentives

As of this printing, federal income tax credits are not available for solar pool covers or solar pool heating systems. State income tax credits and sales tax exemptions, however, are available in many states. They vary greatly. Louisiana, for example, provides an income tax credit for the purchase and installation of solar heating systems, including solar pool heating, equal to 50 percent of the first $25,000 of the cost. That's currently the most attractive incentive in the country. At the other end of the scale is Florida, which offers an incentive of $100.

Solar electric systems are eligible for the federal tax credit, so the solar electric component of a solar electric–assisted heat pump pool heater would qualify for that credit. To learn what's available in your state, visit the DSIRE database at www.dsireusa.org.

Pool heating aesthetics

Solar thermal arrays for pool heating are often large, and that may bother some homeowners and many architects. Flexible collectors used for solar pool heating are black plastic mats, quite different in appearance from glazed collectors used for domestic water heating or space heating. Mats are placed directly on the roof or on the deck of a mounting frame.

The smallest array typically used for a 16-ft. (4.8-m) by 32-ft. (9.6-m) pool is 256 sq. ft. (22.8 m²). The array for a 20-ft. (6.1-m) by 40-ft. (12.2-m) pool that will triple the length of the swimming season is 640 sq. ft. (59.5 m²). An area that large is hard to hide. If you have east-, south-, or west-facing roofs not visible from the entry side of the house, collectors placed there may not be objectionable. But it's a good idea to look at several solar pool heating systems before deciding to have one installed.

PASSIVE SOLAR HEATING & COOLING

Passive solar design is a way of designing buildings to convert solar energy directly into heat without mechanical assistance. It's not so much a system as it is a way of configuring the envelope of the building, particularly the south side, so the house captures and stores solar energy. (Active solar heating, which includes the use of solar collectors and other equipment to capture the sun's energy, is discussed in Chapter 6.)

Passive solar design should start with high levels of insulation, thermal storage, and building techniques that make the house tight. When passive solar strategies are added to a well-insulated envelope, the energy needed for space heating is substantially less, even in cold climates. It is important to realize, however, that a passive solar house probably won't provide 100 percent of the heat requirement, simply because there may be extended periods of time when overcast skies block too much of the sun.

While passive solar heating can be used in both existing and new houses, it's far easier and less costly to build in solar features as the house is designed than it is to modify a house after it has been built. Passive cooling, which is discussed later in the chapter, involves keeping out as much of the sun's heat as possible while enhancing natural cooling strategies during the summer.

 ARCHITECTS TEND TO DESCRIBE PASSIVE SOLAR HOMES IN GLOWING, QUALITATIVE TERMS. It is much less common to hear of results of their design efforts in quantitative terms. Or, as Sir William Thomson (Lord Kelvin) put it in the 19th century, "When you can measure what you are speaking about, and express it in numbers, you know something about it; but when you cannot measure it, when you cannot express it in numbers, your knowledge is of a meagre and unsatisfactory kind."

Effect of Passive Solar Direct Gain on Heating Costs

Adapted from Passive Solar Buildings *by J.D. Baloomb (MIT Press, 1992)*

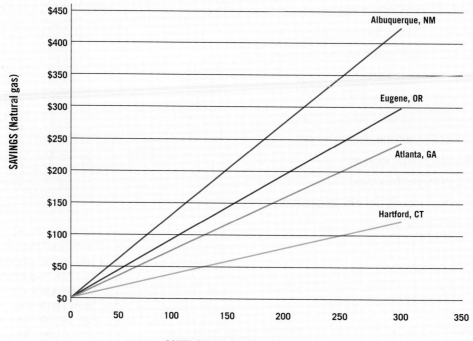

SAVINGS (Natural gas)

Albuquerque, NM

Eugene, OR

Atlanta, GA

Hartford, CT

SOUTH-FACING GLASS AREA (sq. ft.)

From the designer's point of view, combining passive solar heating and passive cooling in the same house is a challenge. Simply put, the house in winter should lose the minimum amount of heat yet admit and store the maximum amount of solar heat; during the cooling season, it should lose the maximum amount of heat and admit the minimum amount of solar heat. While this tension exists, the experienced designer has a number of tools with which to work.

PASSIVE SOLAR HEATING

Just outside a 10-sq.-ft. (0.92-m²) south-facing window there's the equivalent of about 1kW (3,413 Btu/hr) of energy at noon on a clear winter day. Over the entire area of the south side of the house, that's a lot of energy. The challenge for the designer is getting as much of that heat as possible into the house and storing it without incurring the penalties of overheating, excessive brightness and glare, and excessive heat loss.

Two elements are necessary for all passive solar designs. One is reasonably transparent glazing in south-facing exposures. This is to allow solar radiation to enter. The other is an adequate amount and proper placement of mass to absorb and store solar radiation. There are a number of ways these two basic elements can be configured architecturally to produce a successful passive solar design.

FACING PAGE: This 3,000-sq.-ft. (278.8-m²) passive solar home, designed by architect Maryann Thompson, incorporates a grid-tied solar-electric system, gray water collection, and a pellet stove. ABOVE TOP: Deep eaves shade second-story windows from strong summer sun. In winter, the sun's low altitude allows light to shine directly through the windows. ABOVE BOTTOM: The mass of the concrete floor provides thermal storage. The decorative surface has been etched with acid and polished.

DIRECT GAIN

At the most basic level, passive solar heating occurs as sunlight enters through south-facing windows and warms up the interior spaces. Unless controlled with thermal mass in the winter and shading in the summer, solar gain leads to overheating. In winter, moveable insulation applied to glazed areas is highly desirable to prevent heat loss at night.

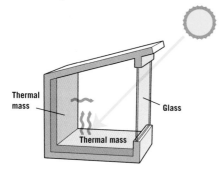

Thermal mass

Glass

Thermal mass

PASSIVE SOLAR FEATURES

Well-designed passive solar houses of today bear little resemblance to most of those built during the 1970s. The houses of today are generally comfortable year-round, have generous amounts of natural light, and cost less to heat than conventional houses with the same floor area. While south-facing glass area is still important, proportionally less glass is used now than 30 years ago.

Energy conservation is an essential ingredient of good passive solar design. This means designing the envelope of the house to lose the least amount of energy of any type, nonrenewable or renewable.

Floor aspect ratio

Passive solar houses are usually rectangular in shape with the long sides facing north and south and the shorter sides facing east and west. Configured this way, sunlight entering the south side can reach deep into the house. Floor aspect ratios (the ratio between width and length) of between 1:1.5 and 2:5 are common.

Glazing

Choosing the right windows is critical to good passive design. They should be selected based on the direction they will face. On northern and western exposures, the main concern in winter is to stem heat loss since at that time of year there is not a significant amount of passive solar gain through western exposures and none at all from the northern. To minimize heat loss on those exposures, the window area should be small and have as high an R-value as you can afford. An average-quality double-glazed window rated at R-2 loses about 10 times as much heat per square foot as an average builder-quality wall. Although current mass-market windows seem to be rated only up to R-3.2, better-made windows are available with R-values of between 5 and 10. These should be used in the eastern, western, and northern exposures.

On eastern exposures, windows can be larger to help the house warm up faster on winter mornings. But care should be taken to ensure that trees and other objects don't shade that side of the house during the winter.

On the south side of the house, there are two glazing-related concerns: the loss of heat 24/7 and heat gain during the daylight hours. If maximizing daytime heat gain were the only objective, single-pane glazing would be the choice because it will admit more solar energy than will double-pane glass. But in colder climates

especially, it loses about twice as much heat. If minimizing heat loss were the only objective, triple-glazed argon-filled units with multiple low-e coatings would be the choice. But that kind of glass will admit much less solar radiation than will clear single or double glass.

One of the characteristics of glass is its solar heat gain coefficient (SHGC). The higher the coefficient, the greater the solar energy transmitted by the glass. For south-facing glazing, SHGCs should be in the range of 0.70 to 0.78 for clear single glass, 0.60 to 0.70 for clear double glass, and 0.55 to 0.62 for clear triple glass. For east-, west-, and north-facing glazing, the solar heat gain coefficients for triple glass with two low-e coatings will be in the 0.25 to 0.40 range.

If you're willing to use moveable insulation over the windows at night, single-pane glazing

ABOVE TOP: The flip side of passive solar heating is solar shading. This British Columbia home controls sunlight with deep overhangs and carefully sized and positioned windows. ABOVE BOTTOM: Concrete floors and exterior walls store heat in winter and help maintain cool temperatures in summer.

THE HISTORY OF PASSIVE SOLAR HOMES

Passive solar heating took off shortly after the OPEC oil embargo of 1973–1974. It seemed that just about every architect or builder not already busy with tract homes or high-end houses was designing or building passive solar houses. Solar design was the subject of many books, magazine and newspaper articles, conferences, and research.

Unfortunately, what passed for a passive solar home at that time often included large areas of south-facing glass and little or inadequate thermal mass. The rationale seemed to be that if a modest amount of glass was good, more must be better. Houses usually had a long east–west axis with south-facing windows and little else, making them uncomfortably hot on clear winter days and virtual ovens during the summer. Interiors were often blindingly bright in the winter. Fabrics faded. Exposed wood dried and

split. Some were even more costly to heat than a well-insulated house without passive features.

Another serious shortcoming was the absence of reliable data on performance. Few people knew how much energy the houses really used. The only way to determine this reliably is to install instruments that monitor performance over the course of a year, which is costly and time-consuming. It was not until the early to middle 1980s, after public interest in solar technology had peaked and waned, that performance data of any quality began to appear.

Since the mid-1970s, a relatively small group of dedicated U.S. architects has continued to refine the technology. Some passive homes have been monitored by universities and engineering firms, and the combined effort is building a solid resource of data for future designers. Significant progress has been made.

ABOVE LEFT: This early passive solar home, by architect Douglas Kelbaugh, was the first in the United States to incorporate a Trombe wall in its design. Behind the glass facade is a concrete wall designed to store heat for the night. Today's passive solar designs typically use less glazing to the south to avoid overheating in summer. ABOVE RIGHT: The Trombe wall of the 1975 Kelbaugh house as seen from the living area. Openings at the top and bottom of the wall facilitate heat distribution via convection.

Low-e coatings on window glazing can significantly reduce solar heat gain in summer. Unlike site-applied low-e films, they are microscopically thin and not visible.

does not mean the elimination of conventionally fueled heating systems, although with super insulation and good passive solar design those systems can be smaller—sometimes a lot smaller.

is the best choice in much of the southern United States. In spite of the significant reduction in heat loss due to moveable insulation, it has not been something many homeowners seem to use consistently. Thus the preferred material for south-facing glazing in most passive solar homes is double-glazing with clear glass (untinted glass without a low-e coating).

Thermal storage

Thermal storage, also known as thermal mass, is the capacity of a material to store heat. Low-mass materials, such as drywall on wood-frame construction, have relatively low heat storage capacity, whereas high-mass materials such as water and concrete have much more.

Without thermal storage, inside temperatures in a passively heated house would rise quickly and result in uncomfortable spaces and increased heat loss. If interior surfaces in direct sunlight are relatively dark in color and have

adequate mass, the sun's heat can be stored more effectively.

Thermal mass may be incidental, such as the mass in drywall, the wood structure, and furniture. It may be intentional, such as in the masonry walls or floor, or it may be apart from the structure, such as stacks of blocks, or tubes filled with water. While all mass is good, relying exclusively on incidental mass in a passive solar house will limit the south-facing glass area and thus the fraction of the house heating load handled by the passive gain. If the glass area is not limited, and only incidental mass is used, overheating is almost certain.

In most climates, thermal mass should be thermally isolated from fluctuations in outside temperatures so that stored heat is lost only to interior spaces. The mass can be in a concrete slab floor 4 in. (10.2 cm) to 6 in. (15.2 cm) thick and capped with dark tile or in concrete block interior walls. But exterior walls should be thermally massive only if they are insulated from outside temperatures. This usually means some type of rigid insulation should be applied to the outside of the walls.

In the hot, dry climate of the Southwest, exterior walls of indigenous homes are traditionally made with adobe, which has high thermal mass. During the day, the outside of the adobe

Traditional architecture from around the world has made use of passive solar design principles. The massive walls of adobe houses, for example, moderate interior temperature swings.

For a window shade to be effective, it should be sealed around the perimeter, such as this one from Window Quilt Insulated Shades. Made with five layers, this material can triple the R-value of a double-pane window or glass door.

is heated by the sun. Heat is conducted inward over the next 8 hours to 12 hours, or longer, depending on the wall thickness. Overnight, the interior wall surface temperature continues to rise, radiating heat to interior spaces. The next day, the cycle begins anew. Little supplemental heat is needed. This works well in climates where most winter days have clear skies.

Window insulation

Since the south-side glazing of a passive solar house should have a high shading coefficient, those windows will have a lower R-value than on the other three exposures. To limit the heat loss through the glazing, moveable insulation for the windows is a good idea. This single feature, provided you use it faithfully during the winter, can save more energy than any one of a number of other energy-conserving features.

Moveable window insulation is usually installed on the inside of the window. During the heating season, it is put in place at night and

R-VALUE VS. SOLAR HEAT GAIN

There are two properties of glass to be concerned with. One is the R-value, and the other is the solar heat gain coefficient (SHGC).

Most homeowners know that R-value is a measure of heat loss. The higher the R-value, the lower the rate of heat loss. Not everyone, however, is aware that the higher the R-value of a window, the lower its SHGC. The lower the SGHC, the less sunlight the window allows in. And the less sunlight that's transmitted, at least through south-side glazing, the less solar heat enters the building.

For successful passive solar design, south-facing glass area and thermal mass are inextricably linked. Provide too much glass area in relation to thermal mass, and the interior spaces will overheat, wasting the collected heat, causing an uncomfortably warm interior, and ultimately causing the passive solar contribution to be smaller than it could be. Provide too much mass for the glass area installed, and the opportunity for a successful design with a higher solar fraction is missed.

Two critical aspects of passive solar design are the ratio between south-facing glass and the heated floor area and the ratio of south-facing glass to thermal mass. The first is convenient for architects and builders to use since it avoids an analysis of the mass needed to store the incoming solar heat. But, in order to use that relationship responsibly, some interior thermal mass must be assumed. The second is less convenient because it requires that the designer know the thermal mass of the space being designed. Tables have been developed to compute the heat stored per unit of mass area. The ratios resulting from this effort vary between about 3 sq. ft. (.28 m^2) and 9 sq. ft. (.84 m^2) of mass per square foot of glass area.

A guideline for adequate thermal mass is as follows: Floor areas exposed to direct sun should be 4-in.- (10.2-cm-) to 6-in.- (15.2-cm-) thick poured concrete; exterior walls exposed to the sun should be 8-in. (20.3-cm) to 10-in. (25.4-cm) concrete block with filled cores. Both surfaces should be insulated on the side away from the living spaces.

removed during the day (it can be left in place all the time on some east, west, and north windows if the view out is not essential). Coverings that do not seal at the edges of the window opening, including heavy drapes, make relatively poor insulators.

Moveable window insulation comes in a variety of forms. One is Window Quilt®, a roll of fabric with insulation and a heat-reflective layer sandwiched between the outer layers of the fabric. The insulation can be retracted into a roll at the top of the window. When the insulation is put in place, the edges slide in tracks along the sides of the window. The bottom of the shade also is sealed to the window frame when the shade is drawn. Depending on the type of glazing, Window Quilt will result in an aggregate R-value for the window plus drawn shade of between about 6.0 and 7.0. In the summer, the shades can be used to help reduce heat gain.

Finally, insulating shutters can be installed on the inside of the window. During the day, the shutters can be open. At night they are closed. The shutters must be tightly sealed at the edges when closed to be effective. Depending on the choice of insulation board, this approach can yield the highest R-value combination.

Any of these measures can be effective. But some people have found it a nuisance to cover the windows nightly and tend to be inconsistent about doing it. For those folks, investing in windows with the highest available R-value is the only alternative, albeit a costly one.

PASSIVE SOLAR HEATING DESIGNS

A variety of passive solar house designs has been devised. Some are more immediately recognizable as passive solar structures than others. Some passive solar features don't lend themselves to traditional architecture.

Sunrooms are often incorporated in passive solar homes as ways to collect solar heat. Sunspaces kept separate from living spaces, such as the one in this Olympia, Washington, home, allow homeowners to manage heat gain better than when such spaces are part of an open floor plan.

Another approach is to build pockets in the walls next to the windows for storing rigid insulation. At night, the insulation can be moved over the window. The insulation must be sealed at the edges to work effectively. One disadvantage to this approach is a compromise in the insulation value of the wall where the pocket is located.

Direct gain

A house configured for direct solar gain is designed to allow the sun to enter the south-side living spaces of the house directly through south-facing windows. It's probably the easiest passive solar feature to integrate into traditional house designs, and it can be applied to existing construction as a retrofit.

Building components should have high thermal capacity for storing heat. If thermal

ABOVE and BELOW RIGHT: The clerestory windows at the top of the wall in this passive solar home in Taos, New Mexico, allow daylight to penetrate deep inside the house, offsetting glare from the south-facing glass.

capacity is small and the glass area is large, interior spaces will overheat quickly and heat losses will be high. Offsetting the loss of heat through south-facing glazing by using windows with a high R-value will reduce solar heat gain.

Glare and excessive brightness can be a problem when there is too much south-facing glass, although these undesirable consequences can be reduced with clerestory windows. Direct sunlight also can damage finish materials. Shades help, but they also reduce solar gain.

Overhangs on the south side or other exterior shading devices that block sunlight during the summer are a critical part of good passive cooling design (discussed later in this chapter).

Carpeting should never be used to cover thermal mass directly exposed to sunlight. Carpeting prevents the thermal mass of the floor from absorbing the sun's energy. If you can't

live without carpeting, then look at some other type of passive solar configuration—one of the indirect gain choices, for example.

Indirect gain

In the category of passive-indirect gain, interior spaces aren't exposed to direct sunlight. Instead, a building feature or component collects and stores the sun's energy and warms living spaces indirectly. There are several ways of doing this.

TROMBE WALLS The Trombe wall, named after French engineer Felix Trombe, is a thermally massive wall that forms the south wall of the house. It's usually made of poured concrete or concrete block with the cores filled with concrete. The wall is dark on the exterior and separated from outside air by a layer of glass. During the winter, the wall is warmed by the sun, and the heat is conducted through the wall to the interior of the house. By the end of a sunny day, the sun's heat is noticeable on the interior

TROMBE WALL

A high-mass wall (often called a Trombe wall) is typically located a short distance behind a glazed wall. During a winter day, the concrete wall absorbs solar radiation. At night, the stored heat moves to the interior by radiation and convection.

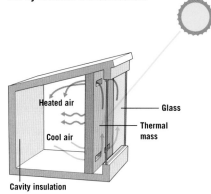

Heated air

Cool air

Glass

Thermal mass

Cavity insulation

side of the wall, much as it would be with adobe construction. The house is heated well into the night by radiation and convection from this wall.

Some designs include vents at the top and bottom of the wall that connect the space behind the exterior glass layer with the interior of the house. Cool air from the house enters the air space through the lower vents, is heated as it rises to the top of the wall, and enters the house through the upper vents. At night, vents are closed to prevent cooling. If the vents are not sealed at night, the unvented wall design has been found to be superior. Another variation includes windows in the concrete wall. The windows allow a view to the south and permit some direct solar gain in the living spaces.

What prevents the house from overheating in summer? Vents at the top and bottom of the glass wall. These are closed during the heating

season. In summer they are left open so that whatever heat gets through the glass can easily be lost to the outside air. A roof overhang above the glass wall also helps by blocking some of the summer sun.

Having the option of moving a layer of insulation between the glass and the wall makes this design even more effective. The insulation prevents heat loss through the cold glass at night or during long stretches of cloudy weather. During the day, the insulation is retracted so the sun heats the wall. One major limitation is that a sizable storage space must be supplied for the insulation when it's not in use.

WATER WALL A water wall, like a Trombe wall, is a way of storing the sun's energy during the day for release at night. Water is attractive as a heat storage material because it has a much higher heat storage capacity per unit volume than concrete. Water can be stored in rectangular containers or translucent fiberglass tubes placed along the south side of the house just inside a glass wall. During the day, sunlight warms the water in the containers. The containers begin to release heat to the space sooner than a concrete wall would. Sometimes the containers are spaced several inches apart to allow some views to the outside as well as some direct solar gain. Daylight enters the room through the gaps between the tubes and also is scattered as it passes through the water. Vents at the top and bottom of the glass wall prevent overheating during the summer.

In another configuration, hollow glass blocks (glass bricks) are filled with water and made into a wall just inside from the outer glazed wall. The water in the blocks stores the sun's heat and

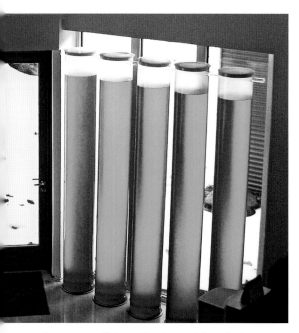

In a water wall, large fiberglass-reinforced tubes can be used to hold water and provide thermal storage. The water can be tinted, as shown, to increase energy absorption.

WATER WALL

A water wall is similar to a Trombe wall but uses water-filled tubes or stackable containers instead of masonry for thermal storage. The advantage of a water wall is that more heat can be stored per unit volume in water than in concrete; the water wall also does not block as much daylight.

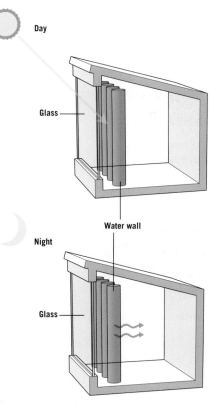

releases it to the occupied spaces in the house. Some of the sunlight passes through the glass block and provides natural light. Glass blocks come in a variety of sizes, colors, and textures.

As with a concrete storage wall, moveable insulation between the exterior glazing and the tubes will reduce heat loss at night. The large space needed to store the insulation is a limitation.

ROOF PONDS The roof pond is a clever design that can, depending on the climate, provide 100 percent of the space heating and cooling needs of a house. The concept was originally that of Harold Hay, who called it the Skytherm House. Elongated plastic bags of water are placed on the roof. The water is heated directly by the sun in the winter and cooled by night sky radiation in the summer. The bags are clear to allow the sun's energy to pass through to the water.

During the winter, at the start of the day, a layer of insulation over the bags is removed, allowing the sun to warm the water. At night, the insulation is replaced. The heated water conducts heat to the ceiling below, and the warmed ceiling radiates heat to the spaces below. In

ROOF POND

A roof pond heats the house in winter and cools it during the summer. On a winter day, water encased in plastic bags on the roof absorbs solar energy. At night, insulation is moved over the bags and heat from the bags is conducted to the ceiling below. The warmed ceiling then radiates heat to the spaces below. During daytime in summer months, the insulation covers the bags of water and the cooled water in the bags absorbs heat from the space below, thereby cooling it. At night the insulation is removed and the water in the bags is cooled by radiation to the night sky. The system is quite effective since the houses require no supplemental heating or cooling, but weight is an obvious disadvantage.

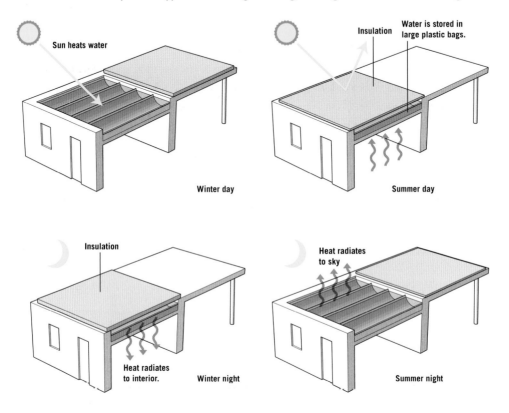

Sun heats water

Winter day

Insulation — Water is stored in large plastic bags.

Summer day

Insulation

Heat radiates to interior. Winter night

Heat radiates to sky

Summer night

summer, the schedule for moving the insulation is reversed. During the day, the insulation layer covers the bags so they are not heated by the sun or the surrounding air. At night, the insulation is removed so the bags of water are exposed to the night sky. In hot, dry climates, heat loss to the night sky can be considerable. Overnight, the water in the bags is cooled. Heat from the space below is conducted upward into the water in the bags, thereby cooling the ceiling. Air close to the cool ceiling becomes denser than the surrounding air, and therefore falls to the spaces below, cooling them.

It is a very impressive, simple heating and cooling concept. Some versions of this design have required no supplemental heating or cooling. Roof ponds work best in hot, dry climates and are generally used on single-story houses.

ICE MAKING IN THE DESERT

Before the advent of refrigeration, ice could be made during the summer in hot, dry climates by exposing shallow dishes of water to the sky at night and taking advantage of radiation cooling. The water was put in glass dishes, and the dishes were set in trenches to protect them from warming by surrounding breezes. The dishes were insulated from the ground by a bed of straw. Sometimes more than one harvest of ice was possible per night. The ice formation occurs even when ambient air temperatures are above freezing.

Unlike some passive designs, the scheme involves some regular human intervention or the use of an automatic control and motor to cover and uncover the bags. The bags of water are heavy so the roof must be reinforced, but no more so than a green roof.

Isolated gain

Because direct gain and indirect gain designs have a significant impact on the architecture of the house, both approaches are best suited for new construction. In contrast, an isolated gain design removes most architectural constraints. It's well suited to new or existing construction.

EXTERIOR SOLAR COLLECTOR Conventional solar heat collectors (see Chapter 2) capture the sun's heat, and a fluid, either air or a liquid, is used to circulate the heat between the collector array and heat storage. It is considered a passive solar system because the circulation of heat between the collector and storage is due to gravity. No motor-driven fan or circulator is used. When the sun heats the fluid in the collector, it becomes less dense than the fluid in the heat storage and rises to replace the storage fluid.

This type of system can have minimal affect on the architecture of the house, although it requires the collector array to be located below the spaces that will be heated. If the system uses air to carry the heat from the collector, the heat storage media can be a bed of pebbles adjacent to the occupied space. Better yet, it can be integral with the house, such as a precast concrete floor slab with air passages through the slab. If a liquid, such as an antifreeze, circulates between the collectors and storage, heat can be stored in a water-filled container located in the living space. The tank can release heat to the space by convection and radiation.

The collectors are usually covered during the summer months.

SUNSPACES While passive solar heating is more applicable to new construction, solar greenhouses or sunspaces have been added to the south side of many existing homes. A sunspace is often a separate structure attached to the south wall of an existing house. It usually has glazed walls on the east, south, and west sides and, in some cases, a glass roof.

Sunspaces have been promoted as a way to provide supplemental solar heat to existing houses, as a place in which to grow plants, and as an extended living space. On sunny winter days, these spaces can be quite comfortable, even too warm, and often produce a surplus of heat that can migrate into the house. Heat also

Sunspaces, sometimes called sun porches, can be added to an existing home. They are available in many sizes, styles, and glazing options.

SUNSPACE

Sunspaces, another variation of passive indirect solar gain, capture the sun's heat. Natural or forced convection can be used to move the heat to living spaces, and the sunspace is closed off from the house at night. Sunspaces are subject to extreme overheating in summer unless the roof is shaded.

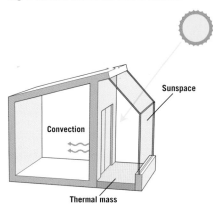

Sunspace

Convection

Thermal mass

can be drawn in living spaces by a fan or drawn into a return duct of a forced-air heating system and distributed uniformly throughout the house.

Sunspaces aren't, or at least they shouldn't be, heated by a conventional heating system. Doing so defeats their purpose. Further, during the winter they should be closed off from the house, often by a sliding glass door, to prevent heat loss from the house at night. In spring and fall, they can serve as an extended living space, a place to grow plants, and a source of heat for the house. During the summer months, especially if they have a sloped glass roof, they are uncomfortably hot during the day for both plants and people.

Unfortunately, many homeowners extend heating systems into their sunspaces so they're more useful in winter. But this essentially eliminates any net contribution of heat to the house. If they are used as intended, and without a glass roof, they can produce a modest net heat gain to the house.

If the sunspace has a glazed roof, overheating during the summer can be extreme. Exhaust fans, operable vents, exterior roof shade, and sometimes all three, are needed to keep the space moderately comfortable. If the sunspace has a conventional opaque roof, overheating is much less of a problem. Often, by opening a sliding door to the outside, or windows on opposite sides, the sunspace with a conventional roof can remain comfortable.

Double-envelope houses

A double-envelope house is a house within a house. The outer shell has passive solar features that allow the sun to warm the space between the inner and the outer walls. This results in a

HOW TO FIND A PASSIVE SOLAR DESIGNER

When searching for a designer, first make sure to choose an architectural firm or design-build firm with lots of passive solar design experience. The designer should be able to provide a visually attractive product, do the analysis required to size the glazing, calculate the amount of thermal mass that will be needed, and determine heating loads.

To ensure that you are getting an experienced passive solar designer:

🏠 Check with a local renewable energy association for recommendations.

🏠 Ask to visit several houses a prospective designer has done and talk with their owners.

🏠 Ask the owners if they will share their energy bills.

🏠 If they heat with wood, ask how many cords they use during a heating season.

🏠 If you like the work of someone who doesn't specialize in passive solar design, ask if he or she is willing to retain an architect or designer who does. Expect to pay extra for the specialist's fees.

warmer environment surrounding the inner, heated house, which in turn results in lower heat loss from the inner house.

Some homeowners claim very low energy use for heating the inner house. Finding independent third-party test results for this house design is very difficult. Also, the design is not

DOUBLE-ENVELOPE HOUSE

In a double-envelope house, the space between the outer and the inner walls captures heat, just as a greenhouse does. In the summer, the heated air is vented to the outside. In the winter, the heated air circulates through the envelope between the inner and the outer houses. Thermal mass serves to moderate both summer and winter temperature swings.

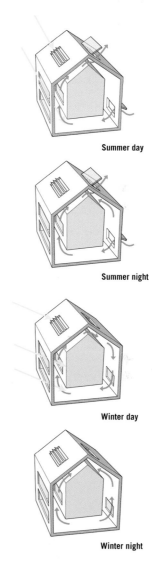

Summer day

Summer night

Winter day

Winter night

easily analyzed by the computer programs that are available for residential design.

There are some shortcomings to this approach. Insulation levels can be lower than they would in single-wall designs, which means some cost savings, but double-envelope houses require a lot of extra building materials and labor. A major concern is the opportunity for fire and smoke to spread rapidly within the space between the inner and the outer envelopes. In some instances, fire marshals have required that fire dampers be placed in the envelope space. Dampers remain open during normal operation and close when fire or smoke is detected. Fire dampers can be expensive.

To avoid the need for dampers, the envelope can be lined with fire-resistant material, such as type X drywall, and the inner house can be sheathed in fire-resistant material. Often, fire marshals have required that a sprinkler system be used between the envelopes. Any of these solutions can add significant cost to the house.

Louvers or shutters over the south-facing windows of the outer envelope or moveable

Passive solar space heating is often combined with point source heating, such as a masonry wood heater or woodstove.

shades in the outer envelope have been used to prevent overheating of the inner house during the summer months.

LIVING WITH PASSIVE DESIGN

By living in conventionally heated homes, we've grown accustomed to an almost steady indoor temperature. A good thermostat can keep the temperature to within a degree or less of its setting. Don't expect that in a passively heated house.

Passive solar heating uses a relatively short burst of solar energy, only 6 hours or so, to do 24 hours of heating. Interior spaces, especially those on the south side of direct gain designs, will increase in temperature over the period that the sun is shining. By how much depends on how well the house can store solar heat. Efficient heat storage means lower peak temperatures and less heat loss. On the other hand, a house with low storage capacity will see higher internal temperatures and proportionally higher heat loss.

Be willing to accept wider interior temperature swings than occur with conventional heating equipment. Doing so will allow passive solar features to work better for you. If the interior temperature goes up 10°F (5.5°C) above your 68°F (20°C) thermostat setting, don't open a window or turn on an exhaust fan. That heat will increase the temperature of the floor, walls, and furnishings. And if the temperature drops 5°F (2.8°C) or 6°F (3.3°C) below 68°F (20°C), don't turn on a heater. The solar heat stored in the floor and walls is keeping the house from cooling even faster. It's payback time. Take advantage of it.

There are two ways for an architect or builder to reduce the energy requirement for a new house or renovation of an existing house. The first is to develop an energy-saving envelope design in the earliest stages of the design process. The second is to simply specify an efficient heating/cooling system after the design is complete.

Both approaches are important, but smart envelope design is by far the more effective. It can reduce total energy use by 75 percent over a conventional design. An efficient heating system, specified after the design is complete, may reduce the house's energy use by only 10 percent to 15 percent. While there are notable exceptions, the vast majority of architects and builders opt for the latter approach, either because they don't know how to or don't want to pay for the analysis required for the former.

At the very least you should see a design heat loss analysis for the house along with an estimate of how much energy it will use. The design heat loss analysis is an indication of the energy required to maintain a comfortable interior at near worst case outside design (winter) temperatures. The winter interior design temperature in the United States is 68°F (20°C). The exterior design temperature varies with the climate. For Boston, for example, it's 5°F (-15°C). The size of the furnace or boiler is based on the design heat loss analysis using those temperatures.

The energy requirement analysis indicates how much energy is required to heat the house on a month-by-month basis or for the heating season.

A passive solar analysis would indicate, at the least, the solar heat gain to the house for the glazing area provided, the net amount of energy entering the house due to solar heat gain and heat loss through that glazing, and the approximate per-centage of the total heating requirement that can be met by the proposed passive solar design.

An analytical procedure that is widely accepted for passive solar house design is the *SLR method.* You should expect your architect to use that method or a vali-dated computer model, such as Energy-10™, for the design of the house.

Supplemental heat

Point sources of heat, such as a gas stove or woodstove, are frequently used in passive solar homes. So are hydronic or forced-air central heating systems. Hydronic systems use much less energy than forced-air systems to distribute heat from the boiler to the house. Forced-air systems, however, circulate air and provide an even distribution of passively collected heat. Hydronic systems are not capable of providing that same passive heat distribution.

Ideally, the passive house designer will be able to maximize the passive gain and distribution throughout the house, thereby minimizing the hours of operation of any type of conventional heat.

Cost of passive solar heating

There may be no added cost of integrating passive solar features into new construction. It's one of the best investments in solar energy technology a homeowner can make.

The cost of altering an existing house to include passive solar heat varies widely, depending on such factors as the architectural style, its orientation, the presence of thermal mass, and the quality and type of existing windows. No passive features should be attempted without also increasing the insulation.

Adding thermal mass to an existing house and increasing the area of south-facing glazing is often so expensive that passive solar heat alone is rarely worth the cost. Passive solar heat is easier and less expensive to add during a renovation.

Lowering the Demand for Heat

As energy conservation measures increase, the cost of heating a house goes down. This chart shows the effects of progressively more insulation levels and tighter construction techniques on heating loads for a 1,000-sq.-ft. (93-m²) house in the northeastern United States. Conservation can be much less costly than providing the same amount of heat with a solar system, passive or active.

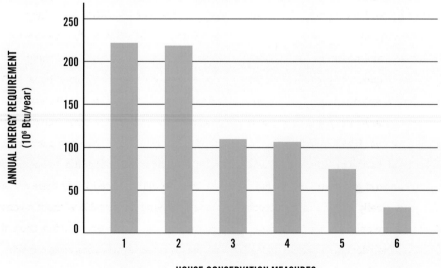

Savings due to passive solar heating

Many variables affect the savings afforded by a passive solar heating system. The graph on p. 100 shows the savings that can be realized by passive solar heating systems in various parts of the country. The savings are a function of the glass area and climate. The figures are based on using natural gas as the fuel.

INTRODUCTION TO PASSIVE COOLING

In a literal sense, passive cooling includes strategies that cause a building to lose heat. It doesn't include those that prevent heat gain. Pragmatically, however, any strategy that causes a building to lose heat or prevents it from gaining heat is considered passive cooling.

There is more to passive cooling than just keeping out the sun's heat. It also minimizes internal heat gain, enhances cooling by natural means, and is capable of storing coolness. Like passive solar heating, passive cooling does not rely on motor-driven fans or pumps (or the use of solar electric panels).

While passive cooling can be used in both existing and new houses, its greatest benefits and lowest cost come with new construction. As with passive solar heating, it is far easier to optimize passive solar features while the house is being designed than to modify the house later.

Except for general guidelines on natural ventilation, there really are no analytical tools that have been developed for passive cooling. Good passive cooling design is an aggregate of measures that keep the sun's radiation out of the

house, reduce transmitted heat gain from the exterior to the interior, and limit internal gains. Most designs make use of thermal mass and natural ventilation and, in the case of roof pond designs for passive solar heating, nighttime radiation cooling.

Our overreliance on mechanical cooling

The wonderful thing about air-conditioning is that by shear brute force it can make just about any house in the country comfortable during the summer months. The unfortunate thing about air-conditioning is that it can make just about any house in the country comfortable during the summer months.

We've come to rely on conventional air-conditioning far too much. For many homeowners, it's considered a necessity. By *air-conditioning*, we mean the typical compression cycle appliance, either in the form of a window unit or in a central cooling system. The compressor is powered by an electric motor. Air is cooled in the evaporator and blown around the house by a fan. Another fan blows outside air over the condenser. Together, those three motors consume a considerable amount of electrical energy. In some hot, humid climates, conventional air-conditioning is considered the only way to maintain interior comfort even though passive-cooling strategies could greatly reduce the number of hours of air-conditioner operation.

In most of the United States, there are other ways of staying comfortable without mechanical cooling. One is to use a room fan. Often the increased rate of evaporation from our skin caused by increased air movement can keep us

Fans can go a long way toward making living spaces more comfortable in hot weather. As a bonus, they also can be used during the heating season to move downward hot air that tends to stratify near the ceiling.

quite comfortable without mechanical compression cycle cooling. In other instances, passive cooling strategies are enough without a fan.

Our excessive dependence on mechanical cooling is due to a combination of factors. Marketing by air-conditioner manufacturers is one; status is another. But perhaps the most significant factor is the design of the houses in which most of us live. Before the 1950s, about the time when the use of residential air-conditioning in the United States began to grow rapidly, houses were designed to keep the sun out during the summer and to allow or encourage cross-ventilation and natural ventilation; where necessary, homeowners used electric fans for comfort.

This is not to say that in some parts of the country, the Gulf Coast states for instance, con-

ventional air-conditioning isn't a virtual necessity. But even there, older house designs were far more comfortable. Houses today are built to be air-conditioned. Sun shading, cross-ventilation, coolness storage in internal mass, natural ventilation, even the use of fans are not considered during the design.

As long as electrical energy was cheap and there was no perceived disadvantage to mechanical cooling, houses could continue to be built with a disregard for passive cooling techniques. We need to relearn the techniques of the past. In doing so, we can reduce the need for mechanical cooling and, in many parts of the country, eliminate it.

Understanding human comfort

While engineers and HVAC installers strive to maintain precise interior comfort conditions, tests have shown most people aren't that fussy. Numerous studies reported by the American Society of Heating, Refrigerating, and Air-Conditioning Engineers (ASHRAE) find people are comfortable in a far wider range of temperature and humidity conditions than household mechanical systems maintain.

Clothing is important to comfort. While fashion designers might disagree, clothing is basically thermal insulation from the environment. What type and how much clothing we wear should be adjusted for the season and our level of activity. Simply by living within an expanded comfort zone, by opening the windows and dressing appropriately, many hours of air-conditioner operation can be avoided, if not eliminated altogether.

PASSIVE COOLING STRATEGIES

Many passive cooling strategies are climate dependent. There are four broad climate zones in the United States and Canada (although climatologists may argue there are more). Different climates require different architectural responses.

🏠 HOT, WET. High humidity and uncomfortably warm temperatures characterize much of the summer. There's usually only a relatively small variation between daytime and nighttime outside air temperatures. This zone includes the southeastern coast and Gulf Coast states. It's the most difficult climate type to design for summer comfort without mechanical cooling.

🏠 HOT, DRY. This zone sees generally low humidity but high daytime temperatures and low or very low nighttime temperatures. It includes most of the Southwest and is perhaps the easiest climate type to design for summer comfort.

🏠 TEMPERATE. Here, there are relatively brief periods of high humidity and high temperatures during the summer. This zone includes much of the mid-latitudes of the United States and even parts of southern Canada. In this climate, it is moderately difficult to design for summer comfort without mechanical ventilation or some mechanical cooling, although the hours that either device are required to operate can be reduced greatly by passive cooling strategies and forced ventilation.

🏠 COLD. Periods of high humidity and high temperatures are even shorter. The northern tier states and much of Canada are included in this climate type. Natural ventilation is desirable, but generally, mechanical cooling is not required.

Keep the heat out

One obvious element of passive cooling design is to keep as much heat out of the house as possible. There are a variety of ways to accomplish that.

MINIMIZE DIRECT SOLAR GAIN THROUGH WINDOWS
The size and orientation of windows has a significant bearing on solar heat gain. In general, heat gain through south-facing windows is greater in

Simply by living within an expanded comfort zone, by opening the windows and dressing appropriately, many hours of air-conditioner operation can be avoided.

Awnings work better than interior shades to prevent unwanted heat gain in the summer because they block the sun's rays before they enter living areas.

winter than in summer because the sun is lower in the sky. Also, during the summer the sun rises and sets much farther to the north than during the winter, increasing the hours of exposure to windows facing east and west. Consequently, the south side still requires protection, but eastern and western exposures require much more careful shading.

In summer, it's better to block the sun's energy before it gets through a window than to reject it once it's inside. Interior shades, blinds, or drapes serve mostly to delay the heat gain to the interior. Exterior shading provisions work much better.

Fixed overhangs above south-facing windows can prevent direct sunlight from entering the house during the summer. If the overhangs are sized correctly, they can keep out the summer sun yet allow the winter sun to enter. Even better than fixed overhangs are moveable awnings or external roll shades. These can be adjusted to keep the sun out of the interior of the house in summer and retracted to allow full exposure to the sun in the late fall, winter, and early spring when the heat is needed.

Vertical fins along the south edges of east or west windows are much more effective in blocking the sun than are overhangs on these orientations. On eastern and western exposures, windows with a low SHGC minimize direct solar gain but not as effectively as vertical fins. Windows with a low SHGC are not desirable on southern exposures because they block solar energy during the winter.

MINIMIZE INDIRECT SOLAR GAIN THROUGH WINDOWS, WALLS, AND ROOF Indirect solar heat gain is due to reflected solar radiation through windows that are shaded from direct sunlight as well as to direct and indirect exposure of the walls and roof to sunlight. The latter affects a much larger area of the building envelope than windows alone. On a per square foot basis, indirect gain is not nearly so great as direct gain through windows, but over the total envelope area it can be significant.

To minimize indirect heat gain, glass with a low solar heat gain coefficient should be used in east- and west-facing windows. To minimize indirect heat gain through the opaque surfaces of the house, thermal insulation should be used in the walls and attic floor. Choosing light or white shingles can result in much lower attic temperatures and thus lower heat gain to the interior spaces. Solar collectors mounted above the roof also can reduce solar heat gain to the attic. As much direct and indirect sun as possible should be kept off all exterior building surfaces.

Trees provide shade, which would seem to make them desirable for passive cooling, but they can screen south-facing glazing during the winter when maximum solar gain is desired. In general, trees, even deciduous trees, should be avoided on the south side of passive solar heated houses.

REDUCE TRANSMITTED HEAT GAINS Heat flows from a region of higher temperature to one of lower temperature. During the summer, at least during the day, the outside air temperature is usually higher than the desired interior temperature, so the hot outside air is pushing heat into the house.

The only thing that deters transmission heat flow is insulation. Thermal insulation is useful in minimizing heat flow from the building during the winter months and into the build-

Green roofs, such as this one on Martha's Vineyard (ABOVE TOP), help keep the house cooler in summer. It also will help protect the roof from UV radiation, lengthening its life. An alternative way to prevent heat gain is with vegetation. The growing wall (ABOVE BOTTOM) stays cool in summer thanks to the shade and evaporative cooling it creates.

Extra-thick walls, filled with insulation, are a key feature in homes that depend on solar energy for some or all of their cooling or heating needs. These walls were constructed with two rows of 2×4 studs spaced about 10 in. (25.4 cm) apart. The cavity between the rows was filled with insulation.

ing during the summer. Thermal insulation takes the form of resistance insulation (such as fiberglass or foamboard) and capacity insulation (such as concrete or adobe). In general, the resistance insulation levels for good passive solar heating design are adequate for limiting this source of heat gain for passive cooling.

REDUCE INTERNAL GAINS When it comes to passive solar heating, internal heat gains work in your favor. They reduce the supplemental energy needed to heat the house. But when it comes to passive cooling, internal gains add unwanted heat to the interior.

Internal gains come from people, appliances, and lights. While it is difficult to minimize the number of people in a house, appliances and lights are more controllable. Efficient lighting, such as compact fluorescent lights (CFLs) and light-emitting diodes (LEDs), helps reduce internal heat gain since the more efficient the lighting, the more lumens per watt.

A number of homes have more than one refrigerator and some have a separate freezer. These contribute heat to the house, not only the heat removed from the interior of the appliance but also the heat from the compressor. If they are absolutely essential, then locate them in a space that is not normally occupied—a basement, garage, or laundry room, for example.

Cooking also adds heat. If the heat can be exhausted to the outside through a range hood, that can reduce the need for mechanical cooling, provided the kitchen is isolated from the central cooling system for the rest of the house. Other options include not cooling the kitchen mechanically and cooking on a grill outside in the summer. Years before the widespread use of air-conditioning, many houses had summer kitchens to keep cooking heat outside.

Other sources of internal gains are dehumidifiers. Try natural or mechanical ventilation instead. That may work nearly as well and contribute far less to the heat buildup inside. One or more computers (count desktop computers at 150w each) left on all day or a plasma TV (700w) also contribute significantly to internal heat gains.

Storing coolness

Coolness storage implies there is some coolness to store and something in which to store it. In most cases, the coolness comes from the night-time air and the place to store that coolness is in the interior mass of the house. This is one place where passive solar heating and passive cooling strategies overlap.

In hot, dry climates, the temperature swing between day and night can be between 30°F (16.7°C) and 35°F (19.4°C). Imagine a living space that is 100°F (37.8°C) late in the afternoon of a hot day. Simply with nighttime ventilation, the temperature can be dropped within a few hours to between 65°F (18.3°C) and 70°F (21.1°C). With adequate thermal mass in the house and effective measures to minimize direct and indirect solar gains, the interior of the house can be kept comfortable throughout the next day, without mechanical cooling.

In temperate and cold climates, the same technique works, although the day–night temperature differences are not so extreme. Open the windows during the evening, leave them open all night, and close them in the morning to trap cool air. Make sure exterior sun shades or other means are used to keep the sun out of the house. The greater the internal heat storage capacity of the house, the longer the effect will last.

In a hot, wet climate, however, there is only a small swing in outside air temperatures between day and night, as little as 8°F (4.4°C) to 12°F (6.7°C). With such a small temperature difference, it does not make sense to add thermal mass to the interior of a house to store coolness —quite the opposite, in fact. Natural ventilation-enhancing strategies, however, are essential to interior comfort in this climate type.

NATURAL VENTILATION Using the winds and relying on the fact that warm air rises will make your house more comfortable during the summer. Positioning windows and interior doors so prevailing breezes can enter on one side of a house and push warm, stagnant air out the other side has worked in homes for centuries. To take advantage of this phenomenon, study the build-

One nice aspect of thermal mass is its duality; it can be used for enhancing both passive solar heating and passive cooling.

ing site before construction to determine the direction of prevailing winds during the summer and then position the house and configure the envelope accordingly.

Another way to encourage natural ventilation is by configuring the house to function as a chimney. Consider a ventilating cupola on the roof of the house, the same feature found on the iconic American barn. The barn cupola is louvered and open to the space below the roof, allowing warm air to be vented. The same type of ventilating device can be used on a house roof. It will create an updraft in the house that will draw fresh air into the lower part of the house. Open the lowest windows in the house at night to

> If a new house is designed from the outset for passive cooling, building costs don't have to be any higher than they would for conventional construction.

allow cool outside air to be drawn in, close those windows the next morning to trap the coolness inside. Note that during the winter the interior throat of the cupola must be tightly sealed and well insulated to prevent the loss of heat. (For an example of a cupola, see the house on p. 129. The openings in that cupola are on the north side.)

An operable skylight can be another means of encouraging natural ventilation, although a skylight is more detriment than benefit. The skylight can be opened during the summer to let heat out, much like a cupola. Unfortunately, an unshaded south-side skylight also will allow unwanted solar gain during the summer. Put it on a north-sloping roof to avoid direct solar gain and it can ventilate spaces below, but it will not supply any useful heat during the winter and lose much more heat than a well-insulated roof area. If a skylight is to be used, it should be on the south-sloping roof and have louvered sun shades on the exterior. Louvers should be angled to block the summer sun but allow winter sun in.

If natural or forced ventilation is to be used to maintain interior comfort, then conventional cooling systems should be shut down until the space is unpleasantly warm again. Before turning on the mechanical cooling system, close windows, skylights, and cupolas.

Passive cooling costs

If a house is designed from the outset for passive cooling, building costs don't have to be any higher than they would for conventional construction. If an existing house is to be retrofitted, the cost will depend on what passive cooling strategies are used. For example, adding thermal mass can be expensive, while beefing up insulation in the attic can be relatively inexpensive. High-performance windows, exterior sunshades, and adding a venting cupola all are examples of retrofits that can be expensive. On the other hand, choosing light-colored shingles instead of dark ones when the roof needs to be replaced doesn't necessarily cost more.

Mechanical ventilation, while not a passive cooling strategy, may be a less costly way to provide interior comfort in existing homes than passive cooling. It certainly is a less-energy-intensive solution than air-conditioning. The use of room fans can make most rooms comfortable for much of the summer without air-conditioning. Whole-house exhaust fans can make an entire house comfortable during the night and much of the next day for most, if not all, of the summer. At the least, these strategies reduce the hours an air-conditioner must be operated.

6 ACTIVE SOLAR SPACE HEATING

In many regions of the country, space heating accounts for most annual household energy use. In New England, for example, it is 59 percent, more than electricity and domestic water heating combined. So it's no surprise that many home-owners, builders, and architects show a great deal of interest in active solar space heating.

Heating your home with an active solar system, however, is far more challenging than heating a swimming pool or domestic water and a lot less cost-effective. First, you are trying to achieve the maximum solar benefit at the time of year when there are fewer hours of sunlight, less intense sunlight, more cloudy weather, and colder temperatures (and often snow cover) than at any other time of year. In addition, as air temperatures go down, so does the efficiency of solar collectors.

Heat produced by solar collectors for space heating is needed only about half the year, so the system takes longer to pay for itself than a domestic water heating system that saves fuel

(money) year-round. To make matters worse, there is a scarcity of experienced system design-ers and installers and a shortage of experienced technicians, particularly for emergency service.

An array of liquid-cooled collectors on the main roof of this net zero energy house in Killingworth, Connecticut, supplies hot water for supplemental space heating. The smaller array supplies domestic hot water. (Additional photos of this house are shown on p. 128.)

ABOVE TOP: An east view of the house on p. 127. Architect Whitney Huber positioned the entrance so the collectors would not be visible on the approach to the front door. ABOVE BELOW: Solar electric arrays on the barn behind the house provide power for household needs as well as for a ground-water heat pump.

Homeowners often wonder whether they can eliminate their existing boiler or furnace or install a much smaller one by installing a solar space heating system. This is not the case. Even if the solar system were sized to provide 60 percent of your annual house heating load, there will be periods during the heating season when there is no useful solar energy for 3 days to 5 days at a time. So you'd still need a conventional heating

system, and it would have to be capable of handling 100 percent of the heating load. If the existing heating system is in need of replacement, go ahead and replace it, and then consider the solar system. If you really want a smaller conventional heater, then reduce the need for heat by implementing conservation measures.

ACTIVE VS. PASSIVE SYSTEMS

An active solar space heating system uses an array of solar thermal collectors to convert the sun's energy directly into heat. Collectors are cooled by a fluid—usually air, water, or a glycol-water solution—that is moved by a motor-driven fan or circulator through the collectors. The fluid transports the collected heat to the house, where it can be delivered directly to the occupied spaces or stored for later use.

Most passive solar heating, on the other hand, involves south-facing windows as solar collectors and interior surfaces that have thermal mass, rather than mechanical equipment to capture and distribute solar energy. One type of passive solar heating system does use mechanical equipment of the type used in active solar heating but relies on the sun's heat and gravity to cause the circulation between collector and storage. Approaches to passive solar heating are discussed in Chapter 5.

Direct use vs. heat storage

Direct-use systems supply the sun's heat directly to the house. They tend to have a small collector array area because excess heat can't be stored, and if it can't be stored, it will cause overheating.

This New Hampshire house, designed by architect Thomas P. Hopper, includes vertically installed evacuated tube collectors that supply an active solar spacing heating system. The advantage to the vertical installation is that they remain free of snow when winter storms blow—unlike the roof-mounted thermal and solar electric arrays, which sometimes need clearing with a snow rake.

A heat-storage system, on the other hand, can meet a larger portion of the heating load but it's more complicated to design and install. Thermal storage is a desirable component of a solar thermal system. It enables solar heat energy collected on sunny days to be available when there is cloud cover and at night.

In an active space-heating system with a large array, more heat is collected during the day than can be used to heat the house at that time, necessitating heat storage. A coolant carries the heat from the collectors to a storage medium. As stored heat is needed, a motor-driven blower or circulator distributes it around the house.

This Rhode Island house, designed by architect Don Watson, incorporates a number of solar features, including an off-grid solar electric system, passive solar design, active solar space, and domestic water heating systems with a 600-gal. heat storage tank. A cupola brightens the interior while providing ventilation during the summer.

CONSERVATION FIRST

As with other types of solar system installations, the first dollar you spend should be on conservation. A 50 percent reduction in heat loss can result in a corresponding reduction in the size of the solar system to provide the same solar fraction. The following suggestions are listed by their payback.

SEAL AIR LEAKS. Use caulk and weather-stripping at all doors and windows. They will reduce both heating and cooling costs and pay for themselves in the first winter. Also address air leaks at foundation sills, fireplace flues, sill cocks, dryer vents, bathroom exhaust fans, range exhausts, and attic hatchways.

LOWER THERMOSTAT SETTING. Employ strategies that make you feel warm at lower temperatures. A simple one, of course, is to wear warmer clothing. Use ceiling fans to move the warm air near the ceiling down to where people are. Divide your home into heating zones, heating only the rooms you're using.

UPGRADE INSULATION. The significance of thermal insulation cannot be overstated. Investing in passive or active solar heating does not make sense if all the sun's energy that goes into the home leaks out quickly. It's far more cost-effective to reduce the need for any type of energy with proper insulation than it is to install a renewable energy system to help offset a very large heating load. An insulation retrofit can be expensive, but it will likely be more cost effective than installing a solar space heating system.

INSTALL A HIGH-EFFICIENCY FURNACE OR BOILER. Today's super- and ultra-high-efficiency models (sometimes called condensing furnaces) have annual fuel utilization ratios of over 90 percent. And while you're at it, insulate heat distribution ducts or pipes to reduce the heat that is lost to unheated spaces.

CONSIDER REPLACING EXTERIOR DOORS AND WINDOWS. Newer windows and doors are often easier to operate, need less maintenance, and have higher R-values. You may even choose to eliminate windows that are unnecessary and to downsize windows that are larger than needed, especially on the east, north, and west sides of the house.

CONSIDER MOVEABLE WINDOW INSULATION. If used regularly at night during the winter, window insulation can reduce heat loss by one third. Some types of insulation can be built right into the window frames. Heavy drapes and roller shades that do not seal at the sides and bottom of the window are relatively ineffective.

AVOID THE USE OF CONVENTIONAL FIREPLACES. While they do provide a pleasant ambience, the open damper is a major source of heat loss. Close the damper before the fire goes out and the house fills with smoke.

There are two classes of heat-storing materials, *sensible* and *latent*. Sensible materials, which are widely used, include water, rock (usually in the form of pebbles), concrete, and sand. Latent heat storage materials include eutectic salts and waxes. These materials have yet to gain much of a foothold in the marketplace, but eutectic salts in particular hold great promise. As of yet, however, no one has developed a durable scheme for their use.

HEAT DISTRIBUTION FOR SOLAR SPACE HEATING

Many factors help determine which heat-distribution system is best. Climate is one. In warmer parts of the country where air-conditioning is typical, most central heating and cooling is done with forced air. In colder parts of the country, where air-conditioning is not needed or is less common, hydronic systems are used for heat distribution. In regions between hot and cold climates, there's a mix of both types.

If the solar project is for an existing home, the heating and cooling equipment already in place will often dictate distribution, for reasons of budget. If the project is for new construction or includes a retrofit of the existing heating system, there are fewer limitations. Another factor is whether you want to use liquid-cooled or air-cooled collectors. What follows are some general recommendations. Choose the one that best suits your situation and collector preference.

🏠 If new construction and liquid-cooled collectors are preferred, a separate radiant-floor heat distribution system has the

(*continued on p. 135*)

Radiant flooring is an ideal form of heat distribution for solar-sourced space heating systems because it heats more effectively at lower supply temperatures than conventional radiators.

Homeowners who ask about solar space heating systems often wonder if they can eliminate their existing boiler or furnace by installing a solar space heating system. This is not the case.

Even a well-designed solar system probably isn't going to supply all the space heat you need; some type of supplemental heating system will be required. Conventional heating sources to supplement solar systems can be divided into three main groups: point source, such as a wood or coal stove; a central source (the most common) using a boiler, furnace, or heat pump; and electric resistance heating.

Heat is distributed from the point sources to adjacent spaces by radiation and natural convection. Heating or cooling is distributed from the central source by a forced hot water or forced warm air system. Heat from the electric resistance source is distributed by forced hot water or forced warm air or by wiring to radiant surfaces with embedded resistance coils in the occupied spaces.

Each type of heat distribution system has pros and cons. Here are some of the more significant ones.

RESPONSE TIME. Point sources can warm a space in 15 minutes to 20 minutes. At night, setting back the thermostat that controls the central system can save energy. But if the system takes hours to bring the temperature back up in the morning, conservation benefits are lost. Forced-air systems have a faster response time than other systems. Depending on the house, they are capable of raising the temperature by 10°F (5.5°C) in 10 minutes to 15 minutes. Radiant floor systems with concrete floors are the slowest. If the radiant coils are in a 4-in. (10.2-cm) slab, it may take 12 hours or more to make the house comfortable. When radiant coils are stapled to the underside of a wood frame floor, response times are much faster.

COMPATIBILITY with air-conditioning. Point sources of heat don't supply cooling. Point sources of cooling, such as a window air-conditioner, do not supply heating. Central forced-air systems are used in most single-family homes where cooling is desired because ducts can supply both hot and cool air. Hydronic heat distribution systems are seldom used in houses for cooling unless the house is large. In those cases, chilled water is usually distributed from a central chiller to fan-coil units in the individual spaces. Electric resistance heating systems do not provide cooling, unless a forced-air system is used to distribute heated or cooled air.

HUMIDITY CONTROL. A stand-alone dehumidifier or window air-conditioner can be used to lower relative humidity. A central forced-air system can be used to raise or lower relative humidity. Hydronic heating systems supplying baseboard heaters or radiant surfaces, widely used in colder climates, can't do either.

FILTRATION. If the air in a home must be filtered, either a stand-alone, floor-mounted air filter or a forced-air system with central filtration can be used. A hydronic heat distribution system cannot provide central filtration, unless it distributes heat to fan-coil units. The fan-coil units usually have filters, but these are only particle filters with limited efficiency.

FIRE AND SMOKE SPREAD. Forced-air systems are more conducive to the rapid spread of fire and smoke in a house. Fire dampers and smoke detectors should be used in forced-air systems to minimize that risk. Fire and smoke distribution are not concerns with hydronic systems.

ENERGY REQUIRED FOR HEAT DISTRIBUTION. Energy is required to move heat from a central source of heating to the spaces to be heated. The less energy required to move that heat, the less energy used in that house. Forced-air systems require six to seven times more energy than hydronic systems to deliver the same amount of heat. This is an important consideration in homes that hope to approach net zero energy use.

ZONING. Dividing a house up into separate temperature zones can help save energy. Hydronic systems are easily zoned. Forced-air systems can be zoned, but the dampers and fan speed controls that are needed are relatively expensive.

NOISE. Hydronic systems are much quieter than forced-air systems. Sound can travel through air ducts much more readily than through the piping of hydronic systems. Even duct lining will not completely eliminate the problem.

LONG-TERM THERMAL STORAGE

Just about anyone who has contemplated heating their home with solar thermal energy has wondered whether there's a way to capture solar energy that's so abundant during the summer and store it for winter use. This has been accomplished in single-family homes in a limited number of prototype installations, but it has yet to find widespread application.

The main limitation has been the cost and size of the storage container that is needed. For a poorly insulated house in the Northeast, the storage tank would have to be very large, approaching the size of the house. The lower the heating load, the less heat that must be stored, so well-insulated houses would require smaller storage. But before long-term storage is attempted for even very well insulated houses, much more can be done with passive solar heat and moveable window insulation than is being done today.

Where long-term, or seasonal, heat storage has been successful is at the community scale as well as in commercial applications. There are a number of such projects in western Europe and Canada. When the project is residential, homes in the communities are typically close together and connected by a district heating system. Where solar heat is stored, arrays of solar thermal collectors are tied into the heat distribution system. Both short-term and seasonal thermal storage are used in the same installation.

The location of the heat store depends on site-related conditions. Heat can be stored in water-filled tanks above ground; in aquifers, caves, and pits; and in holes drilled (bore holes) into the ground. This storage means is also used for storing other sources of heat, such as that from heat pumps and co-generation facilities. Seasonal storage of winter cold for summer cooling is also done this way. For more information on a Canadian project, see the Drake Landing Solar Community website (www.dlsc.ca).

The Drake Landing planned solar community in Okotoks, Alberta, Canada, uses a communal solar thermal system for 90 percent of its space heating and 60 percent of its domestic hot water needs. Liquid-cooled collectors for space heating are mounted on the garages of the 52 homes. Collected heat is stored underground during the summer months and is distributed to the homes in winter. The houses are designed to use about 30 percent less energy than conventional houses.

(continued from p. 131)

advantage of requiring much lower supply water temperatures than conventional radiators and of using less energy to distribute heat than forced-air system types.

🏠 If new construction and air-cooled collectors are preferred, a separate forced-air distribution system for the solar array is usually a good idea due to service issues described later.

🏠 When retrofitting an existing forced-air system with liquid-cooled collectors, using solar heat to preheat the return air to the air handler or furnace makes the most efficient use of the collected solar heat. Integrating two systems, however, complicates emergency service.

🏠 When retrofitting an existing hydronic system supplying baseboard radiators, some other separate type of heat distribution should be used for the solar heat—one or more small fan coils, for instance.

🏠 In most houses, central air-conditioning requires a forced-air system, so the solar system can employ either air-cooled or liquid-cooled collectors. But when the conventional heat distribution system and the solar system are integrated, the service issue described later in the chapter can be a deciding factor.

The supply temperature

The supply temperature from a solar array is an important consideration in system design. For a given outside ambient temperature and solar ra-

FORCED-AIR DISTRIBUTION SYSTEMS HAVE ONE BIG ADVANTAGE OVER HYDRONIC SYSTEMS. A heat-exchange coil installed on the return (suction) side of an air handler can use solar-heated liquid to warm the returning air stream. If the solar-heated liquid is hot enough, the solar system will supply all the heat and the burner will not turn on. If the solar-heated liquid is not hot enough, solar heat can still be used to preheat the returning air to the furnace, thereby lessening the amount of conventional fuel needed.

diation level, the higher the supply temperature from a collector, the lower its efficiency. Collector arrays with lower supply temperatures will operate more efficiently than those with high temperatures. If possible, for optimum efficiency of flat-plate collectors during the heating season, the collection loop temperatures should not exceed 120°F (48.9°C).

Forced-air distribution systems

Different types of heat distribution systems have different supply temperature requirements, which can have a major bearing on the system's compatibility with solar collectors.

If the conventional heat distribution system is a fuel-fired, forced-air system, the temperature of the supply air is typically 140°F (60°C). If it is a ground-source heat pump, supply air is between 110°F (43.3°C) and 120°F (48.9°C); with an air-source heat pump, supply air temperatures as low as 90°F (32.2°C) to 95°F (35°C) are not uncommon.

For a given heating load, when the supply air temperature is low, the supply air volume must be high. When this occurs, and the location of supply grilles was not well planned, the air coming out of the grilles will feel cool or cold. When supply air volumes are high (because supply temperatures are low), supply registers must be carefully positioned. Low-temperature supply air also needs larger ducts.

A drawback to forced-air heating is the amount of energy it takes to run the blower. It can use six to seven times as much electricity as the circulator for a typical hydronic system. An advantage to the forced-air heat distribution system is its ability to use solar heat directly from a liquid-cooled array or from the heat storage tank to preheat air returning to the central air handler. This preheating can't be done with a hydronic heat distribution system.

Hydronic heat distribution

Many homeowners with hydronic heat distribution systems that supply baseboard or cast-iron radiators believe an active solar system should be a good fit with their heating systems. That's not often the case. Supply water for baseboard radiators and conventional cast-iron radiators is typically 180°F (82.2°C), with return water 10°F (5.5°C) or 20°F (11.1°C) lower. Lower supply water temperatures can be used, but the surface area of the radiator must be increased to meet the same heating load. Because of that, this type of heat distribution is not suitable for use with liquid-cooled solar thermal systems in a retrofit. If it's new construction, this is possible, but the baseboard radiation area would have to be increased three to five times to use supply water at 100°F (37.8°C) to 110°F (43.3°C).

In radiant-floor heating, supply water is usually between 85°F (29.4°C) and 120°F (48.9°C), depending on outside temperatures. Typically, the lower the outside air temperature, the hotter the supply water. This temperature range is well suited to the efficient operation of liquid-cooled solar thermal systems. If the radiant coils are embedded in the ceiling, a higher temperature is required, typically 120°F (48.9°C) to 160°F (71.1°C), which considerably lowers the efficiency of flat-plate collectors. By spacing the tubing in the radiant surface closer together, somewhat lower supply temperatures can be used.

If the solar heat distribution system is hydronic and multiple small fan coils are used, supply water at the relatively low temperature of 85°F (29.4°C) to 105°F (40.6°C) can be used. This makes these small fan coils particularly attractive for use with solar thermal systems. One advantage they have is quick response time. Air at that temperature can feel cool, though, so fan coils should be located so they don't blow directly on people.

TYPES OF ACTIVE SOLAR SPACE HEATING SYSTEMS

There are a variety of active solar space heating systems and many ways to incorporate them into a home. Some include thermal storage; others don't. Solar heat distribution can be integrated

SOLAR COLLECTORS AND ANY SUPPLEMENTAL HEAT SOURCES should have separate distribution systems. This adds to installation costs but greatly simplifies service—and makes emergency service far easier to get.

This 1,400-sq.-ft. house, designed by Charles W. Moore with Richard B. Oliver, was an early attempt at near net zero design. Heavily insulated, the house has most of its windows on the south side for passive gain. A 4-in.-thick floor slab and thermally massive exterior walls retain passive heat gain. Insulated shades cover the windows and glass doors. In summer, south-side overhangs keep out the sun, and a ventilating belvedere is opened to maintain comfort.

with a conventional system. Other systems are designed so solar and conventional components supply heat independently. (An industry convention is to call them solar integrated and solar separate.)

Some designs work better than others, and some designs are easier to service than others, as discussed next.

The following five active solar system types are the most common. The systems contribute from less than 5 percent to about 60 percent of the annual space heating load, depending on the size of system and the heating load of the house. The ratios of collector area to heated floor area cited here apply mainly to existing houses with the code-minimum levels of insulation and tightness of 10 years to 15 years ago. Extremely tight and well insulated houses, with moderate to significant passive solar provisions, will require fewer collectors (some none at all).

An active space-heating system and water-filled coil behind the fireplace supply heat to the solar storage tank visible in the photo. Heat is distributed through an underslab pebble bed to supply grilles at the periphery of the house, producing a forced-air and radiant-floor effect. The energy systems, designed by author Everett Barber Jr., also include a separate SDHW system.

Small air-cooled array without storage

A small air-cooled array without heat storage is low cost and ideal for heating one or two rooms that are used extensively during the day, such as a home office on the north side of the house where there is no passive solar gain. The array is usually small (less than 5 percent of the total heated floor space). Heat gathered by air-cooled collectors is blown directly into the living space. These systems are simple and trouble-free. There are no heat exchangers, heat storage tanks, or pebble bins and no plumbing tie-ins to a solar domestic water heating system. On the downside, the system sits idle for half the year and provides only a small portion of the total space heating load. Attempts to use these systems to heat domestic water during the nonheating season haven't been very successful.

Small liquid-cooled array without storage

Similar in concept to air-cooled arrays are the small liquid-cooled arrays without storage. These systems use liquid-cooled collectors and can be used year-round. During the heating season, the heated liquid, usually a glycol-water solution, is circulated through a small fan-coil unit (a liquid-to-air heat exchanger with a blower) to supply heat to the house. During the nonheating season, the system can be used to heat domestic water. On the upside, this is a simple, easy-to-maintain solar heating system that, if the array is big enough, can supply all of the domestic hot water during the summer. On the downside, the system provides only a small portion of the total space heating.

 MANY HOMEOWNERS AND ARCHITECTS DON'T LIKE THE APPEARANCE OF BASEBOARD RADIATORS. With forced-air systems, all you see are supply and return registers. To many homeowners, that's visually more appealing. But other factors should be considered. Piping used in a hydronic system takes up much less building space than does the ductwork for a forced-air system. For example, assuming standard temperature differences, a ¾-in.- (1.9-cm-) dia. copper tube can carry about the same amount of heat as a 12-in.- (30.5-cm-) dia. duct.

Two air-cooled collectors blow heat directly into the second-story rooms of this home. Such an arrangement is ideal for rooms that are heavily used during the day, such as a home office or family room, but get little direct solar gain. These collectors contribute only a small fraction of the home's heating needs.

SMALL AIR-COOLED ARRAY WITHOUT STORAGE

An air-cooled collector can be ducted directly to the room or rooms it is meant to heat. A fan blows heated air into the room from a collector mounted on the roof or a wall of the house. A fan intake removes air from the room and returns it to the collector to be reheated.

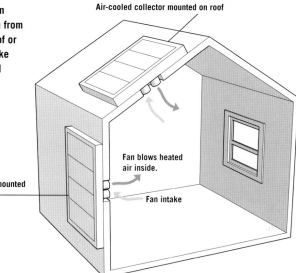

Air-cooled collector mounted on roof

Fan blows heated air inside.

Air-cooled collector mounted on side of house

Fan intake

USING EXISTING DUCTS FOR SOLAR HEAT

An air-cooled system also can be connected to existing heating ducts. The conventional heating system acts as a backup for cloudy days and at night.

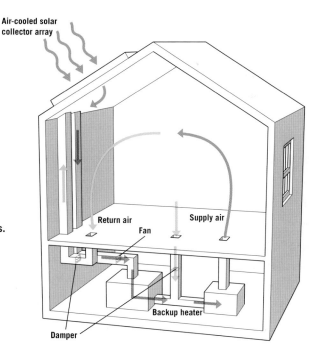

Air-cooled solar collector array

Return air

Supply air

Fan

Backup heater

Damper

AVOID INTEGRATED SOLAR SPACE HEATING SYSTEMS

In an integrated system, solar heat is distributed through the conventional heating system. Installers generally prefer that arrangement because there can be a significant cost savings. But there is an important reason to consider a separate solar system: service, especially emergency service.

Unless the same installer puts in both the solar and the conventional heating systems, it may be very difficult to get emergency service on either one. Most likely, the solar system installer will be unable or unwilling to service the conventional heating system and very few conventional heating system contractors will touch the solar system. At 2 A.M. on a winter night, this is not a problem any homeowner needs. This has been a common and bitter complaint from the owners of integrated systems. Until the industry develops to the point that either contractor can competently service the other's system, stay away from integrated systems.

Medium liquid-cooled array without storage

To satisfy a larger share of the heating load, and to help heat domestic water, a medium array (up to 10 percent of the heated floor space) of liquid-cooled collectors can be used. Heated glycol can be circulated through radiant-floor tubing, where some heat storage is provided, or to one or more small fan-coil units. The system doesn't heat domestic water when it's supplying space heat. In the off-season, it supplies most

if not all of the domestic hot water. These are simple, easily maintained systems, but they still provide a relatively small percentage of the space heating. A drain-back collection loop helps minimize the risk of overheating in summer.

Large air-cooled array with storage

A large air-cooled array with storage has a relatively large array (up to 20 percent of heated floor space) of air-cooled collectors. Heat distribution is by forced air. Heat can be sent directly to occupied spaces as needed or stored, typically in a bed of pebbles or crushed stone. When the returning air from the collectors is directed to storage, heat is transferred directly to the pebbles. No heat exchanger is required to transfer the heat from the air to the pebbles.

These systems often include a separate, smaller array of liquid-cooled collectors to preheat domestic water year-round, which is better than using an air–water heat-exchange coil in

Large liquid-cooled array with storage

Similar to the air-cooled system is the large liquid-cooled array (up to 20 percent of the heated floor space) with storage. When heat is needed, the array can feed one or more fan-coil units. When there's no call for space heat, the system stores heat from the array in a tank of water. To minimize collection energy costs, a separate small array of liquid-cooled collectors can be used for domestic water heating year-round.

These systems collect more heat than an array of forced air-cooled collectors of the same area because liquid-cooled collectors are currently more efficient than air-cooled collectors. But provisions must be made to prevent the coolant in the system from freezing or overheating. The storage tank will probably need to be replaced after 25 years to 30 years.

FACING PAGE and ABOVE: This Maine solar home, designed by architect Robert Knight, includes active space heating. The collector array is ground mounted in an open field for maximum solar exposure.

the return air stream from the collector loop to heat domestic water. The reason is that heat exchangers placed there have a strong tendency to suffer freeze damage, and considerable damage can be done to the house by the leaking water.

Large air-cooled arrays can provide as much as 40 percent to 60 percent of space heating. As long as they are used for space heating only, they do not require protection from freezing or overheating, and the systems have proven reliable. On the downside, some system owners complain of a musty odor from the pebble bed, especially when the system starts heating the house in the fall. The ductwork is much larger than the tubing required for a similarly sized array of liquid-cooled collectors. Energy required to run the fan motor is much greater than that required to run circulators in a comparably sized hydronic solar system.

Thermal storage for an active space heating system is often a liquid-filled steel tank, such as the one shown here during installation. Afterwards, it was insulated with 6 in. of sprayed-on polyurethane foam and enclosed.

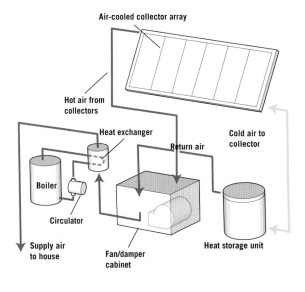

LARGE AIR-COOLED ARRAY WITH STORAGE

This active air-cooled space heating system can operate in four possible modes: solar heated air to the house, solar heated air to storage, storage to the house, and backup heat to the house.

Air-cooled collector array

Hot air from collectors

Heat exchanger

Return air

Cold air to collector

Boiler

Circulator

Supply air to house

Fan/damper cabinet

Heat storage unit

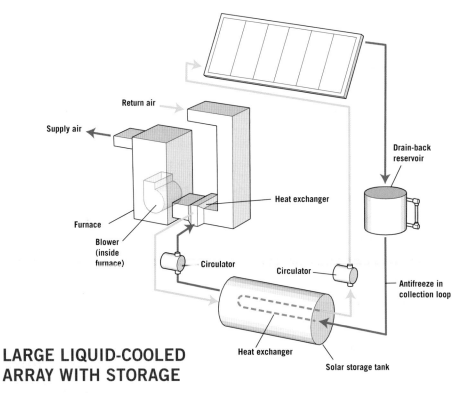

Return air

Supply air

Drain-back reservoir

Heat exchanger

Furnace

Blower (inside furnace)

Circulator

Circulator

Antifreeze in collection loop

Heat exchanger

Solar storage tank

LARGE LIQUID-COOLED ARRAY WITH STORAGE

This active liquid-cooled system stores heat in a large tank of water. Heat can be distributed to the house via radiant flooring or through air ducts, as shown. A liquid-to-air heat exchanger moves the heat from the water in the storage tank to return air entering the furnace.

> I strongly favor solar space heating systems that use a distribution system separate from the conventional heat distribution system just so the system owner can be ensured of emergency service. —E.B.

Solar fraction goes up as heating load goes down

The proportion of space heat a solar array can provide depends, among other things, on how the house is built. At one end of the spectrum are super-insulated houses, built by a very limited number of contractors. At the other end are older, poorly insulated homes with big heating bills. Clearly, the better insulated a house is, the tighter the construction, the less energy of any sort is needed to heat it. The less energy needed to heat the house, the smaller the collector array needed to provide a significant solar fraction. In fact, with good passive design and highly energy efficient construction, there comes a point where an active solar thermal system may not be worth the added cost.

In recent years, some solar installers have been trying to use relatively small arrays, sometimes no larger than would be used to heat domestic water, to provide a significant share of the heating load. In the few cases when house energy consumption and system output have been carefully monitored, the installed solar systems have not come close to their expectations.

SYSTEM COMPONENTS

Three types of collectors can be used for active solar space heating systems: flat plate air-cooled, flat plate liquid-cooled, and evacuated tube liquid-cooled. Each has merit. Air-cooled collectors are less costly and immune to overheating and freezing. But they require relatively large diameter ducts to move heated air and are less efficient than currently available liquid-cooled collectors. Liquid-cooled collectors have a slimmer profile, are more efficient, and use relatively

An air-cooled solar thermal array was added to this well-insulated, 1,200-sq.-ft. (111.5-m²) house on the Connecticut shore. The array can supply heat directly to the house or store heat in a pebble bed. A separate liquid-cooled solar domestic water heating system supplies most of the domestic hot water. Supplemental heat was originally provided by electric resistance coils and later by an oil-fired boiler.

small diameter pipes to move the heated fluid. In addition, liquid-cooled collectors, either flat plate or evacuated tube, are a better choice if the system is going to be used for domestic water heating when space heating is not required. For a more complete review of collectors, see Chapter 2.

Liquid-cooled collectors have the potential for freezing and overheating, whether they are used for space heating or heating domestic water. For a discussion of these problems and their solutions, see Chapter 3.

Collector mounting

Collector arrays for space heating differ from those used for heating domestic water in their tilt angle, orientation, and size. Because a solar space heating system is primarily used in the winter, the ideal angle of tilt will be the latitude of the site plus 15 degrees (see the chart on p. 146). If the roof angle is not that steep but is no less than the local latitude, it may be more economical to mount the collectors parallel with the roof and live with somewhat lower performance than to invest in tilt correction.

An array for space heating also can take up a lot of area. If the roof isn't big enough for the array, a smaller array or a ground-mounted array may be necessary. (For more, see Chapter 2.)

Heat storage tanks

Heat storage tanks for liquid-cooled solar space heating systems store the sun's heat in water at atmospheric pressure. This is significant because this kind of tank is much less costly than one designed to be pressurized. Steel fuel oil tanks and concrete septic tanks have both been widely used to store solar heat. Fuel oil tanks should be made with steel of at least 7 gauge and do not require a lining. Concrete tanks are heavy, but if handled carefully during placement, are quite durable. Many installers either apply an epoxy coating to the inside of the concrete tanks at the seam between tank halves or install an EPDM liner inside the tank.

Heat storage tanks also have been made from sheet metal with steel or wood frames. While heavy polyethylene liners for above-ground swimming pools have been used to line these tanks, the plastic liners become brittle and crack over time. A far better material is 60-mil EPDM rubber, the same material used for roof membranes.

Some tanks are made of sheet metal or fiberglass and a liner. They are usually collapsible, simplifying retrofit installation. Molded polyethylene tanks are not a good choice. They aren't suitable for water temperatures over 140°F (60°C), and water in a well-insulated solar heat storage tank can easily reach 180°F (82.2°C) to 190°F (87.8°C) at some times of

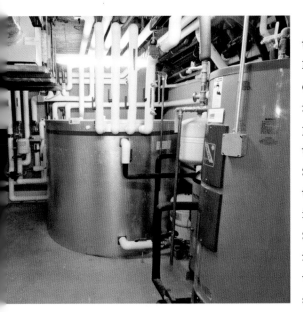

FACING PAGE: Roofing penetrations for ducts from a large air-cooled solar collector array are much larger than those for liquid-cooled collectors. ABOVE: Heat storage tanks can be constructed from sheet metal and a heavy liner, such as this one installed in a basement. One advantage to such tank designs is that they can be installed after the basement is complete.

the year. Polypropylene tanks can handle water temperatures up to 212°F (100°C), but they're more expensive than some other options.

Tank construction depends to some extent on where it is to be installed. If the tank is to be buried (not recommended due to difficulty of access for service), use a rigid tank that can withstand the pressure of the surrounding earth, such as a fuel oil or concrete septic tank. If the tank is to be placed above ground, other types can be used.

All tanks must be well insulated. As a general rule, the thicker the insulation the better. If the tank is to be installed below grade, the insulation must be a closed-cell foam and the tank and insulation should also be protected from ground water.

If the tank is to be installed above ground, then other types of insulation can be used. Fiberglass is the least expensive but loses its effectiveness when compressed or wet. Rigid foam insulation withstands the highest load per square foot, which is important for certain locations (beneath the tank, for example). Sprayed-on polyurethane foam insulation gives the highest R-value per inch thickness but also is the most expensive on a per-board-foot basis. Sprayed-on polyurethane foam is not suitable for long-term exposure to water. If exposure to water is a concern, then a closed-cell insulation, such as expanded polystyrene, is recommended.

Pebble beds

A pebble bed is the most common means of providing heat storage in solar thermal systems using air-cooled collectors. The bed is placed in a sealed, insulated enclosure. Air flow through the bed can be either horizontal or vertical. If horizontal, a plenum is needed at both ends of the bed. If it's vertical, a plenum is needed at top and bottom.

The size of the bed is variable. The air volume passing through the bed, the quantity of heat to be stored, and the cross-sectional area of the bed in the direction of the air flow determine the size of the bed, the diameter of the pebbles, and the type and horsepower of the fan needed to push air. If the air-flow path is long, larger pebbles are used to minimize the air pressure drop. If the air-flow path is short, smaller pebbles are used.

Beds can be designed so air flows in the same direction whether heat is being charged or discharged. Other beds are configured so air

Optimum Tilt and Orientation

In this example, for 40 degrees north latitude, a solar array gets the best winter output when it faces due south at a tilt of 50 degrees to 55 degrees. Other numbers represent the percentages of optimum performance with different tilt angles and orientations.

(Adapted from F-Chart by Emaan Amaar.)

TILT

AZIMUTH	0	5	10	15	20	25	30	35	40	45	50	55	60	65	70	75	80	85	90
South 0	50	59	67	74	81	86	91	95	98	99	100	100	98	96	92	88	83	76	69
20	50	58	66	73	79	84	84	84	84	84	84	84	84	84	84	84	84	84	84
40	50	57	63	69	74	78	78	78	78	78	78	78	78	78	78	78	78	78	78
60	50	54	58	63	66	68	68	68	68	68	68	68	68	68	68	68	68	68	68
80	50	52	53	54	55	56	56	56	56	56	56	56	56	56	56	56	56	56	56
East–West 90	50	50	50	50	50	49	49	49	49	49	49	49	49	49	49	49	49	49	49

HIGH   **LOW**

100–98   97–90   89–80   79–70   69–60   59–50   49–40

flows in one direction for charging and in the opposite direction for discharging. Same-direction beds are simpler but require many hours of fan operation. Opposed-direction beds are more complex but require less fan operation because the last heat stored in the bed is available to the house more readily.

The size and shape of the bed is quite flexible, although they are usually rectangular. It might be a 4-ft. (1.2-m) by 6-ft. (1.8-m) by 8-ft. (2.4-m) bed, for example, or a 2-ft. (0.6-m) by 10-ft. (3.1-m) by 30-ft. (9.1-m) bed. Because of their weight, they usually go in a basement or on a concrete floor slab.

A container for the bed can be made of wood; concrete block; or galvanized, corrugated culvert pipe. It should be well insulated on all sides. Rigid insulation such as polyisocyanurate boards or a closed-cell insulation such as expanded polystyrene is recommended since neither compresses easily. In addition, the pebble bed should be wrapped in a vapor barrier to keep out moisture and prevent the growth of mold.

Collector coolants

Air-cooled collectors use air, exclusively, as the coolant. Liquid-cooled collectors usually use water or a glycol-water solution. Some installers use water in drain back systems, but there's the risk of freezing damage to the collectors. Glycol, when used in a drain-back system, should be mixed with water to have the highest freezing point consistent with the climate. That's because the more dilute the glycol, the better it transports heat.

Other liquid collector coolants that have been used with good success are silicon oil and Brayco 888. The advantage to both is that they have a high boiling point and won't, in fact, boil in flat-plate collectors. However, they are more expensive than glycol-water, don't transport heat as well, and will boil in evacuated-tube collectors.

Heat exchangers

In air-cooled systems, a heat exchanger to transfer the sun's heat from the air to the pebbles in a heat storage bed is not necessary. In most liquid-cooled active space heating systems, however, a heat exchanger is used to transfer heat from the collection loop fluid to the heat storage container.

When distributing stored heat, most liquid-cooled systems don't need a heat exchanger to transfer heat from heated water in the storage tank to the heat distribution system. The water in the tank can simply be circulated through the heat distribution system as needed. However, if the water from the tank must pass through an unheated space or below grade, then a

glycol-water solution should be used in heat distribution piping. If glycol is used there, a heat exchanger is required between the water in the heat storage tank and the glycol. While the heat storage tank could be filled with a glycol-water mix, this is rarely done due to the cost of that much glycol.

Heat dumps

Excess heat is not a problem for air-cooled solar thermal systems, but it can be a problem for some liquid-cooled solar space heating systems, especially during the off-season. If at all possible, some use for heat from the array should be found during the summer to improve system economics. If that's not possible, the system must be able to cope with the heat it can't use.

The most common type of liquid-cooled solar heat collection loop is an indirect type filled with a glycol-water solution. If there is no flow

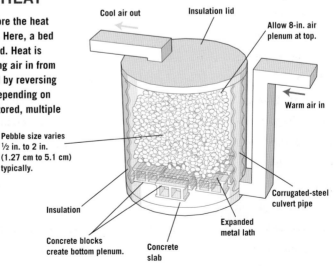

PEBBLE BED FOR STORING HEAT

Pebbles can be used to store the heat from air-cooled collectors. Here, a bed of pebbles is being charged. Heat is stored in the bed by blowing air in from one direction and removed by reversing the direction of air flow. Depending on the amount of heat to be stored, multiple beds may be required.

Cool air out

Insulation lid

Allow 8-in. air plenum at top.

Warm air in

Pebble size varies ½ in. to 2 in. (1.27 cm to 5.1 cm) typically.

Insulation

Concrete blocks create bottom plenum.

Concrete slab

Expanded metal lath

Corrugated-steel culvert pipe

HEAT EXCHANGER IN SOLAR STORAGE TANK

Heat exchangers move heat from one fluid to another. In this example, the heat exchanger at the bottom of the solar storage tank is filled with a heat-transfer liquid that has been heated by an array of liquid-cooled collectors. As the liquid passes through the coil, it transfers heat to the liquid in the tank. The heated liquid is then used to heat the water in the heat exchange coil in the upper part of the tank. The water returning from the space heating system is either heated in the heat exchanger in the upper part of the tank or diverted directly to the instantaneous heater.

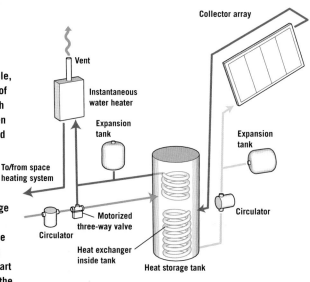

Collector array

Vent

Instantaneous water heater

Expansion tank

Expansion tank

To/from space heating system

Motorized three-way valve

Circulator

Circulator

Heat exchanger inside tank

Heat storage tank

---

through a flat-plate collector on a hot summer day, a collector absorber can top 400°F (204.4°C). The absorber of an evacuated tube collector under the same conditions can exceed 600°F (315.5°C). At these temperatures, the solution in the absorber will boil, often venting through the pressure relief valve, and will gradually break down. After enough fluid leaves the system there will not be enough in the collector loop when heat is needed.

The most common way to deal with excess heat is by using a heat dump. When the temperature of the fluid in the collectors exceeds about 250°F (121.1°C), the collection loop circulator moves the coolant to a place where the heat can be wasted, such as a fan-coil unit. Lengths of fin-tube baseboard radiators located outside or in a basement, or coils of tubing buried in the ground also have been used. In some instances, stored heat can be dumped through the collec-

tors at night by operating the circulator 24/7. This can work well with solar domestic water heating systems but is less successful with solar space heating systems due to the larger collector area.

Air-cooled collector arrays don't overheat. They can simply be switched off for the summer.

Also unaffected by overheating are indirect drain-back systems partially filled with glycol-water solution. When there's no call for heat, the collection loop circulator shuts off and the antifreeze drains to a reservoir.

Other system components

A variety of other parts and pieces are needed to complete space heating systems:

🏠 CIRCULATORS AND BLOWERS. Motor-driven circulators move the collector coolant through the collectors to a point of use or to thermal storage. Circulators also

Differential temperature controllers with a digital display allow the homeowner to see the collector and storage temperatures for both the SDHW system and the space heating system.

are used in hydronic heat-distribution systems to move heat from solar heat storage to radiators or through radiant surfaces. In air-cooled systems, blowers do the same job.

DAMPERS. Gravity-operated and motorized dampers are used in air-cooled space heating systems to control the flow of air through ducts, collectors, and thermal storage beds.

DIFFERENTIAL THERMOSTATS. In its simplest form, a differential thermostat has two sensors, one at the collector array and one on or in the heat store. When the temperature in the array reaches 20°F (11.1°C) or so above the storage sensor, the thermostat switches on the blower or circulator. When the collector sensor cools to within about 5°F (2.8°C) above the storage sensor, the thermostat turns off the blower or circulator. Most differential thermostats also have a high-limit setting that will stop

heat collection if the heat store becomes too hot. Many of the thermostats presently on the market have optional digital displays that show the collector and storage temperatures.

THE ECONOMICS OF SOLAR SPACE HEATING

First, some generalizations. If a solar space heating system is used only for space heat, and not for domestic hot water in the summer, recouping your investment with avoided fuel costs will take longer. Also, systems that include heat storage are more expensive than systems without it.

The installed cost of a solar space heating system is usually expressed in terms of dollars per square foot of collector area. That includes all system components, plus the labor to install them. At the low end of the cost spectrum, a system that includes two 4-ft. (1.2-m) by 8-ft. (2.4-m) air-cooled collectors but no heat storage could cost between $60 and $120 per square foot ($645 and $1,290 per square meter) installed. It would heat a few rooms on sunny days. At the high end of the spectrum, a system with twenty 4-ft. (1.2-m) by 8-ft. (2.4-m) collectors, plus heat storage, might cost between $90 and $160 per square foot ($968 and $1,720 per square meter) installed but it would provide a substantial amount of the heat in a moderately well insulated house.

These numbers don't include rebates or incentives. But even with the most generous incentives available, a solar space heating system is difficult to justify economically if the heat is used only in winter. Your money is better invested in conservation.

SYSTEM MAINTENANCE

For the most part, maintenance for solar space heating systems is similar to that required on conventional forced-air and hydronic heat systems. But it varies somewhat, depending on what type of system you have.

ALL SYSTEMS

If the system is mounted on the roof, check the seals at all roof penetrations at least once a year. After several years, flashing boots have a tendency to leak. The best place to check for leaks is on the underside of the roof deck.

AIR-COOLED COLLECTORS

Filters in the heat collection loop (and any in the heat distribution part of the system) should be checked for dirt buildup at least twice a year. If they are dirty, they should be cleaned or replaced, depending on the type of filter.

Make sure that any dampers in the system operate and that seals are intact.

Check any roof penetrations for leaks.

LIQUID-COOLED COLLECTORS

Confirm that the collectors are delivering heat. This is an important test. It's easily made by checking the temperature of the heat storage tank at the start and end of a clear day. If the temperature has increased during the day, the system is most likely working.

If a glycol-water solution is used in the collection loop, check the fluid freeze point annually. For optimum heat transfer, it should be slightly below the lowest likely winter temperature for the region. This is usually done with a refractometer. If a heat transport oil is used, this test is not necessary.

Check the pH of the glycol-water solution annually. It should be 7.0 or higher when copper tubing is used. If a heat transport oil is used in the collection loop, pH is not a concern.

Don't change the fluid every few years just because you've heard that is needed. Unfortunately, a common practice of a few solar service companies is to change the fluid every 2 years to 3 years. A stable glycol, such as Dowfrost™ HD, can last for 20 years or more.

FILLED SYSTEMS ONLY

Check the pressure in the collection loop at least every 2 months or 3 months. The pressure should be high enough to minimize air migration into the piping loop and to suppress boiling to at least 250°F (121°C). Gauge pressure is typically between 30 psi (2 bar) and 75 psi (5 bar). If it's below about 10 psi (0.7 bar), a pressure boost is likely in order.

Setting up a service agreement with a reputable solar service company is a good idea. Arrange to have the system inspected at least once a year. The inspection should be made some time before or early into the heating season. An experienced service technician is much more likely to spot problem areas than a homeowner.

IT IS UNLIKELY THAT YOU WILL find anyone who can correctly size a solar thermal system simply by looking at the house. A quantitative analysis is needed. If a contractor or salesperson is unwilling or unable to perform one, find another installer.

SIZING A SYSTEM

The size of a solar space heating system is typically discussed in terms of its solar fraction, which is how much of the heating load it can handle.

Heating loads are based on the construction of the house, including the heated floor area, insulation, windows, doors, and air-tightness. Once the design heat loss has been calculated, then a solar heating system output analysis is made. This is usually done with a computer program such as F-Chart. The program accounts for the local climate and produces tables showing the monthly solar fraction for the proposed system. Typically, the F-Chart analysis is made several times with a different system size plugged in each time. The size that fits the owner's budget is usually the one chosen.

A large, leaky house without much insulation will need collectors equal to 10 percent of the heated floor area to provide no more than 10 percent to 15 percent of the annual heating load. If a similar-size house is very well insulated, construction is tight, and passive solar heating is used as well, the same collector area might provide 60 percent to 70 percent of the annual heating requirement. There is no way to reasonably predict the solar fraction without someone doing a careful analysis.

As a practical matter, the size of the solar space heating system that a homeowner eventually installs has more to do with the homeowner's budget than with anything else.

HOW LONG WILL THE SYSTEM LAST?

Provided good-quality components are used, a well-installed solar thermal system should last about as long as a hydronic or forced-air heating system. That said, you can expect good flat-plate solar thermal collectors to last at least 50 years. That's significant because the collectors can represent 60 percent to 70 percent of the material cost of the system.

Circulator and fan motors can be expected to last 20 years to 25 years, but it might be advantageous to replace them sooner as more efficient motors become available. Dampers, motors, and thermostats may last 15 years to 20 years. Circulators and circulator motors and motor-operated valves and thermostats can be expected to last

If a large solar space heating system is desired, then the system will return greater savings if the energy it supplies can be put to use during the summer months, by heating a swimming pool, for example.

Calculating Payback

This chart shows payback for a residential space heating and domestic hot water system where fuel oil is the supplemental fuel. It assumes hot water usage of about 64 gal. (242 L) a day in a well-insulated house of 1,500 sq. ft. (139 m²) in the northeastern United States. The solar array is 160 sq. ft. (15 m²). Estimates include a 30% federal income tax credit.

(Analysis by Everett M. Barber Jr.)

RESIDENTIAL SPACE and DOMESTIC WATER HEATING (YEARS TO PAYBACK)*

	ANNUAL RATE OF FUEL COST INCREASE		
Annual Rate of Electricity Cost Increase	5%*	10%	15%
$100/sq. ft. ($1,070/m²)	19	14	12
$120/sq. ft. ($1,290/m²)	20+	16	13
$140/sq. ft. ($1,500/m²)	20+	17	14
$160/sq. ft. ($1,720/m²)	20+	18	15
$180/sq. ft. ($1,940/m²)	20+	19	15
CO_2 saved (lb./year)	3,965	3,965	3,965
Estimated annual savings (year 1)	$491	$491	$491
Estimated annual savings (year 10)	$762	$1,158	$1,728

*1970 to 2000 rate for New Hampshire 5.1% (EIA data)

Avoided cost of fuel oil displaced by solar: (No 2) $2.80/gal ($0.74/L)

System will not provide 100% of space heating load for any month of heating season.

System will provide 100% of domestic water heating load for non-space heating season.

15 years to 20 years. If thermal expansion tanks are used in the hydronic solar thermal system, they typically last 5 years to 7 years.

SOLAR ELECTRIC HEAT

So far, we've discussed the use of solar thermal systems to heat homes. But many homeowners are curious to know if a solar electric system can be used for space heat. After all, the reasoning goes, electricity has been used for decades to heat homes with baseboard electric heaters or radiant walls or ceilings, so why can't it be done with electricity generated by the sun?

In fact, it can, but due to the much lower efficiency of solar electric collectors compared to solar thermal collectors, the array must be quite large to provide even a modest portion of the electrical energy consumed by an electric resistance heater. A large array of solar electric collectors is expensive.

A heat pump is a much more efficient way of using electricity to provide space heating, requiring about one third as much electrical energy through a heating season as resistance heaters. Depending on the climate, the heat pump can use the ambient outside air or the earth as its source of heat. If you are determined to use solar electric modules to heat your home, then it should be done with a heat pump.

As yet, we've seen no third-party data to confirm that a solar electric system/heat pump combination is a more cost effective way to heat a house than a solar thermal system. Before choosing such a system, check the incentives available to you. The combined effect of federal and local tax credits and rebates may result in a lower cost solar electric system/heat pump than a solar thermal system, which does not enjoy all of the incentives.

SOLAR FRACTION is the portion of the annual heating load that will be met by the solar system. A solar system that is said to have a solar fraction of 0.5 means that it will provide about 50 percent of the annual space heating need. The conventional heater still must be sized to provide 100 percent of the design heating load because there will be days when the solar system will produce no useful heat.

TECH CORNER | BOOSTING SYSTEM PERFORMANCE

One way to get significantly more heat out of a given size solar array is to lower the collection temperature. That's because for a given ambient temperature, the hotter a collector is made to operate, the lower is its efficiency.

In a conventional active solar thermal system, the lower end of the collection loop temperature is limited by the lowest temperature that can be used to satisfy the demand for heat from the house. In a performance-enhanced active solar system, a reasonable supply temperature to the house can be maintained and the collection loop temperature can be lowered. This can be done by using a heat pump to take heat from the solar heat storage container and boost the temperature to normal heating supply temperatures.

During the coldest time of the winter, the heat pump will maintain the heat storage container at well below the temperatures that are encountered in conventional solar thermal systems. By collecting heat at those reduced temperatures, the heat collected by a given array size can be increased significantly, sometimes as much as doubled.

A drawback to this type of system is the need for service technicians who are competent to service solar thermal and heat pump based systems. If they are readily available, this is a good marriage of technologies. If they are not, once the system fails, it is worthless.

7

CONVERTING SUNLIGHT TO ELECTRICITY

Solar electricity has been in the news a lot in the last few years. In some parts of the country, in addition to a sizeable federal income tax credit, significant state tax credits, rebates, and leasing programs are now available. Largely as a result of those incentives, over the past 5 years the installed cost of solar electric systems has dropped by almost 30 percent. There's also the promise of lower utility bills, a hedge against future rate hikes, and a smaller carbon footprint.

There is, however, more to solar electricity than most salespeople will tell you. First, unless a lease program is available, even with incentives a solar electric installation represents a significant investment. Second, for solar electric systems to satisfy a sizable percentage of your energy requirements, you'll have to take a hard look at how much electricity you consume and whether you're willing to break old habits of consumption. That said, this chapter will help you decide what sort of solar electric system will work for you and give you a clearer picture of what the installation entails.

ABOVE TOP and **BOTTOM:** Solar energy has long held a fascination and promise with consumers. At the solar exposition in 1955, the first solar electric collector, then called a solar battery, was unveiled.

ABOVE LEFT and RIGHT: This off-the-grid house in Dorchester, New Hampshire, was designed by architect Stu White. It is powered by two thin-film laminate solar electric arrays, which were applied to the standing-seam metal roofs of the main house and to a small barn. Heat is supplied by a wood-fired boiler.

A LITTLE HISTORY

The first photovoltaic cell was invented at Bell Labs in 1954. Following that discovery, solar electric applications of the late 1950s and early 1960s were limited to space programs. As time passed, the technology evolved, and terrestrial applications were developed as well. These early uses included calculators, charging batteries for highway signs, navigation aids, and communication stations.

During the 1970s, interest developed in using solar electric systems to provide power for marine use, recreational vehicles, and off-grid homes (those not connected to a utility electric grid). Most of those off-grid systems were small because solar-module costs were high and off-grid houses used propane appliances to minimize electric loads. The increasing availability of solar modules prompted a rapid development of appliances that use the direct current (DC) that solar modules supply.

As the off-grid movement grew, many converts wanted the alternating current (AC) appliances they had grown up with. But to get the DC electricity from the solar electric modules to AC electricity, a device called an *inverter* is needed. For many years, electromechanical devices called *rotary inverters* were available. In the early 1970s, the first solid-state inverters came on the market. Urban legend has it that what drove sales for the first solid-state inverter manufacturer were California marijuana growers. They lived off the grid . . . far off the grid! These devices produced AC electricity that, while not as clean as utility power, was good enough to power most off-grid residential appliances. As the inverter industry began to produce inverters for solar applications, *(continued on p. 158)*

CONSERVATION FIRST

By making a concerted effort, most people can reduce the amount of electricity they consume by 50 percent without changing their lifestyle. Consider a solar electric system only after those changes have been made. After conservation, that $65,000 solar system you thought you needed will cost only $32,500.

LIGHTING

🏠 Get the family into the habit of turning out lights when they leave the room or install occupancy sensors that do it for them.

🏠 Use dimmer switches where possible.

🏠 Substitute compact fluorescent lights (CFLs) for incandescent lights or, better yet, swap them for light-emitting diodes (LEDs). CFLs use about 75 percent less energy than incandescent lamps; LEDs use between 90 percent and 95 percent less energy than incandescents. In both cases, costs are higher but so is lamp life.

🏠 Install a timer or motion detector for outside lights. For lights that must be left on, use LEDs, or try solar-powered security lights.

LED-powered entry lights reduce electricity consumption by 90 percent compared to incandescent lights and will dramatically reduce the frequency of bulb changes.

HOUSEHOLD APPLIANCES

🏠 If your house is heated with electric resistance heat, replace it with an appliance that burns natural gas or propane. If you live in a mild climate, consider an air-source heat pump instead of electric resistance heat.

🏠 Augment an electric water heater with a solar thermal system or replace it with a gas- or oil-fired water heater.

🏠 If you have an electric range, replace it with a gas range. Remember that a microwave oven cooks more efficiently than an electric range.

🏠 Turn off the dry cycle on your dishwasher. Prop open the dishwasher door to allow the dishes to dry.

Occupancy sensors are a convenient way to have lights turn off automatically when a room is no longer occupied.

- Replace an electric clothes dryer with a gas or propane model, and hang clothes to dry outside when you can.

- Replace appliances with inefficient motors with high-efficiency models.

- Clean refrigerator condenser coils a couple of times per year, and don't set the thermostat lower than it needs to be.

- Use the yellow EnergyGuide^{SM} labels for quantitative guidance when replacing appliances. The much touted Energy Star® labels do not provide quantitative data on energy consumption.

- Avoid buying a refrigerator too big for your needs. Top-freezer models are more efficient than side-by-sides or models with the freezer on the bottom.

COOLING

- Replace older air-conditioners with models that have high seasonal energy efficiency ratios (SEERs).

- Consider a whole-house exhaust fan as a way to eliminate or at least reduce the amount of time an air-conditioner must run.

- To keep attics cooler and lower the cooling load in the house, install a wind-assisted turbine vent in the roof or install a power vent in the gable.

- When reroofing, consider white or light-colored shingles. They will make a huge reduction in attic temperature compared to dark shingles.

ELECTRONICS

- Shut off computers when not in use. A single laptop computer running 6 hours a day can use 7.2kWh a month; a desktop 18kWh.

- Upgrade your television. An older model drawing 145W of electricity will consume more than 52kWh a month if it runs 12 hours a day. A big plasma TV will use more than 250kWh per month if on for 12 hours.

- For easier control, plug computers, peripherals, televisions, and other electronic equipment into a power strip with a pilot light and an on/off switch. When the equipment isn't being used, turn off the power strip. This prevents the device from drawing any power in standby mode, which is sometimes called a *phantom load.*

- Plug the adapters for calculators, cell phone chargers, and other devices into a power strip, and turn on the strip only when the device is being used. Many power adapters draw power even when they're not on.

OVERALL ELECTRICITY USE

- Consider a whole-house energy monitor as a way to focus your attention on all the electrical loads in your house. The monitor will display the energy being consumed at any given time. That information is very helpful in ferreting out individual, unwanted, loads. By diligent use of such a tool, users have been able to reduce their electrical loads by 75 percent to 80 percent. Several such devices are available. For starters, look at The Energy Detective™ products (www.theenergydetective.com). Other, more elaborate meters are available.

(continued from p. 155)

the number of off-grid houses using the unrefined form of AC grew rapidly.

The idea of using a solar electric system to connect to the utility company lines so that house loads could be shared with the utility company had been around for decades, but until the early 1990s, no one had been able to develop an efficient solid-state inverter that produced AC electricity of a quality acceptable to the utilities. In about 1993, an electronic inverter that produced high-quality AC electricity became commercially available. With this innovation, the grid-tied house became possible. While that development was significant technologically, the number of grid-tied houses increased slowly, due mainly to the high cost of the solar electric systems. Then, in the middle to late 1990s, electric utility company restructuring occurred throughout much of the United States. One of the byproducts of restructuring was incentive programs set up to stimulate the use of solar electric systems. The incentives greatly improved the affordability of solar electric installations. As the incentives became available across the country, the number of grid-tied solar electric installations increased dramatically.

SOLAR ELECTRIC SYSTEMS FOR RESIDENTIAL USE

There are three basic types of residential solar electric systems:

- off-grid
- grid-tied without batteries
- grid-tied with batteries

Off-grid solar homes aren't connected to the utility's grid. Solar-generated electricity is stored in batteries. Owners of these systems usually have a supplemental source of thermal energy, such as propane, and a fuel-fired generator. In a few instances, they may supplement electricity from the solar system with electricity from wind or microhydro.

Grid-tied systems without batteries are used in homes that connect (inter-tie) to the utility grid. During the day, when the sun is shining, the solar system produces most, if not all, of the electricity needed. Electricity that is not used in the house is fed into the grid. At night, the grid supplies whatever electricity is needed. The majority of grid-tied systems are of this type.

Grid-tied systems with batteries are used in homes that connect to the utility grid and are found mostly where power outages are common.

WHAT WE SPEND ON ELECTRICITY

In the average U.S. home, electricity accounts for about 20 percent of total annual energy use. The actual percentage depends on how many people live in the household, what appliances they have, where the house is located, and how actively conservation is practiced. Across the country, the cost of electricity ranges from about 7¢ a kilowatt hour to 25¢. According to the U.S. Energy Information Agency, the average residential consumption is 888kWh a month, meaning average bills range from $62 to $222, not including service charges and other fees.

Installing the modules is best done on a roof that has many years of life left. It's not a job you want to do more often than necessary.

Because this type of system is more costly, it is used much less often than grid-tied systems without batteries.

In utility districts that offer net metering for renewable energy systems, homeowners get credit at the retail rate for electricity they produce, up to the net zero point, which is the point at which the solar system generates as much power as the house consumes. Beyond that point, and depending on the company, the utility may or may not provide further compensation. When added compensation is provided, it is often at the wholesale rate (that is, at the rate the utility company buys power from its suppliers). In effect, the grid serves as storage for the solar electric system without batteries, in somewhat the same way that batteries serve as storage for the off-grid systems. As a storage medium, however, the grid is a much more efficient way to store electricity than are batteries. Once batteries are fully charged, there is no place for the additional electricity to be stored. Any excess production is wasted.

Off-grid systems

Most nonsolar, off-grid homes rely on propane and fuel-fired generators to meet their energy needs. But as off-grid solar electric systems become less costly, more homeowners are installing solar electric systems for household loads, such as lights and many appliances, and relying on propane for their heavy thermal loads.

The primary attraction of off-grid solar electric systems is that they allow people to build on less expensive, underdeveloped parcels of land that are not close to utility lines. To compare the cost of an off-grid solar electric system with that of utility company power, consider how much

OFF-GRID SYSTEM

Off-grid systems use solar electric modules to charge the battery bank via a charge controller. The DC current from the batteries can then be changed to modified sine wave AC by the inverter, or by omitting the inverter, simply used as DC, in which case appliances and lighting fixtures must be DC compatible.

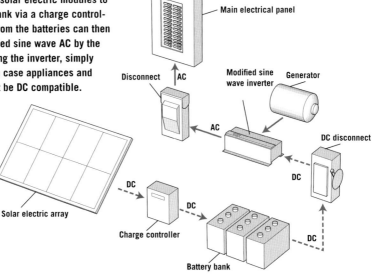

Main electrical panel

Disconnect | AC

Modified sine wave inverter | Generator

AC

DC disconnect

DC

DC

Solar electric array

DC

DC

Charge controller

Battery bank

DC

it costs to get power to the site. Typical rates for running above-ground power lines to a building site range between $10 and $25 per foot ($32.81 and $82.02 per meter). For example, if you are a half mile from the nearest power line and the utility charges $15 per foot ($49.21 per meter), the cost of the solar electric system would have to be less than $39,600 to justify on an installed cost basis. (Below-ground rates for electric utility connection are generally much higher and depend greatly on subsurface conditions.)

Unlike utility company power, electricity from the solar electric system, once installed, is free. And, if you have been off-grid for some time without a solar electric system, you will find that you won't need a noisy generator running 24/7 or the maintenance or fuel deliveries that go along with it.

For some sites, an off-grid solar electric system is the only feasible way to provide electrical service.

If, as a homeowner, you are determined to install a solar electric system and disconnect from the grid, that can certainly be done, but it may involve some lifestyle changes as well as deep pockets.

Grid-tied systems

The vast majority of the more than 100 million dwelling units in the United States are connected to the electric power grid. Consequently, most homeowners considering solar electric systems will be interested in a grid-tied system.

Homeowners opt for solar electric systems for a variety of reasons: incentives and rebates that make the systems more affordable, lower power bills, concern for the environment, and less reliance on foreign oil. But cost is a major consideration. Many homeowners can't afford a system that will supply all the electricity they use (on average, 888kWh a month in the United States in 2001). Regardless of the depth of your pocket, reducing your electrical loads before buying a solar electric system makes good sense.

Grid-tied systems are still beholden to the grid. The inverter, which converts DC electricity coming from the array to grid-quality AC electricity, constantly checks the quality of power

ABOVE TOP: This roof-integrated PV system is part of a grid-tied development in San Jose, California. The PV slate placement is well above the dormers that might otherwise shade and degrade the system performance. ABOVE MIDDLE: This grid-tied Massachusetts development features solar-electric systems on each house as standard equipment. ABOVE BOTTOM: This solar electric home in Milton, Massachusetts, boasts an 8.4kW system. It was installed by groSolar®, one of several companies that lease equipment to homeowners through a power purchase agreement (see p. 181).

(see p. 181)

GRID-TIED SOLAR ELECTRIC SYSTEM

Grid-tied systems supply AC electricity to the main circuit breaker box that is also served by utility company power. Thus wired, the house can get electricity from either its solar electric modules or when that is not possible, from the utility grid. Most homeowners choose this type of solar electric system.

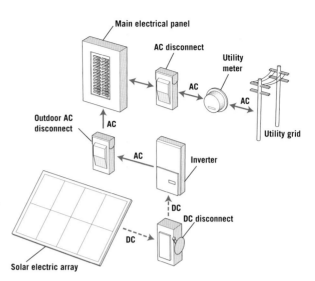

GRID-TIED WITH BATTERY BACKUP

A grid-tied system with battery backup supplies AC electricity to the main electrical panel that is also served by utility company power. Thus wired, the house can get electricity from either its solar electric modules or when that is not sufficient, from the utility grid. When utility company power fails, the solar electric system switches from the main electric panel to supply AC power to a separate critical loads panel. This type of system is chosen in places where frequent utility company power failure occurs.

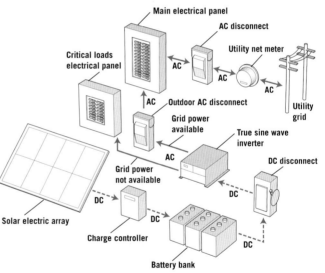

Seldom does anyone install a grid-tied solar electric system with battery backup to provide 100 percent of the electricity for the house. The cost is usually prohibitive.

from the grid. If the grid falters or fails completely, the inverter immediately shuts off. It does not restart until grid power has been on and normal for 5 minutes. If there is a power outage, your grid-tied solar electric system without batteries does not produce power. This feature helps protect utility workers who may be working on nearby power lines.

Grid-tied with battery backup

Grid-tied systems with a battery backup supply power for critical household loads when utility power fails. Because the batteries and charge controller are an extra expense, these systems are found mainly where grid power failures are common. These systems have more of the characteristics of an off-grid system than of a grid-tied system. They include batteries, a charge controller to properly charge the batteries, a true sine wave inverter, and a separate emergency loads circuit breaker box.

When grid power is available, the solar array charges the batteries and the batteries feed the inverter, which supplies power to the main distribution panel for the house. When grid power fails, the inverter automatically switches its output to supplying AC power to the critical loads circuit breaker box. This separate distribution panel is connected to selected loads, such as the heating system, well pump, and refrigerator.

You pick the critical loads when you install the system. You also decide how many days of autonomy (days without sun) the battery bank should be sized for—the more days

of autonomy, the bigger the battery bank. Most homeowners settle on 3 days or less.

Seldom does anyone install a grid-tied solar electric system with battery backup to provide 100 percent of the electricity for the entire house. The cost is usually prohibitive. If you want to have all household electrical loads met when the utility company fails, the most feasible solution is to install an auto-start, fuel-fired generator.

SYSTEM COMPONENTS

Solar electric collectors are available in a variety of types, either as glazed modules or as unglazed flexible laminates. (For more information, see Chapter 2.) At present, glazed modules are three or four times more efficient than laminates and are the most widely used.

At the same time, laminates have some characteristics that make them a better choice in certain situations. First, they are light in weight, which is critical when the roof can't handle a lot

In an innovative dual usage, solar electric modules can be used to build the roof of a carport.

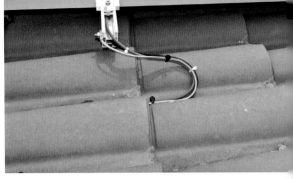

This California home's solar electric array was installed on a pergola, which shades the deck below.

of extra weight. Second, they are available in roll form and can be installed between the seams of a standing seam metal roof. This feature appeals to some homeowners who don't like the look of modular collectors.

Another form of laminate-type collector that has received considerable media attention is the solar shingle. They look much like traditional shingles and are integrated with traditional shingles on the roof.

Other solar roofing products use solar electric modules operating at higher efficiency. They're attached to the roof, much like traditional slates or tiles. They are more costly than modular collectors, but because they're integral to the roof, some owners find them more appealing visually.

ABOVE TOP: Flat-plate solar electric modules can be mounted on almost any type of roof, including tile (shown), slate, wood, and asphalt. ABOVE BOTTOM: Solar slates help mitigate qualms some homeowners have about the appearance of roof modules.

Inverters change DC current from the solar electric collectors to AC current to power standard household appliances and lighting. All grid-tied solar electric installations require an inverter.

allows the solar electric system to provide more power with fewer solar modules. Most newer inverters offer this feature. Old-style inverters do not.

INVERTERS FOR OFF-GRID APPLICATIONS In cases in which an off-grid system includes an inverter, it's likely to be a modified sine wave inverter. The wave form it produces is not a perfect sine wave but it's acceptable for virtually all AC household loads and it's less expensive than a true sine wave inverter. An even less expensive option is a square wave inverter, which can be used for some individual loads, such as incandescent lights, power supplies, and small heaters. The square wave inverters are usually low-wattage devices and are seldom used for whole-house loads. True sine wave inverters (discussed later) must be used for grid-tied applications, but their extra cost is hard to justify for off-grid use.

Most off-grid inverters are available with an integral battery charger. These have terminals that allow them to be connected to an AC generator. When the inverter is operated in charger mode, the AC generator can be used to charge storage batteries and power loads in the house at the same time. Generally, these are very powerful chargers and well worth the small extra cost.

INVERTERS FOR GRID-TIED SYSTEMS True sine wave inverters are one of the more significant innovations in the electronics industry of the

Inverters

Although an inverter is required for all grid-connected systems, they are optional for off-grid applications and in many cases aren't used at all. Instead, appliances run on DC power. While this may seem odd to many homeowners, a good selection of DC appliances is available. Eliminating the inverter makes the system less expensive and that much more reliable because there's one less costly part to fail.

A particularly important feature of a good inverter is the ability to provide maximum power point tracking (MPPT). This feature uses software that allows the inverter to search for the point where the current and voltage of the photovoltaic module produce the maximum power output available regardless of cloud cover or ambient temperature. Basically, this feature

Several types of batteries can be used in solar electric systems. By far the most common is the deep-cycle lead-acid battery. *Deep cycle* means the battery can be deeply discharged and then recharged many times before it will no longer hold a charge. While many neophytes try to use them, car batteries are inappropriate for use in solar electric systems. They are intended to provide a large flow of current for a short duration. If you deeply discharge a car battery just a few times, it will no longer hold a charge and must be replaced.

Deep-cycle batteries can go through as many as several thousand charge–discharge cycles before they fail. They are available in three types: wet cell (flooded cell), gelled cell, and absorbed glass matt (AGM). The last two are known as sealed or maintenance-free batteries. The AGM battery is relatively new compared to the gelled-cell battery. In an off-grid house, wet-cell batteries are a better choice because the state of charge can be determined accurately with a hydrometer at any time. They also last longer, have greater storage capacity, and are about half the cost.

Typical battery bank voltages for off-grid houses are 12V, 24V, and 36V. A few systems use 48V battery banks. The voltage of individual batteries ranges from 2V to 12V DC. Individual batteries for off-grid systems are arranged in series and parallel combination to produce the desired voltage. The higher the battery bank voltage, the smaller the wire needed to carry the same amount of power. Smaller wire is less expensive.

The inverter is chosen to match the battery bank voltage on the input (DC) side of the inverter. If the battery bank produces 12V DC, house wiring is very likely to be DC, although inverters with 12V DC input are available. If the battery voltage is 24V, 36V, or 48V, then the distribution system is likely to be AC.

last 20 years. The AC power they produce is at a frequency, voltage, and quality acceptable to utilities so the power can be supplied directly to the grid.

Some manufacturers offer small inverters that are integral with solar modules. These module–inverter combinations produce 120v AC and can be connected directly to the house distribution system. While at first glance there is undoubtedly some merit to this approach, reliability is a concern. Now, instead of one or two inverters that can fail, there might be 20, 30, or 40 modules in the system, each with its own inverter that can fail. A gradual loss of output from the solar array caused by the failure of several small inverters could be difficult to detect.

Most inverters for grid-tied residential systems can be located outdoors or indoors. However, not all inverters for off-grid systems can be located outdoors without a separate enclosure.

Charge controller

A charge controller regulates how batteries are recharged. When batteries are discharged and sun is on the array, the charge controller begins recharging with a constant current charge. This is also known as the bulk charge, which is the highest level of charge. As the battery voltage or state of charge increases, the charge controller transitions to a constant voltage charge, also known as the absorption level charge. Finally, it transitions to the float level of charging, which offsets the battery's tendency to self-discharge.

Modern solar charge controllers include an equalizing charge feature. This provides a higher-than-normal charge rate to reduce the

A charge controller regulates charging of batteries in off-grid systems and in grid-tied systems with battery backup.

IN GRID-TIED SYSTEMS, the inverter is connected to the grid via one or two circuit breakers in the main panel. When the solar system is delivering electricity to the circuit breaker box and the electrical loads in the house are less than the inverter output, surplus electricity goes into the grid. When there is no electricity available from the solar system, the grid supplies the power.

buildup of sulfur on battery plates and extend battery life. The equalizing charge is applied for a short time, usually a few hours, sometimes monthly and sometimes no more than twice a year, depending on the battery. Another important feature of a good charge controller is MPPT, the same function most newer inverters have.

Combiner boxes

Solar electric modules for grid-tied applications are connected in strings. There may be as few as one or two modules in a string or as many as eight, depending on the rated voltage of the module and the required input voltage to the inverter. A combiner box combines the output of multiple strings of modules. Usually the box is located as close as possible to the solar array so a single pair of wires runs from the array to the inverter. The box is mainly a way to use less wire. Each string circuit also is fused to protect the inverter and charge controller from lightning.

Converters

A converter is used only in DC wiring systems and is not always required. It steps DC voltage up or down, like a transformer in an AC system.

Additional grid-tied components

Some utilities allow traditional bidirectional meters to keep track of electricity consumption. This type of meter can turn in both directions, running forward when the house is on utility power and backward when solar arrays are producing more power than is being used. At the end of the billing period, the electric bill is based on the net result. If more power was supplied by the solar system than consumed, the utility may credit the system owner for the power supplied above zero net. Some utility companies provide that credit at the wholesale rate they pay for electricity; others give no credit at all.

In recent years, many utilities have replaced bidirectional meters with two one-directional digital meters, commonly called "buy" and "sell" meters. The buy meter registers the electricity used by the house. The sell meter registers the electricity sold by the house to the utility.

Another component of a grid-tied installation is the manual outdoor disconnect for the inverter's AC output. The disconnect is usually located close to the electrical service entrance to the house and is required by utilities as a back-up safety device. If switched off by the utility company, it prevents electricity supplied by the solar system from flowing into the grid when there is a power outage that requires linemen to work on the lines in the neighborhood.

SIZING A GRID-TIED SYSTEM

There are four key variables that determine the size of a grid-tied system:

- How much electricity is required (the load).
- The capacity of the solar electric system needed to meet the load.
- A rough estimate of the cost of the system.
- Your budget.

Determining the load is relatively easy. Just look at your utility bill after making every effort to conserve. For example, if your monthly bill averages about 1,000kWh, you are using about 12,000kWh per year.

To determine the output of an array of solar electric collectors in your part of the country, you can use a user-friendly interactive program called PVWatts™, which is maintained by the National Renewable Energy Laboratory and is available on the Internet (www.pvwatts.org). PVWatts version 1 is strongly recommended for first-time users.

An interactive online computer program maintained by NREL and called PVWatts can help you estimate how much electricity a solar electric system would produce at your house. Here's an example of how to use the program. Let's assume you live in Albuquerque, New Mexico.

1 Go to http://rredc.nrel.gov/solar/calculators/PVWATTS/version1.

2 On the U.S. map that appears, select New Mexico, then select Albuquerque.

3 Under the heading "PV System Specifications," find "DC Rating (kW)." Enter 1.0 in the block provided.

4 Find "DC to AC Derate Factor" and accept the default value (0.77).

5 Find "Array Type" and accept the default, "Fixed Tilt."

6 Find "Array Tilt (degrees)" and accept the default, 35. (That's the latitude for Albuquerque.)

7 Find "Array Azimuth (degrees)" accept the default, 180 (true south).

8 Find "Cost of Electricity (cents/kWh)" and accept the default, "Default = State Average."

9 At the bottom, click on the "Calculate" button.

10 On the screen that appears are two tables, "Station Identification" and "Results." Read down the "AC Energy" column under "Results" to find the monthly output of the 1kW array. At the bottom of that column is the AC energy produced by the system for a year.

You can select "back" on your browser, return to system specifications, and plug in new values for the system, changing the DC capacity of the collectors, for example, or the tilt of the array.

Some utilities don't make it easy to determine your monthly consumption of electricity. They will provide the kilowatt hours consumed for only the month of the billing, and you may have to go to some effort to determine the total monthly consumption because the rate charged may vary, depending on the number of kilowatt hours used. If you are diligent, you should be able to figure your monthly consumption. Another option is to contact the utility company and ask them to send a statement showing your monthly and annual consumption. If you keep your old bills, of course, you won't have a problem.

The size of the array will depend on the load, available sunlight, and the efficiency of the collectors. As of this writing, the better solar

For this example, let's assume you're going to install the system in Atlanta. Start by determining how much electricity you use in a year. Some utility bills include a chart giving the kilowatt hours you normally use in a day or a month. Make a small table, listing the months and the kilowatt hours used. Total the kilowatt hours used in a year. For argument's sake, let's suppose the total is 12,000kWh.

To determine the cost of a solar electric system you first must determine the DC capacity of the solar array. As of this writing, systems cost between $6 and $7.50 per installed watt, before incentives.

Following the example in "Using PVWatts to Estimate PV Output" on p. 169, go to the PVWatts website and select Atlanta, enter 1.0 for the DC capacity, and accept all of the other defaults. Then select "Calculate" and check the AC energy for the year. The result is 1,345kWh per year. Divide 12,000 by 1,345 to get 8.92kW.

Now return to the system specifications page on the website and enter 8.92 for the DC rating. Accept the defaults. Select "Calculate" and check the AC energy for the year. This time, the result is 11,999kWh per year. Based on an installed cost of $6.50 per watt, that solar electric system will cost $57,890 installed, before incentives.

That is a start. Here are some questions to consider as you further refine the system: Will shade reduce the amount of electricity the array produces? Is the house roof large enough for the array? How much is my share of the total cost? Are incentives limited to a maximum system size? What is my budget?

modules have an efficiency of 16 percent to 18 percent. To be conservative, assume that a 1kW array of present-technology modules covers an area of about 65 sq. ft. (6.0 m²). The 8.9kW system we sized for Atlanta in "Sizing a Grid-Tied System" above would cover 578 sq. ft. (53.7 m²). Once the collector area is known, check your roof. If it's too small for the collectors, making the array smaller using less electricity or mounting it on the ground are your alternatives.

Another way to estimate what your home will be able to produce is to use the In My Backyard (IMBY) program offered by the National Renewable Energy Laboratory (www.nrel.gov/eis/imby). It is a map-based interface that allows you to find an aerial photo of your home, sketch in the array location and approximate size, and enter other variables. The calculator will then estimate system costs and the electricity production you can expect for the system. Note that this service is not available in all parts of the United States.

Budget, of course, is another limiting factor. You may decide that, even after rebates and tax credits, you can afford to produce only a portion of the electricity that you consume. A leased system may be an option if a leasing program is available.

SIZING AN OFF-GRID SYSTEM

The size of the collector array for an off-grid system is based on both the electrical loads and the number of days of overcast weather the system can handle before you have to run a back-up generator. To do this, you'll have to itemize different loads, their wattage (watts = amps × volts), and the hours per day each will be used. With these calculations in hand, refer to *Stand-Alone Photovoltaic Systems: A Handbook of Recommended Design Practices,* from Sandia National Laboratories. It includes a system sizing method, worksheets, and examples; download it from the Sandia website (www.sandia.gov).

Once the size of the array is known, the location can be determined. The roof is usually the least costly option, provided it's large enough and oriented correctly. Otherwise, some type of ground mounting will be in order.

BATTERIES

The bank of batteries for an off-grid home is sized based on the calculated daily load, the size of the array, the solar energy available, and the number of days you want to be able to go without using a back-up generator. A larger battery

ABOVE TOP and BOTTOM: A battery box can be located indoors or out. This one, shown with the lid open and closed, was built from dimensional lumber and ¾-in. (2.0-cm) plywood. Its outside location eliminates the need for venting.

bank gives you more time without the generator, but the maximum most owners choose usually is 5 days. Where a generator is used with an off-grid system, it must be run at least once a month to be sure it will start when it's needed.

The size of the footprint for a battery bank for an off-grid home can be as small as 3 ft. (0.91 m) by 4 ft. (1.2 m) or as large as 8 ft. (2.4 m) by 12 ft. (3.7 m), depending on whether it's part of a grid-tied or an off-grid system. Since flooded-cell batteries are much more economical for this application, the tops of the batteries should be low enough to allow you to inspect the liquid levels in the batteries and add water as needed.

Batteries can be located indoors or outdoors. The location depends largely on available floor space, proximity to the solar array, the strength of the floor, and the climate. Batteries are heavy; some banks can impose a floor load of as much as 300 lb. per square foot (1,464 kg per square meter), many times above normal design loads for wood-frame residential construction. Because of their weight, batteries are usually located on a concrete floor or structurally reinforced wood floor. When placed on a concrete floor the batteries should be placed on wood planks to reduce their tendency to self-discharge.

When batteries are indoors, they are typically placed in a sealed room or site-built, vented plywood enclosure. Indoor installations are especially desirable in colder climates because battery capacity is temperature sensitive, and keeping batteries at or near room temperature will maximize their capacity. Other advantages include a shorter distance between a roof-mounted array and the batteries (thereby limiting the size and cost of the connecting wiring), and the fact that, indoors, batteries are more likely to be inspected regularly. Disadvantages to indoor installations include the loss of living space and the need for a sizable floor area that's strong enough to support the weight. Venting also is a must if flooded batteries are used because they give off hydrogen, a flammable gas, when they are being charged.

An option for avoiding the need for a sealed battery bank enclosure is to use absorbed glass matt (AGM) sealed batteries. They don't require the vented enclosures, but are about twice the cost of the flooded cell batteries for the same ampere-hour capacity.

When batteries are placed outdoors, they can be located in a shed or outbuilding. If there are no sources of ignition in the building, flooded cell batteries don't need to be in a sealed, vented enclosure. The advantages to the outdoor enclosure are no loss of living space and it is often easier to construct a floor of adequate structural strength in an outbuilding. This works well in warmer climates where the loss of battery capacity during the winter months is not as significant as it is in colder climates.

Disadvantages to the outdoor placement include the necessity for sealing the batteries from the rest of the structure and venting them if the outdoor structure has any sources of ignition; the higher cost of the DC wiring due to longer runs, trenching, and underground conduit; and battery capacity reductions of 50 percent or more during cold weather.

Of all the components in a solar electric installation, the battery bank is potentially the most hazardous. In addition to the hazard posed by hydrogen gas, which is released when the battery is charged, battery terminals also pose a risk. If a conductor is accidentally put across the battery positive and negative terminals, the battery will short through the conductor and very likely explode. Since lead-acid batteries contain sulfuric acid, a battery explosion is a very hazardous event!

CHOOSING A COLLECTOR LOCATION

Before deciding on any type of mounting location, roof or ground, it's important to perform a shade analysis. Shade can significantly reduce the energy produced by the array. In most instances, the closer to the ground an array is mounted, the greater the potential effect of tree shade during the winter when the sun is low in the sky and shadows are long.

Glazed modules can often be mounted parallel to and slightly above the roof. Modules are usually mounted on a series of rails that run across the tops of short piers. The piers, which are secured through the roof membrane to the roof structure, hold the collectors 4 in. (10.2 cm) to 5 in. (12.7 cm) above the roof. The modules

These ground-mounted collectors are sited in an open area where there is no shading, 30 yd. (27.4 m) or 40 yd. (48.8 m) from the house.

HOW STRONG IS YOUR ROOF?

Can your roof support the added weight of a solar array? A square foot of modular collector weighs about the same or a bit more than a square foot of asphalt shingles. Most building codes allow about 2.5 lb. per square foot (12.2 kg per square meter) for a layer of shingles. Usually, building codes permit no more than two layers of shingles on a roof.

If there are already two layers of shingles on the roof, adding a solar array is comparable to adding another layer of shingles—probably forbidden by code. Several options are available. One is to reinforce the roof. Your local building official may require you to retain a licensed structural engineer to decide what reinforcements are needed. Another option is to remove the two existing layers of roofing and install one new layer plus the solar modules.

must be held above the roof so there is room for air flow on the backside of the module. The air flow cools the modules and allows them to operate more efficiently. Brackets are available for attaching modules to a standing-seam metal roof. Alternatively, laminate, flexible, unglazed collectors can be glued in the spaces between the standing seams.

If the roof is not oriented adequately or if the roof angle is too low, modular collectors with a different kind of mounting system are used. Like the parallel-to-roof mounts, tilt-correction frames have rails to which the solar modules are secured. The frames are tipped up to face the sun more directly. When multiple rows of modules are installed, rows should be separated

Tracking arrays can be mounted on one or two poles, depending on size.

in the north–south direction so one doesn't cast a shadow on another to the north. Shading as little as 10 percent of a solar electric module will greatly reduce its output.

There are a variety of frame designs for mounting modules on the ground. The most basic is a metal frame, either galvanized steel or aluminum, that holds collectors at the desired tilt and orientation. The metal frame is typically secured to concrete piers sunk into the ground or to concrete grade beams. Arguably, the most visually attractive type of ground-mounted frame is the pole mount. A single, large-diameter pole is used to support an array. Since the number of collectors that can be attached to one pole is limited, multiple poles may be needed. The pole is secured to a thick, reinforced concrete slab buried 4 ft. (1.02 m) to 5 ft.(1.3 m) below grade.

Some pole-mount systems allow the modules to track the sun. Whether a tracking array is worth the added cost depends on where you live. In the Northeast, a sun-tracking array that adjusts in one axis, azimuth only, delivers about 25 percent more electricity over a year than a fixed array of the same area. A sun-tracking array that tracks the sun in two axes, altitude and azimuth, delivers about 28 percent more electricity. In the Southwest, the single-axis tracker produces about 31 percent more electricity than the fixed array, and the two-axis tracker delivers about 38 percent more electricity.

In general, roof installations are less expensive. Even if the roof is not exactly at the right orientation and tilt, the savings from the simpler installation usually make up for the compromise in performance. At some point, however, the wrong orientation and tilt can severely compromise performance. See "Estimating Annual Power Output" tables for information on optimum orientation on pp. 176–177.

The choice of mounting location for the array can have a bearing on whether glazed modules or laminates can be used. If the roof is to be used, either modules or laminates can be used. If some type of ground mounting is to be used, modules are preferred over laminates since they are much more efficient and therefore require smaller and simpler ground-mounting frames. Further, laminates are flexible; thus for ground mounting, they require a frame that provides more support than is needed for the modular collectors.

Other factors that affect the decision on where to mount the array are the roof structure itself, and the effect that modules will have on attic temperatures. Local building officials may ask that the roof be checked by a structural engineer. If modules are used, then the attic

SOLAR ARRAYS AND ATTIC TEMPERATURE

Another factor to consider in the debate over locating the array on the roof vs. the ground is the effect it will have on temperatures in the attic or living spaces immediately below the roof.

Solar modules are installed at least several inches above the roof, allowing air to circulate beneath them. This not only helps preserve the efficiency of the module but also can make a significant reduction in the temperature of the space below the roof. Lower attic temperatures increase indoor comfort and reduce cooling loads.

An air space of several inches between the roof and the back of a solar electric collector allows ventilation and helps keep the module cool. Modules lose efficiency when they become too hot.

Laminate collectors that are secured directly to the roof are nearly black in color, so they absorb heat. If the present roof membrane is light in color, the application of laminate collectors can result in a much hotter attic than before. However, the performance of laminate-type collectors is much less affected by high temperatures than most modular collectors.

temperatures can be reduced considerably since there is an air space between the underside of the modules and the roof. If laminates are used, attic temperatures will be no different than if dark shingles cover the roof.

Optimum Tilt Angles

Solar electric arrays perform best when the tilt angle is adjusted for latitude.

SOLAR ELECTRIC ARRAYS

Latitude (Degrees)	Optimum Tilt*
32	30
36	30
40	35
44	40

*Tilt measured from horizontal.

Setting the collector tilt

If your system is grid tied, you want the maximum output for maximum electricity savings. That is available from an array oriented to the south and mounted at a tilt as indicated in "Optimum Tilt Angles" at left.

If your system is off grid, and the electricity is needed year-round, you want a south-oriented array and a tilt higher than a grid-tied system would have. That configuration will provide more electricity during the winter when loads are usually greater, there are fewer hours of sun, and snowfall can be heavy. As a rule of thumb, use a tilt of at least 15 degrees plus the latitude for maximum winter solar gain.

Estimating Annual Power Output

Among factors affecting the output of a solar electric array are the direction the array faces (the azimuth) and the array's tilt angle. Arrays facing due true south, or close to it, yield the most electricity. The optimum tilt angle depends on the site's latitude. These charts summarize the best orientation and tilt for four cities around the United States. The four-digit number near the center of each chart is the total estimated annual output of electricity in kilowatt hours. The two-digit numbers represent percentages of optimum performance based on different orientations (azimuth) and tilt angles.

(Adapted from www.PVWatts.org by Emaan Ammar.)

PERCENTAGE OF OPTIMUM TILT/ORIENTATION FOR 1KW DC ARRAY

HARTFORD, CT

TILT

AZIMUTH		0	5	10	15	20	25	30	35	40	45	50	55	60	65	70	75	80	85	90
East	90	84	84	84	83	82	81	79	77	75	73	71	68	66	63	60	57	54	51	48
	100	84	85	85	85	85	84	83	82	80	78	76	73	71	68	65	62	59	55	52
	120	84	86	88	89	90	90	90	89	88	87	85	83	80	77	74	71	67	63	59
	140	84	87	90	92	94	95	95	95	95	94	92	90	87	84	81	77	73	68	64
	160	84	88	91	94	96	98	99	99	99	98	96	94	92	89	85	81	77	72	66
South	180	84	88	92	95	97	99	100	1200	100	99	98	96	93	90	86	82	77	72	66
	200	84	88	91	94	96	97	98	98	98	97	95	93	91	88	84	80	75	70	65
	220	84	87	90	91	93	94	94	94	93	92	90	88	85	82	79	75	71	66	62
	240	84	86	87	88	89	89	88	87	86	84	82	80	77	74	71	68	64	60	56
	260	84	84	85	84	83	82	81	79	78	76	73	71	68	65	62	59	56	53	49
West	270	84	84	83	82	81	79	77	75	73	71	68	66	63	60	58	55	52	49	46

ATLANTA, GA

TILT

AZIMUTH		0	5	10	15	20	25	30	35	40	45	50	55	60	65	70	75	80	85	90
East	90	89	89	88	88	86	85	83	81	79	76	74	71	68	65	62	59	56	52	49
	100	89	89	90	89	89	88	86	85	83	80	78	75	72	69	66	63	59	56	52
	120	89	91	92	93	93	93	92	91	89	87	85	82	80	76	73	69	65	61	57
	140	89	91	94	95	96	96	96	96	94	93	91	88	85	82	78	74	69	64	59
	160	89	92	95	97	98	99	99	99	98	96	94	91	88	85	80	76	71	65	60
South	180	89	92	95	97	99	100	1300	100	99	97	95	92	89	85	81	76	71	65	59
	200	89	92	95	97	98	99	99	98	97	96	93	91	87	84	80	75	70	65	59
	220	89	91	93	95	95	96	96	95	93	92	89	87	84	80	77	72	68	63	59
	240	89	90	92	92	92	92	91	90	88	86	84	81	78	75	71	68	64	60	56
	260	89	89	89	89	88	87	85	83	81	79	76	74	71	68	65	61	58	55	51
West	270	89	89	88	87	86	84	82	80	77	75	72	69	66	63	60	57	54	51	48

	100–98	97–90	89–80	79–70	69–60	59–50	49–40	
HIGH								**LOW**

ALBUQUERQUE, NM

TILT

AZIMUTH		0	5	10	15	20	25	30	35	40	45	50	55	60	65	70	75	80	85	90
East	90	86	86	86	86	85	84	83	81	80	77	75	73	70	67	64	61	58	55	52
	100	86	87	87	88	88	87	87	85	84	82	80	77	75	72	69	66	63	59	56
	120	86	88	90	91	92	93	93	92	91	90	88	86	83	80	77	73	69	66	61
	140	86	89	92	94	96	97	97	97	97	95	94	91	89	86	82	78	73	69	64
	160	86	90	93	96	98	99	100	1700	100	99	97	95	92	88	84	80	75	69	63
South	180	86	90	93	96	98	99	100	100	100	99	97	95	92	88	84	79	74	68	62
	200	86	89	92	95	96	98	98	98	97	96	94	92	89	85	81	77	72	67	61
	220	86	88	90	92	93	94	94	93	92	91	89	86	84	80	77	73	69	64	60
	240	86	87	88	89	89	89	88	87	86	84	82	79	76	74	70	67	63	60	56
	260	86	86	85	85	84	83	81	80	78	75	73	70	68	65	62	59	56	53	50
West	270	86	85	84	83	81	80	78	75	73	71	68	65	63	60	57	54	52	49	46

EUGENE, OR

TILT

AZIMUTH		0	5	10	15	20	25	30	35	40	45	50	55	60	65	70	75	80	85	90
East	90	89	88	87	85	84	82	80	77	75	72	70	67	64	61	58	55	52	49	46
	100	89	89	88	87	86	85	83	81	79	77	74	71	69	66	63	59	56	53	49
	120	89	90	91	91	91	90	89	88	86	84	82	79	77	73	70	67	63	59	55
	140	89	91	93	94	94	95	94	93	92	91	89	86	83	80	76	72	68	63	58
	160	89	92	94	96	97	98	98	98	97	95	93	91	88	84	80	76	71	65	60
South	180	89	92	95	97	99	100	100	100	99	98	95	93	90	86	82	78	72	67	61
	200	89	92	95	97	99	100	1100	100	99	98	98	93	91	87	83	79	74	69	63
	220	89	92	94	96	97	98	98	98	97	96	94	91	89	86	82	78	73	69	64
	240	89	91	93	94	94	95	94	94	92	91	89	87	84	81	78	74	70	66	61
	260	89	90	90	91	90	90	89	87	86	84	82	79	76	73	70	67	63	60	56
West	270	89	89	88	89	88	87	85	84	82	80	77	75	72	69	66	62	59	56	52

Solar arrays produce very little electricity after the snow cover reaches 2 in. (5.1 cm) to 3 in. (7.6 cm)—a problem in regions where there is appreciable snowfall and roofs are low pitched. When designing an array for a flat roof in a region with heavy snowfalls, mount frames at the optimum tilt (or steeper) so the snow will slide off after a few days. The bottom of the array must be mounted high enough above the roof surface so snow that slides off will not cover the lower part of the array.

When the leaves are off the trees, it's easy to determine whether tree limbs will shade the area where solar collectors might be placed. On a sunny day, look at the sun from the approximate location of the solar collectors between 9:00 A.M. and 3:00 P.M. If you see a similar view to the one shown here, either the trees must be cut or trimmed or the collector location must be changed.

Dealing with snow

Snow is a fact of life in northern and mountainous areas. If the roof is pitched at 35 degrees or more, then it is likely that after several days the accumulated snow will slide off the array on its own. When it comes to shedding snow, the higher the tilt the better. Be careful to locate the array so snow doesn't slide off the array and land on a vulnerable roof below, such as a greenhouse roof.

You can remove snow accumulations with a snow rake. The rakes look something like a wide squeegee, but with a blade of aluminum or plastic rather than rubber. They are relatively inexpensive, lightweight, and can extend up to about 30 ft. (9.1 m), allowing you to stand on the ground while using the rake. If the solar array is mounted on a ground-mounted frame, snow can be easily removed with a broom.

Shade

Shade is a major consideration for virtually any type of solar system, electric or thermal. If the array is even partially shaded for several months of the year, it may not be worth installing the system in the first place. This is especially true for solar electric collectors, which are generally much more adversely affected by shade than are solar thermal collectors. When a single solar electric collector in a string of collectors, or even a single cell within a string of cells, is shaded, the entire string of cells will produce zero electricity. In comparison, the output of a solar thermal collector is simply proportional to the area shaded.

The decision to remove trees is not easy. Trees add value to property in many ways, but some may have to be trimmed or cut down to keep shade off the collectors. If the trees are on a neighbor's property, that probably isn't an option, although it never hurts to ask.

MAINTENANCE

Grid-tied solar electric systems require little maintenance, but a few simple tasks can reap large rewards. It is a good idea to keep a chart of the inverter's monthly output, which will tell you if there is a long-term loss of power. Solar modules seldom fail unless they are hit by lightning or a tree limb, but a connector can come loose due to repeated buffeting in the wind, from the weight of ice on the wires, or when someone walking on the roof trips over an exposed wire. In some areas, squirrels have caused extensive damage to wiring insulation on arrays.

Within the combiner box are fuses that protect the inverter from lightning strikes. If one or two fuses burn out, the entire string of modules to which those fuses are connected will not supply power to the inverter. Inverters fail from time to time as well. The failure may be total, which is easy to identify due to the visual alarm on most inverter displays, or gradual, which is not so easy to identify. By tracking the inverter output over the months of ownership, you will have a convenient means of identifying faults in the system.

Off-grid maintenance

Off-grid systems need more care. They are susceptible to the same problems as grid-tied systems but also have more components that can be a source of trouble. Batteries need maintenance, and charge controller(s) are a potential source of system faults.

Flooded cell batteries must be topped off with distilled water several times a year. The liquid level should not be allowed to drop below the tops of the plates. When the batteries are first installed, and every year thereafter, the specific gravity of each cell in the battery bank should be tested and a log kept. This provides information on the condition of individual cells and batteries. Long-term trends are then evident. Battery terminals should be coated with a deoxidizer when the batteries are installed. Every year or two, the deoxidizer should be reapplied. The charge controller display should be checked on clear days to ensure that the charging level is in the expected range. The display on the inverter(s) should be checked to be sure that the inverter is working.

GRID-TIED ECONOMICS

Solar electric systems are relatively expensive, but they have a long service life. Modules are usually guaranteed to provide 80 percent of their

In areas where dust collects on the module surface and there is little rain, cleaning several times a year will improve system performance.

NET METERING

In addition to rebates and tax credits, net metering has helped spur the growth of grid-tied systems. This arrangement currently allows homeowners in 42 states to be credited for the electricity they produce, at least to the point that production equals consumption.

It works like this: When you produce more electricity than you are using, the surplus is fed into the power grid. When usage exceeds production, you draw power from the grid. At the end of the month, you pay for the net amount of electricity used. In effect, under net metering, you'll be credited for the electricity you generate at the same retail price you pay.

In some states, if production exceeds usage no extra is paid for the electricity produced above net zero. In other states, excess production earns the same rate the utility pays for the electricity (the wholesale rate).

In utility districts with inverted tier electric rates, where homeowners pay increasingly higher rates for kilowatt hour usage over set thresholds, the electricity produced by the solar system will lower the homeowner's rate, thereby saving additional money.

Further, many utilities charge more for power used at times of peak demand. Usually, the time of peak demand coincides nicely with the time of peak output of the solar system, thereby reducing the net cost of power even more.

Most utilities track the monthly net but wait until the end of the year, or the end of a 12-month period, to settle up with the homeowner. Programs vary from state to state. Go to the Database of State Incentives for Renewables & Efficiency (DSIRE) website (www.dsireusa.org) to find whether your state allows net metering and, if so, what rules apply.

nominal output over a 20-year to 25-year period. The exact length of time depends on the manufacturer. It is probably safe to assume that a well-made solar electric module will last at least 30 years; otherwise manufacturers would not risk insuring them for 20 years to 25 years. The other major component of the grid-tied systems is the inverter. Most inverters are now guaranteed for 10 years. Experience over the past 17 years with grid-tied systems indicates that the inverters fail more often than modules. The other components in grid-tied systems are of minimal cost compared to the collectors and inverter.

Incentives

Depending on where you live, grid-tied systems are eligible for a variety of rebates and/or production credits, state tax credits, and lease programs. There also is a federal income tax credit. The source of money for rebates or production credits usually is a small fee assessed on all rate payers in a utility district. Net metering, another incentive, usually is a mandate of the public utility control commission or is in an act passed by the state legislature.

There are currently no rebates for off-grid systems. The argument for this is that utility rate payers contribute to the fund for the rebate given to those who install solar electric systems,

Calculating Solar Electric Payback

The speed at which a solar electric system pays for itself in avoided costs for electricity depends on several factors, including the cost per kilowatt hour of electricity and how quickly power costs go up. These estimates apply to a 5.4kW DC system in Hartford, Connecticut. *(Analysis by: Everett M. Barber Jr.)*

RESIDENTIAL SOLAR ELECTRIC PAYBACK (YEARS TO PAYBACK)*

ANNUAL RATE OF ELECTRICITY COST INCREASE

Installed Cost (per Watt)	5%	10%	15%
$5.50	19	15	12
$6.00	21	15	13
$6.50	22	16	13
$7.00	23	17	14
Annual savings estimate for year 1	$1,062	$1,062	$1,062
Annual savings estimate for year 10	$1,647	$2,504	$3,736

*Estimates include a 30 percent federal income tax credit but no other rebates. Based on an electricity rate of 17¢ per kilowatt hour. From 1970 to 2000, the rate for Connecticut was 5.1 percent (EIA data).

and they benefit indirectly from those who install grid-tied systems. The main long-term benefit to the grid-tied system owner is that fewer new power plants will have to be built. However, rate payers derive no benefit from systems off the grid. The 30 percent federal income tax credit does apply to both grid-tied and off-grid solar electric systems.

Power purchase agreements vs. leases

Leases and power purchase agreements (PPA) represent two ways to have a solar energy system with no down payment. The two are similar in that you must give up tax credits and rebates and there are provisions for buyouts or extensions at the end of the term.

Payment arrangements differ. The monthly payments over the term of a lease are constant. At the outset, they exceed the cost of the electricity generated. But since they are constant over the term of the lease, the lease payments should be less than the cost of the same amount of electricity purchased from the power company later in the lease, as electric rates rise. The monthly payments for the PPA vary since they are based on a fixed rate per kWh produced. At the outset, they exceed the cost of the electricity generated. But since the rate is constant over the term of the PPA, payments should be less than the cost of the same amount of electricity purchased from the power company later in the term. Another distinction: the lessee must maintain the system over the term of the lease, whereas the investors maintain the system over the term of the PPA.

BUYING A SOLAR ELECTRIC SYSTEM

Solar electric is a rapidly growing industry, and many pitfalls await the uninformed consumer. Be sure to read the advice in Chapter 9 on hiring a contractor before you go shopping for a solar electric system. When you're ready to start, go to the websites of manufacturers who make solar modules and inverters. While manufacturers rarely install their own equipment, they often maintain a list of regional distributors who sell their equipment to installers. The distributor will be only too happy to give you the contact information for a local installer. Better yet, contact the organization in your area that issues rebates, if one exists. Many of them maintain a list of vetted installers. Local solar energy groups are another potential source.

This is also the time to contact your utility company about your intent to install a solar electric system. Most utilities have prepared detailed guidelines for supplying power to their grid. At the least, the utility may require access to your property and require you to maintain a minimum level of liability insurance. Installing contractors may or may not give you a copy of these. It is important that you read this document before you sign a contract with an installer.

HOW ARE CARBON DIOXIDE EMISSIONS AFFECTED?

With the exception of nuclear and hydro-electric sources, any electricity produced in a grid-tied solar array offsets the emissions from a conventional power plant burning a fossil fuel.

Conventionally fueled power plants produce a certain amount of carbon dioxide (CO_2), a greenhouse gas. The U.S. Energy Information Agency maintains a list that gives the total pounds of CO_2 per kilowatt hour of electricity for all 50 states. For example, a solar electric system in Vermont saves negligible CO_2 because virtually all of the electricity generated in Vermont comes from nuclear power. At the other end of the scale is a state like North Dakota, which generates about 2.2 lb. (1.0 kg) CO_2/kWh. Thus, a 5kW solar electric system in North Dakota would generate about 6,000kWh per year and prevent about 13,200 lb. (5,987 kg) of CO_2 from being produced at the power plant.

For most areas of the United States, a solar electric system can displace a significant amount of carbon dioxide.

 REBATES VARY IN STRUCTURE. Some are structured so they cover a system supplying no more electricity than is used in the home over a 12-month period. Others set a limit on the maximum kilowatt (DC) system they will fund. If you want a collector area that provides more than the maximum electricity used or is larger than the upper size limit, you will have to pay the full cost, without rebates, for the portion of the system that provides the excess.

8 OTHER USES FOR SOLAR ENERGY

Thus far, the emphasis of this book has been on using solar energy to meet major household needs. That's not to imply there are no other important uses for solar energy in the home. There are more than a few that deserve attention. With one exception, the electric commuter car, most of them are not as energy intensive as the applications we've discussed so far, nor do they cost as much.

COOKING WITH SOLAR ENERGY

People in many developing countries around the world cook with solar energy. The practice is limited mainly to sun-rich areas where alternative fuels, such as wood or animal dung, are scarce. But it will work in your backyard, too. It takes more patience than using a gas grill, but it's safer, will reduce your use of fossil fuels, and will lessen the output of carbon dioxide (CO_2). There are several sizes and types of solar cookers, including curved concentrator cookers, panel cookers, and box cookers. They can be used for everything from frying eggs to cooking a roast. The designs all use reflectors in one way or another to concentrate solar energy.

Concentrator cookers typically focus energy on a cooking surface by means of a curved or parabolic reflector. These cookers achieve temperatures adequate for grilling and frying, but require frequent readjustment as the sun moves.

The Toyota® Prius incorporates a solar electric roof panel. It powers cabin vent fans that keep the interior from overheating on sunny summer days.

RIGHT: The three reflectors for this solar oven focus solar energy inside a black cooking chamber. Glazing helps prevent the heat from escaping, allowing interior temperatures to reach 300°F (148.9°C). MIDDLE and BOTTOM: A portable solar oven can bake, boil, or steam food. With the reflectors open, it can reach temperatures of 360°F (182.2°C) to 400°F (204.4°C).

Panel-type cookers employ simple flat panels—often made of cardboard, and covered with reflective Mylar® or aluminum foil. The solar energy is focused on a cooking vessel, usually black, which is placed inside a transparent enclosure. High-density polyethylene bags (the clear plastic bags found in many supermarkets) or glass can be used for the enclosure.

Box cookers, the earliest type of solar cooker, date to the 18th century. They consist of an insulated box, usually constructed of wood, with a glass cover. Inside the box are one or more cooking vessels with black exteriors. Box cookers may or may not be equipped with a lid that protects the cover glass when it's not being used and doubles as a reflector.

There are numerous variations on all of the solar cooker types described here. For more information on solar cookers and their advantages, visit The Solar Cooking Archive Wiki at http://solarcooking.wikia.com. *Cooking with the Sun* (Morning Sun Press, 1992) by Beth and Dan Halacy is another good resource.

DRYING FOOD

If you live in a sunny climate, you may want to consider solar food drying. Drying (dehydrating) food via the sun, which is one of the oldest food preservation methods known, requires no chemicals, preservatives, fossil fuel, or electricity.

TWO SOLAR OVENS

Concentrator Cooker

A parabolic reflector focuses solar energy on a dark-colored cooking vessel to produce high temperatures. This design is subject to cooling of the pot by the wind.

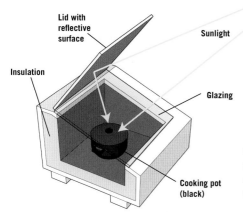

Sunlight

Cooking vessel

Parabolic reflector

Lid with reflective surface

Sunlight

Insulation

Glazing

Portable Box Cooker

Glazed, insulated box-style solar ovens use one or more reflectors to focus solar energy on a cooking pot. In this design, the pot is protected from the wind by the glazing.

Cooking pot (black)

The food to be dried is placed inside an enclosure and supported on trays. Air is heated by the sun in a small collector on the inlet side of the dryer and passes over the food.

Heating the air reduces its humidity. As the dried air passes over the food, moisture in the food evaporates. The temperatures in a dryer are typically 20°F (11.1°C) to 30°F (16.7°C) higher than the air outside the enclosure. The moisture-laden air exits the dryer through a vent. Depending on the design of the solar dryer, the air circulation is accomplished by natural convection or with a fan.

SOLAR DESALINATION

Desalination is the process of removing salt and other impurities from seawater. Solar desalination was used during much of the last century, mainly on inhabited islands where there was little rainfall and potable water had to be brought in by ship. Desalination can provide an alternate source of clean water for drinking and cooking. In addition to converting seawater to potable water, desalination can be used where local sources of water are not potable, as long as they are not contaminated by volatile organic compounds.

In its simplest form, a solar still is an airtight enclosure with a shallow black basin and a tilted

BUILDING A SOLAR DRYER

You can build a simple solar food dryer with as little as a cardboard box, a rack tray, and some netting (to keep out insects and animals). There are many variations; a good place to look for ideas is at the Solar Systems website (www.solarcooking.com; click on the British flag for English).

If stored in a cool, dark dry place, dried food will keep for several months. Don't let your garden's abundance go to waste. Dried vegetables can be added to soups, stews, and casseroles. Dried apples, apricots, grapes, cranberries, cherries, and bananas are delicious snacks and are great for hiking or camping.

Netting

Drying box

Vents

A homemade food dryer moves solar-heated air through a food-drying box, which can be fitted with racks. Screening keeps insects out.

Black paint

Clear plastic sheet

Collector box

Air flow

transparent cover. The basin is filled with water. Sunlight passes through the glass cover and the solar radiation is absorbed by the black surface. As water temperature increases, so does the rate of evaporation. Water vapor condenses on the underside of the cover, which is cooled by the outside air. The condensed water runs down the underside of the cover and is collected in a trough and removed through tubing to a tank. No moving parts are required.

A still is relatively simple to create on your own—and simple to operate. More efficient solar stills exist. While their yield is higher, they

This basin-type solar still is used to provide potable water from sea water.

require more maintenance than the basin-type still. Over years of experience, the basin-type still has proven very reliable and requires little maintenance.

SOLAR-HEATED OUTDOOR SHOWERS

Heating water for an outdoor shower is another low-cost way to use solar energy. For what is perhaps the simplest form of a solar shower, place a coil 50 ft. (15.2 m) of black garden hose on the ground, or mount it on a sheet of plywood or on a roof. Lay it flat so that all coils are exposed to the sun. Allow the hose to fill with water and then stop the flow. Let it sit in the sun for an hour before showering. Be careful not to leave the water in the hose for more than a few hours. On a clear day, the water can become very hot, well above comfortable shower temperatures.

In another variation on a simple solar-heated shower, you can mount a black-painted, 5-gal. (18.9-L) water tank above your shower structure. Fill the tank with a hose. On a clear day, after several hours in the sun, the water will be warm enough for showering. Commercially available solar showers include large (typically 5-gal. [18.9-L] or 7-gal. [26.5-L]) black plastic bags that have a fill cap and showerhead. More streamlined designs incorporate the collector and hot water storage in the stand or the shower base. Most commercial units include a mixing valve that allows you to adjust the water temperature (and avoid getting scalded).

DAYLIGHTING

Daylighting is simply the use of windows to manage natural light inside the house. As with passive solar heating and passive cooling, daylighting is better incorporated in new construction than in existing construction. With the exception of the solar tube mentioned in "Adding Solar Tubes for More Light" on p. 188, daylighting has to be designed into the house.

When done well, daylighting can do many things to enhance the interior of a house. Aesthetically, natural light can define interior spaces; many architects say daylight creates space. It also can create a sense of drama in

Roof windows are a way to allow natural light to reach dark areas of the home but cause unwanted heat gain during the summer and heat loss during the winter.

ADDING SOLAR TUBES FOR MORE LIGHT

Windows, light monitors, and skylights serve a number of purposes in addition to admitting light. Solar tubes, however, are expressly designed for daylighting and are one of the few practical ways to increase natural light in existing buildings without a major renovation. They can also be quite effective in new construction.

Also called solar light pipes, solar tunnels, or daylight pipes, these products consist of a plastic dome mounted on the roof, a reflective tube, and a ceiling-mounted diffuser. A solar tube is ideal for lighting up dark parts of a building that would normally need artificial light even during the day. At the worst, they are aesthetically neutral but can be an aesthetically positive feature.

Per square foot of opening, they bring in much more daylight than a window with less winter heat loss and less summer heat gain. They are also said to help counter seasonal affective disorder, which affects many people deprived of natural light during the winter. These are a manufactured product and can be installed by almost any general contractor.

ABOVE TOP: Solar lighting tubes are a daylighting alternative to skylights. They can be installed at less cost and in smaller areas than conventional skylights. ABOVE BOTTOM: Solar lighting tubes allow light but very little heat to enter rooms. Heat loss is low as well.

GLARE CAN BE MITIGATED TO SOME EXTENT WITH BLINDS, SHADES, DRAPES, AND SHUTTERS. Blinds, for example, can block some direct light or reflect it toward the ceiling where it is diffused. Insulating shades or interior shutters will reduce heat loss through windows during cold months. Shades on the interior of windows, however, do not provide nearly as effective a barrier to heat gain during the summer as shutters or other devices on the exterior. Once the heat is through the window, it is in the building and must be dealt with. Exterior shutters, especially those that are automated or crank operated, can greatly reduce heat gain in the summer.

Shades help control natural light, making it possible to reduce glare, but do little to prevent excess heat gain. Low-e glazing treatments will reduce unwanted solar gain on east, north, and west exposures but should be used on south exposures. Exterior shutters are most effective at preventing unwanted solar heat gain.

Shades and blinds are essential components of any daylighting plan. Automatic controls are necessary when they're installed on roof windows. A reflective surface added to the upper side will further reduce heat gain.

a room or entry or highlight surface texture. Because of the sun's movement during the day and year, it produces an ever-changing visual landscape within the house. Functionally, its main benefit is to reduce the need for artificial lighting.

More often than not, sunlight admitted to houses is not well managed. The result can be too much sunlight with the attendant unwanted heat gain during the summer, which increases cooling loads. In winter, problems associated with daylighting include both intense glare and high heat loss. Glare can make reading or watching TV nearly impossible. Excessive brightness causes visual discomfort. Heat loss during the winter adds to the heating load, increasing heating costs.

A well-known professor of daylight design said, "It's the quality of daylight that is important,

and not the quantity. Quantity causes problems." For many homeowners, improving daylight in a house usually means increasing the quantity of sunlight that enters the interior with more vertical windows, especially on the south side, and with skylights in south-facing roofs.

Windows are important to successful house design, providing cross-ventilation, views, and daylight, but they should be handled thoughtfully. As a generalization, the average double-glazed window (R-2.2 [approx.]) loses about 10 times more heat during a winter night than the average insulated wall (R-21 [approx.]). During the summer, that same window can admit 50 times more heat than a well-insulated wall. By increasing the amount of window area to admit more daylight, the potential for unwanted winter heat loss and summer heat gain increases many fold.

The orientation and size of the glazing makes a major difference. South-facing glass can result in a valuable net gain of daylight and heat, but if the glass area is too big, glare, excessive heat loss, and overheating will result even in winter. East-, west-, or north-facing glazing can admit useful daylight, but these exposures are net heat losers during the heating season. That is, more heat flows out of them than enters over a heating season. During the summer months, east- and west-facing glazing brings in much more direct solar heat than south-facing glazing. That heat is unwanted. North-facing glazing can provide uniform light during the daytime, year round, but during the winter due to its high rate of heat loss, north-facing glazing is a detriment from the standpoint of minimizing heat loss.

With a couple of notable exceptions discussed in the following section, effective daylighting does not involve the use of a device or single-purpose building element, as do most of the other solar applications in this chapter. Rather, it involves the manipulation of building walls, glazing, and interior surfaces to enhance the effect of sunlight entering the building.

Daylighting do's and don'ts

⌂ DO hire a daylighting consultant, not a lighting designer who works mainly with artificial lighting.

⌂ DO reduce glare by locating windows so light comes into a room from more than one direction. For example, if direct sunlight comes in a large south-facing window, then use another high window, or light monitor, or east- or west-facing window to illuminate the north wall of the room. The light from that north wall will do much to offset the glare from the south glazing. An alternative means of bringing light deep into the building is to use a light shelf. This is a shelf installed near the upper part of a glazed area. Sunlight

MORE LIGHT, LESS HEAT

A light shelf, mounted outside a window on the south exposure, reflects light to a white ceiling to help illuminate the room. The shelf also serves as an overhang to help reduce solar heat gain in summer through the larger, lower portion of the window while allowing most of it to enter the lower window in winter.

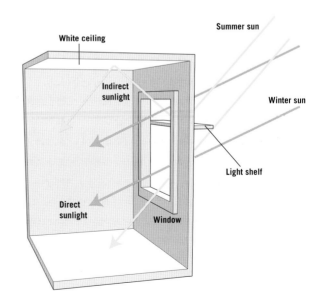

White ceiling

Summer sun

Winter sun

Indirect sunlight

Light shelf

Direct sunlight

Window

reflected off the shelf penetrates deeper into the building and illuminates the underside of the ceiling. That light helps offset the glare from the lower glazed area. Reflective blinds can also be used to bounce light off a ceiling, thereby diffusing the daylight and eliminating glare.

🏠 DO place south windows near east or west walls. Compared to windows located in

Don't let a builder or architect convince you that if a little bit of glass is good then a lot more glass is better.

SKYLIGHTS

Skylights may seem a logical extension of daylighting, but while they admit plenty of daylight, they have other less desirable characteristics. Throughout the U.S., they are net heat losers during the winter months and net heat gainers during the summer months. This has been determined by metered rooms with skylights and by computer modeling. Although all skylights reduce the amount of artificial lighting needed and operable skylights provide some cooling in summer via ventilation, the benefits are far outweighed by winter losses and summer gains. In spite of the negatives, many homeowners like skylights. So, the challenge becomes how can skylights be used in an energy-conscious way?

To reduce heat loss in winter, select a skylight with as high an R-value as you can afford. R-values for the best triple-glazed skylights are in the range of 1.82 to 2.22, although at least one manufacturer claims an R-value as high as 3.45. A second way to reduce heat loss is to install an easily removed, insulated panel over the underside of the skylight. You can use a product like Window Quilt, or an insulating panel made on-site. The site-built panel can be a 4-in. (10.2 cm) thickness of fiberglass duct board insulation (R-16 [approx.]), enclosed in a frame, or a similar thickness of foil-faced and -backed foam board (R-28 [approx.]). Hinge one edge so that it is easily put in place during the night and opened during the day. A third approach is to limit the aperture of the skylight to no more than 4 percent of the floor area of the room, which will limit the heat loss yet allow a useful amount of daylight to enter.

To reduce heat gain in summer, install a louvered sunshade above the skylight on the exterior of the house. (As with any type of shading device, the greatest benefit is achieved by stopping the sun's heat *before* it reaches the interior of the house.) Configure the louvers so they run east west. Tilt and space the louvers so that direct sun does not get through at the time of the summer solstice, yet the maximum amount of direct sun gets through at the time of the winter solstice. This louver becomes a permanent fixture above the skylight.

the center of a wall, this will significantly improve the lighting of the interior by the natural light that is diffused by and reflected from the wall.

- 🏠 DO learn about the different types of glazing materials. Some types have a high solar heat gain coefficient and will transmit a high percentage of the available sunlight. These should be used on the south-facing windows. Other types of windows have a low solar heat gain coefficient, which means they will not transmit much of the incident sunlight. These would normally be used on east-, west-, and north-facing windows.

- 🏠 DO use north light exclusively if you need steady, even light in a space throughout the day. Be aware of the importance of minimizing north-facing glazing since it is a net energy loser during the winter months. Heat loss through north-facing glass, or glass on any other orientation for that matter, can be reduced by using various insulating window treatments, such as Window Quilt. To be effective, however, window treatments must be opened and closed each day. They are a good way to cope with a poor existing design.

- 🏠 DO realize that a skylight rarely brings useful heat into a house at the time of year when it's most wanted. Flare the skylight opening on the inside and paint it white. This will diffuse the light that enters the house. Alternatively, locate a skylight in a south-facing roof close to a light-colored north wall if possible so the light reflects off the wall to the room below.

- 🏠 DO build a large-scale model of the house to study how daylight will affect it. Computer models exist for daylight analysis, but these give illumination levels and do not give an indication of the quality of light in an interior space.

- 🏠 DON'T expect significant energy savings by using natural light in houses. The reduction, if any, will be modest since the daylight is displacing artificial light that is usually not used much during the day, at least not to the extent it is used at night.

DRYING CLOTHES OUTDOORS

Hanging the wash out to dry is a practice that dates to time immemorial. It's an inexpensive way to begin using solar energy and to save money on electricity or gas bills. As a bonus, sunlight gives laundry a fresh smell, bleaches whites, and has a sanitizing effect. The sun's UV rays, however, can fade brightly colored clothing, so you may want to turn these clothes inside out before you hang them to dry.

Clotheslines can be installed on pulleys and run from windows or decks to poles, making it easy to hang and remove clothing. Umbrella-style clotheslines also work well. Some models are installed in a concrete-anchored sleeve that allows the unit to rotate to ease hanging and removing clothes. For best results, install the clothesline outdoors in a sunny spot where there is good air circulation.

Note that this section was not titled "Solar Clothes Drying." The drying of clothing on a line is more a function of the relative humidity of the air surrounding the clothes than it is due to the

LIGHT BY CABLE

Another approach to solar lighting is the use of light collectors and optical cables to bring natural light to windowless areas, or to areas where natural lighting is preferred over electric lights. Natural light is believed to be healthier than artificial light for people, and by reducing the need for electricity produced from nonrenewable sources, it's also healthier for the planet. The downside is that these systems can't store daylight. Further, they are limited to collecting direct sunlight only. When a cloud passes between the sun and the collector, the light goes out, and light output on cloudy days is little or none. Parans Solar Lighting in Sweden is marketing systems worldwide.

LEFT: A glazed light collector consisting of rows of optical lenses captures sunlight. A flexible optical cable then transfers it into a building interior. A switch, that turns the optical lenses from the sun, can be used to turn off the light. MIDDLE: The Parans light collector can be mounted on a roof or exterior wall of new or existing buildings. Mounting hardware is similar to that which is used for conventional flat-plate collectors. RIGHT: The optical cable can be run in the same chases as electrical cables and plumbing. The maximum length is 65.6 ft. (20 m.).

sun. The sun is certainly a factor, but less so than humidity. Clothes will dry on a low humidity night almost as well as on a sunny, dry day. Put clothes out early on a sunny humid day, and they might not be dry by the end of the day. Put clothes out on an overcast, very cold, dry winter day, and the clothes will usually be dry by evening. Hang clothes in a dry basement in the winter, and they will dry overnight, without any sun at all.

SOLAR DEHUMIDIFICATION

In some parts of the country, particularly along the Gulf Coast, high humidity often is more intolerable than high temperature. Many homes use conventional air-conditioners primarily to

Laundry dries surprisingly quickly outdoors as long as the humidity is not high.

lower humidity. Unfortunately, in the process of dehumidifying, this equipment also lowers the air temperature to the point that occupied spaces can become uncomfortably cool. If only the humidity could be lowered to a comfortable level, many people wouldn't need conventional air-conditioning, and energy savings would be considerable.

Solar-powered dehumidification is one way to use solar heat to dehumidify the air without using a conventional air-conditioner. Humid air from an occupied space is passed through a desiccant. The desiccant is a drying agent that absorbs moisture. Once dehumidified, the air is returned to the occupied space. Once the desiccant has been saturated with moisture, it has to be heated to drive off the moisture. Relatively low-temperature heat can be used to drive the moisture from the desiccant. That heat can be supplied by a solar thermal array.

ABOVE TOP: Electric cars will reduce pollution, especially when the electricity they use is produced by a renewable energy source, such as wind or solar and not coal. ABOVE BOTTOM: Solar car designers from around the world compete in cross-country time/distance rallies, such as the American Solar Challenge. In 2010, the course was an 1,100-mile (1,768-km) drive from Tulsa to Chicago.

SOLAR-POWERED CARS

Solar-powered racing cars have been developed and refined for at least the past 20 years. The considerable media attention given these races has stirred public interest in the possibility of solar electric cars for everyday use. But on close examination, it's easy to see that these vehicles aren't ready for commercial use, and it's unlikely one will be developed soon. There simply isn't enough surface area on the vehicle for all the solar cells it would need for everyday use. The efficiency of solar cells would have to increase manyfold for this to be a possibility.

Beyond specialized solar-powered racing cars, there is considerable interest in electric

cars, both from the standpoint of economy of operation and lowered emissions. The type of car now available on a limited basis is a plug-in electric car. Plug-in means batteries in the car are charged when the car is plugged into a conventional outlet.

Charging times on limited-production models using 120V outlets are reported to be 10 hours to 12 hours, depending on the voltage of the charging equipment. Shorter charging times are available with higher voltage chargers. These cars have a maximum range of 80 miles (128.7 km) to 100 miles (160.9 km) and are billed as commuter cars. According to the Department

SOLAR DESICCANT AND EVAPORATIVE DEHUMIDIFICATION

Solar thermal energy can be used to dry desiccants that are in turn used to dehumidify air in homes. In this system, humid outside air is drawn through a slowly rotating wheel containing desiccant. The desiccant in the wheel absorbs the moisture in the air. The dried air then moves to a heat exchanger wheel, which removes excess heat from the air. Next, the dry air passes through an evaporative cooling element that cools the air further. The air leaving the home is heated in a heat exchange coil that receives its heat from a solar thermal array. That outgoing heated air is used to dry the desiccant in the desiccant wheel. In winter, the system is used to supply heat to the home.

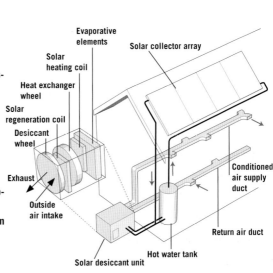

Evaporative elements

Solar collector array

Solar heating coil

Heat exchanger wheel

Solar regeneration coil

Desiccant wheel

Exhaust

Outside air intake

Conditioned air supply duct

Return air duct

Hot water tank

Solar desiccant unit

---

of Transportation, the average commute in the United States is 40 miles (64.4 km) per day.

Some of those who are interested in these cars are also interested in powering them with solar energy. The most feasible way to do this is by plugging them into a conventional outlet either at home or at work or both. At home, the outlet would be powered by the utility grid and by a solar electric array. Parked at home, the commuter car would be charged overnight, entirely by utility power. During the day, the solar electric array would supply power to the house and, because electrical loads are usually low during the day, most of that power would be sold to the utility. Ideally, this would equalize the charge for power from the previous night.

An array of solar electric modules on the roof of the car could be used to provide a small amount of the electricity needed to charge the batteries. But putting an array on the roof would

mean that for charging to occur, the car would have to be parked outdoors and away from shade.

OTHER USES FOR SOLAR ELECTRICITY

If you don't have the time or money—or just aren't ready—to install a photovoltaic (PV) system to power your home or electric car, there are still ways you can use solar electricity.

Outdoor solar lighting

The same PV technology that is becoming a common power source for lights on our roads and in our parking lots can be used in your own yard. Solar-powered lighting has been around for decades, but thanks to improving technology and lower costs, more consumer applications are available than ever. Solar lights, whether functional (path lights, for example) or decora-

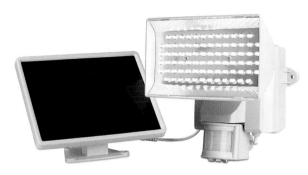

Solar-powered outdoor lights can be used for security (TOP LEFT, lens removed), path lighting (BOTTOM LEFT), and accent lighting (ABOVE).

tive, charge during the day and usually provide light when needed at night. A light with a fully charged battery can keep an efficient light glowing for up to 8 hours.

Many solar lights are sold as an integral unit, including solar cell, battery, and lamp. Others include the battery and lamp as one component and the solar cell as another. If the solar panel is integral to the light fixture, then the fixture must be placed so that the device receives sunlight year round.

You can be more flexible in where you place lighting fixtures with separate solar modules. The panel should be mounted where it will get maximum sun exposure: facing due south and not shaded by trees or other structures. Most lights include a light sensor, so you don't have to worry about turning them on and off manually.

Solar attic fans

Attics are superb, if unintended, collectors of solar heat, especially when roofing surface materials are dark. In summer, this can pose a problem even if you don't visit your attic often. Attic heat is conducted to the rooms below, raising temperatures and increasing cooling costs if you use air-conditioning and discomfort if you don't.

WHEN REROOFING, consider a white or light-colored roof surface. It will greatly reduce the solar heat gain that reaches the attic while lengthening the life of the shingles.

The buildup of heat in an attic can be reduced by use of ridge vents, gable vents, or a series of small, through-the-roof vents; the vents are powered by natural convection and the wind. Solar attic fans provide a means of forcefully ventilating the attic. Usually roof-mounted, they incorporate a solar electric collector, a fan, and stainless-steel screening to keep animals out. Some models allow you to install the fan in a louvered gable opening. Others come with flashing kits and are suitable for shingle, tile, shake, and flat roofs.

KEEPING THE ATTIC COOL

A solar-powered attic vent lowers attic temperatures thereby lessening the cooling load on the occupied spaces and extending the life of the shingles.

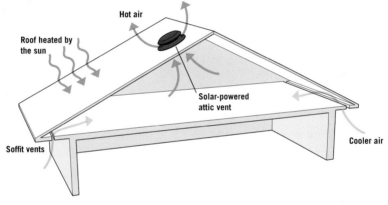

Hot air

Roof heated by the sun

Solar-powered attic vent

Soffit vents

Cooler air

TECH CORNER | RECHARGING A CAR WITH A SOLAR ARRAY

A conservative figure for the amount of electricity required to power a small commuter electric car is 25kWh per 100 miles (160.1 km). Using the electricity produced by a solar array in the Northeast as an example, a 1kW solar electric system would supply about 1,200kWh of a.c. power per year. If the car's owner commuted the full 100 miles (160.1 km) each day and did not charge the car at work, a solar electric system with a capacity of approximately 5kW would be required to recharge the car battery.

As batteries become more efficient, the weight of cars should decline and the energy needed for the same trip should diminish.

9 SHOPPING FOR A SOLAR SYSTEM

When energy costs are rapidly increasing, and handsome incentives for renewable energy are available, many homeowners are eager to get some of that free money. At times of great demand for new products, business owners see opportunities, too. While some are motivated by a mix of idealism and the desire to grow their businesses, others are interested only in easy money.

Don't assume that solar companies new to the market are financially sound, sell proven products, have experienced technicians, or will be around for the long run. Start-up companies selling new technologies, regardless of the industry, have a difficult time of it even in the best of times. Solar companies are no exception. They struggle to find and keep qualified installers. In addition, they're at the mercy of fluctuating energy costs; incentive program managers who change programs, sometimes to the detriment of the industry they are trying to nurture; and shifts in public interest. Learn as much as you can about consumer protection laws in your state and about the businesses that sell solar energy equipment, before buying a system.

 A 1986 U.S. DEPARTMENT OF ENERGY SURVEY concluded that nearly 1 million solar energy systems were installed in the United States between 1973 and 1986. Just 10 years later, an estimated 50 percent of those systems had been abandoned or removed; 20 years later even fewer of those systems remain in use.

MAKE SURE YOU ARE PROTECTED

In most states, plumbers, electricians, architects, and other building professionals are vetted by state licensing boards, which require schooling, rigorous examinations, long periods of apprenticeship, and continuing education to maintain proficiency. In addition, construction

ABOVE and RIGHT: Solar energy is a new field compared to most of the trades involved in residential construction. Extra caution in choosing a contractor is advised. Also be sure your homeowner's insurance policy is in force.

is covered by extensive building codes and by trained local code officials, who are charged with ensuring compliance. All of this helps protect the public's health and safety. Yet this established mechanism for training the labor force, design professionals, and code compliance officials isn't always in place when it comes to new building technologies such as solar energy. Here, consumer protection may be spotty or even nonexistent.

Consumer protection and the solar industry

With a few exceptions, solar system designers, retailers, installers, and code officials are scrambling to gain the experience that consumers, unaware of the scope of the task, assume they already have.

Architects and consulting engineers are rigorously trained in traditional technologies but are rarely as well schooled for work on solar systems. You might assume that plumbing, heating,

or electrical contractors would be ideal candidates for installing solar systems. But although they have skills and experience in related areas, few have shown interest in this emerging technology or have received specialized training. History has shown that without training, they can do as much harm as the untrained and unlicensed, but well-intentioned, solar installer.

In the United States, solar water heating and solar electric systems are rarely sold or installed by licensed plumbing or electrical contractors— the very people who, one would think, are best qualified to put them in. Although some licensed electrical workers are installing solar electric systems, plumbing and electrical contractors often choose to do the work they know best and not seek the requisite training in a new technology. Often, the demand for their existing products and services is such that they are barely able to keep up. And many fear the expense of making a commitment to a new area of technology (remember, solar energy technology made a big splash 30 years ago), only to have it deflated by falling energy costs and loss of incentives.

Compounding the problem, very few trade schools offer instruction in solar electric or solar thermal system installation. Instructors need instruction to teach that material, and states need to require that instruction. As a result of the recent recession, many states are looking for ways to cut costs, and the addition of experienced solar instructors is, unfortunately, not a priority.

There also has been uneven progress when it comes to building codes and the officials who enforce them. The National Electrical Code® has led the way in developing codes for the installation of solar electric systems. In the solar thermal field, the International Association of Plumbing and Mechanical Officials (IAPMO) has developed a Uniform Solar Code. But in most states the training of officials who enforce and interpret those codes lags far behind.

Who are the installers?

For the most part, people who are relatively new to the industry are doing the actual installation work. In general, many are idealistically motivated. They seek out businesses in the solar field and apply for a job. While they don't begin with nearly the same experience or expertise as a licensed tradesman, they are willing to learn those skills and to work for lower wages than licensed tradesmen. That's appealing to company owners because it means better profit margins.

Licensing requirements vary from state to state. Some do not require solar installers to be licensed, but they do require that a licensed electrical or heating contractor be hired to connect the solar system to the conventional power source (or conventional source of water heating). Other states require people who install solar

ABOVE TOP and BOTTOM: Any work done on a roof is particularly hazardous. Be sure the contractor you select carries worker's compensation insurance for its employees as well as liability insurance.

Some companies hire people with a contractor's license just so they can apply for building permits—a practice that is illegal in most states.

systems to have a solar electric license or solar thermal license, depending on what they install. In some states, even traditional trades don't require licenses. In other states, New York, for example, there is no statewide licensing of the trades. It is left to the municipalities.

Some companies hire people with an electrical or heating contractor's license just so they can apply for building permits—a practice that is illegal in most states. In some states, laws limit the ratio of apprentices to journeymen on a job to one to one. With that limitation and the scarcity of qualified journeymen, the business is sorely limited in the number of systems it can install if it follows the letter of the law.

The North American Board of Certified Energy Practitioners (NABCEP) provides training to certify individuals who want to install solar electric systems and solar thermal systems.

Given this lack of uniformity, the first step if you're considering buying a solar system of any type is to find out whether the state or municipality where you live requires installers to be licensed.

DO YOUR RESEARCH

A solar energy installation will certainly be an investment in dollars, and it should also be an investment in your time. If you invest your time wisely, it is more likely your monetary investment will be recovered many times over in avoided fuel costs.

Begin your research by becoming familiar with the various types of solar systems that are available and which ones fit your needs. By all means, read the rest of this chapter. Beyond this book, there are a variety of other resources:

🏠 GOVERNMENT WEBSITES. These can be loaded with information and will certainly expand your knowledge. In general, they try hard to avoid favoring any one type of system over another. One caveat: Based on our experience with these sources, they do not accurately predict the costs of installed systems in all parts of the country; in particular, the fuel costs they use are often out of date or are not representative of those found in many parts of the United States.

Look for a contractor who has been trained in a nationally recognized program, not just by an equipment manufacturer. Here, future installers learn about photovoltaics at the Florida Solar Energy Center®.

THIRD-PARTY TESTING IS KEY

The efforts of two independent and authoritative organizations are of great benefit to consumers shopping for solar energy systems. The first is the California Energy Commission (CEC), which tests solar electric collectors and inverters. A CEC listing is often required for the equipment to qualify for a rebate. Second, the Solar Rating and Certification Corporation (SRCC) tests flat-plate solar thermal and evacuated-tube collectors. The SRCC rating is required for a federal income tax credit.

The impact of testing by these two organizations is hard to overestimate. Testing results can be used in computer models to predict the performance of a system as well as verify a company's claims of equipment performance. The latter benefit is particularly useful. No longer can a salesperson claim that his or her solar collector is twice as efficient as the competition's without fear of a challenge.

MANUFACTURERS' WEBSITES. Information provided by manufacturers is quite different from what you'll find on government websites. Manufacturers will, for the most part, tout the virtues of their products, their installations, and the size of their companies. After all, they are in business to sell their products. Their websites and literature will include eye-catching images of their most attractive installations as well as technical data on their products.

In some cases, this type of information can be useful for comparing different products. Manufacturers, however, are not installers. They typically supply their products to distributors who resell them to installers. Many manufacturers maintain lists of distributors who can be contacted to find a local installation contractor. Don't assume that the first web addresses that come up in an Internet search are going to have the best products. Their ranking in a web search is more an indication of how much money they spent to position their website for early selection by the search engines.

PROFESSIONAL GROUPS. The American Solar Energy Society (ASES) maintains a website (www.ases.org) that offers a wealth of information about solar energy products and applications. It claims to serve professionals and grassroots advocates. It has an online bookstore listing publications on a wide range of solar topics. The ASES website includes a list of local chapters, some of which sponsor monthly or quarterly lectures. A digital edition of *Solar Today* is available from ASES. It is a monthly magazine that will be of interest to anyone who wants to know more about solar energy applications, technology, and public policy. You'll also find links to other sites with relevant information. This website is a very good place to begin.

ISES. Another society, the International Solar Energy Society (ISES), may be of interest to some consumers, but its technical orientation and global audience may be beyond the interests of the average U.S. consumer. It publishes a magazine, *Renewable Energy Focus,* that should be of interest to technically oriented consumers (www.ises.org).

🏠 DSIRE. The Database of State Incentives for Renewables & Efficiency (DSIRE) is a comprehensive source of information on state, local, utility, and federal incentives and policies that promote the use of renewable energy and energy efficiency. Visit their website and look for the incentives for your state (www.dsireusa.org).

If there is a solar energy rebate–issuing organization in your state, contact them about solar home tours. They are usually proud of the systems that they have partially funded and will often sponsor periodic tours of the sites. In addition to locally sponsored home tours, there is the national solar home tour sponsored each year by ASES. Visit the ASES website for information on the tour, and visit some of the houses. If the homeowners are present, find out how they feel about their investment and the installer.

As you research the technology, begin to compile a list of retailers and installers in your area. The Internet, electronic directories, and your phone book's yellow pages are good ways to do this. If there are rebate-issuing organizations in your state, contact them for the names of installing companies. There is a good chance that the rebate organization has vetted the companies on their list of approved installers. Ask if there have been complaints about any of the installing contractors.

FINDING SOLAR DESIGN PROFESSIONALS

At this stage of industry development, a limited number of architects have become quite proficient at energy-conserving design. A few also have entered the field of solar system design, though they are not always easy to locate. Sorting though the online telephone directories may yield a large number of listings claiming solar design experience, but the experience of these professionals may be uneven or slim. A better approach is to contact a local solar energy society or sustainable energy group. They may be able to narrow your search. Always ask professionals for their references and examples of their work.

Engineers, to the limited extent they become involved in house design, are just as proficient as architects in reducing energy use. Most, however, are even further behind than architects when it comes to solar systems. State chapters of professional organizations, including the American Society of Heating, Refrigerating and Air-Conditioning Engineers (ASHRAE) and the Institute of Electrical and Electronics Engineers (IEEE), are places to start looking for engineers who are experienced in solar thermal or solar electric system design.

Some solar design professionals list their services in *Solar Today,* a monthly publication from ASES.

ASSESSING SOLAR RETAILERS AND INSTALLERS

You will encounter a variety of companies, most of which are relatively new to the business, selling and installing solar systems. As a consumer, it's useful to know the various types of companies and to have some idea of their strengths and weaknesses.

Most tend to specialize in either solar electric or solar thermal (hot water) installations. If they offer both, one is likely to be a sideline. Thus a salesperson from a company whose bread and butter is solar electric may try to convince you of the need for a solar electric system even when a solar hot water system or high-efficiency replacement windows are a better investment for you. You may need to go to other sources for that advice.

Sales companies

A company that limits its activities to selling solar systems is usually called a *sales company*. This sort of business requires the least amount of capital. Basically, a salesperson sells the system, and a subcontractor installs it. The installer (or sometimes another contractor) services the system. A sales company needs only to find an installer to serve as a subcontractor, learn something about the product they intend to sell, print some business cards, and figure out how to generate leads. Most sell only solar electric or solar thermal—seldom both.

Since sales companies can get into the business with little capital, they usually don't last long. When the economy is slow, rebates change or disappear, or energy prices fall, sales-oriented companies are more likely than others to move on to more profitable ventures.

The use of subcontractors can pose other problems for the consumer. The subcontractor may be proficient but have no strong allegiance to the salesperson. In fact, the subcontractor may have agreements with several sales companies. Getting the subcontractor back to make a repair may not be easy, especially if the subcontractor's shop is hours away or the sales company owes him or her money.

System integrators

System integrators typically sell, design, install, and service the systems they sell. They are often among the most experienced of the installing companies. A good familiarity with the technology allows them to select among similar components made by different manufacturers. This has pricing advantages for them and minimizes the

Look for a solar contractor who specializes in the type of solar system you intend to buy. The skills required for installing a solar electric system are very different from the ones needed for a SDHW or space heating system.

It is easier to find replacement parts for factory-designed systems made in the United States.

risk of construction delays when delivery is slow from one of their suppliers. System integrators usually employ an in-house sales force and use their employees to install the systems. Many system integrators, however, try to use the lowest-priced labor they can find, increasing the risk of installation issues. There are exceptions. Presently, system integrators tend to specialize in solar electric systems because they believe they are the most profitable. If they sell solar thermal systems, it's usually a sideline to their main business.

Installers who sell factory-designed systems

One fast way to get into the solar business is to install factory-designed systems. The company can concentrate on the business aspects of selling the product and trust that the factory engineers have designed a system that will function correctly. Often the business owner or key employees are trained to install systems by the manufacturer.

Because the system packages are designed for easy installation, the installing company can use lower-skilled workers at lower wage costs. The installing company hopes the manufacturer is providing a system type that has been installed many times before, thus many of the system bugs have been worked out.

Getting a solar contractor involved in the planning stage for a home-improvement project, such as this in-ground pool installation, will save money and ensure better results.

A particular drawback to imported equipment is that the components are built using metric sizes. Heating, plumbing, and electrical supply houses in the United States all sell components with English- or imperial-system sizes. Thus the system owner is limited to a single source for replacement parts. A part might not fail for several years, perhaps longer. If the installer has left the manufacturer for any reason or left the business, you may have to search out someone else for service and may have difficulty finding parts.

On the downside, factory-designed systems may be more costly—and not as good as, or at least no better than, one put together by an experienced system integrator. Many factory-designed systems sold in the United States today are made in Europe, which makes getting replacement parts difficult, especially when incentives disappear and the installing contractor moves on to a different business.

Factory-based design engineers often lack hands-on installation experience, and the long-term performance of their packaged systems may be unknown. Also, these systems may be fine in the climate for which they were originally developed (western Europe, for instance, or China) but not so well suited to the regions where they're installed in the United States.

Experience counts

Not as common are smaller companies that have been in the solar business for a number of years and have a great deal of experience in designing, installing, and servicing solar systems. They have learned to survive, if not prosper, in the solar energy business. They typically specialize in just one type of system, either solar thermal or solar electric, advertise little, and aren't guilty of aggressive sales practices.

Their prices will generally be lower than those of the recent entries because they don't have such high overhead or high profit goals. Most of them will be properly licensed and insured. They are likely to be difficult to find but if you are diligent, you may be able to find one in your area. The search effort will be time well spent.

VETTING SOLAR COMPANIES

You can judge a solar installation company by its experience, seriousness, financial record, and sales representatives, among other things. A good way to begin is to find out how long the company has been around. That may require some digging. Often, the most experienced company will not be the most prominent when it comes to advertising. To differentiate itself from newcomers, a long-established company often states years in business in its ads. Look for a company that's been in business for at least 10 years to 15 years. Their experience will be invaluable. Over that time they will have made lots of mistakes and have had the chance to learn from them.

Ask if the company specializes in a particular type of solar system. Companies that sell solar electric systems may sell solar thermal systems as a sideline, and vice versa. Ideally, you would like to buy from a company whose main business and experience are in the type of system that you want.

The serious quotient

Next, find out how serious the company is about its business. Is it insured? Does it carry worker's compensation insurance for its employees, liability insurance, and vehicle insurance? Have its installers been OSHA trained in safe practices? Remember, the installers are working on ladders and on roofs, which is hazardous work. If these criteria are missing, look for another contractor. Confirm that a principal of the business has a license to do the work (assuming a license is required) and that the installers/service technicians have licenses, too. You can ask the company for the owner's license number over the phone and then check with the state office that issues licenses, usually the department of consumer protection, to confirm that the license number you were given applies to the type of work being done. You also may be able to find out from the same state agency how many years the business has been licensed. In some states, that licensing agency should be able to tell you if there are any judgments against that contractor.

Once you've confirmed that the company is insured and properly licensed, contact your state's secretary of state and ask if the business is registered. An out-of-state company may have an office in your state to satisfy the rebate issuing organization but not be registered with the state. In the event of a dispute, you'll want to be able to settle it in a court in your state. If the contractor is from out of state and is not registered with the secretary of state, you cannot sue him or her in your state. Trying to recover damages out of state can be difficult.

It's also wise to try to get a sense of the company's financial health. If the company is traded publicly, ask for a copy of the latest quarterly financial statement, which it is required by

DON'T UNDERESTIMATE A VEHICLE WITH COMPANY LOGOS. A truck logo can indicate more of a commitment to the business than an unmarked vehicle. While you're at it, look for the contractor's license number on the vehicle. Many states require that the contractor's license number be displayed. Check with the state to confirm that the license number belongs to an active member of the firm.

SHOULD A HOMEOWNER ACT AS THE CONTRACTOR?

Consumers can buy a packaged system from a catalog store and hire a local contractor to install it. But this approach has its drawbacks.

The prospective owner, along with someone at a catalog store, decides which system will suit his or her needs. Usually, the salesperson at the catalog store has never installed a system or lived with a system that he or she designed. Further, the future system owner doesn't know what he or she really needs. It is not like buying a pair of shoes over the phone or online.

Homeowners who choose this option because they are convinced they can save a lot of money must then find a contractor to install the equipment. Contractors who don't know much about solar systems may be willing to do the installation. Contractors who are solar specialists may be less willing because they lose the markup on the components.

There can be problems with the components. For example, they may have been damaged in shipment or during packaging, they may not all fit together properly, threads on fittings may be crossed, or the systems may be undersized for the task. The person at the catalog store doesn't know the actual load the system is to satisfy, and the homeowner may not really be aware of the house's actual load.

The homeowner feels cheated if the system doesn't perform as expected. In such cases, the contractor can't win. Both the homeowner and the catalog company blame the contractor for problems. Most experienced contractors won't touch this sort of installation. If you are lucky, you can save money. If not, you can waste a lot of money and have to contend with a lot of aggravation.

A sure clue to the seriousness of a company is whether it offers emergency service. If you're told you won't need it, find another company.

the SEC to provide. Or go online to any website that offers news about stocks. In addition to quarterly statements, companies often provide audio records of earnings conference calls. If the company tells you they don't yet have financial statements, look elsewhere. They are too new to the business.

If the company is private, getting current financial information may be more difficult. You can try checking the company's Dun & Bradstreet® rating. Businesses use Dun & Bradstreet regularly to check companies they may want to do business with, but few consumers know that a private individual can also check the rating of a company. Call them (800-234-3867) or go visit their website (www.dnb.com) and ask for an assessment of the solar companies you are considering. Dun & Bradstreet offers several levels of data for different fees. Its basic level may be all you need. A word of caution: Some of the companies you're investigating may not update their Dun & Bradstreet financial data on a regular basis.

Another way to determine a company's financial health is to ask whether it's for sale. Its representative may tell you no, even if it is, but it never hurts to ask. If the company is for sale, any warranty they give on their work is very likely to be in jeopardy because a business buyer typically buys the assets of a business and not the liabilities, and a warranty is considered a potential liability. (Manufacturers' warranties on the components should still be in force even if the installer sells the business or goes out of business.)

You may also want to ask about the company's suppliers. Call them and ask how quickly the company pays. Full payment in 30 days (net 30) is standard; 60 days is common. If the company typically takes 90 days or longer to pay, or if their terms are cash in advance or cash on delivery, the company may be short of cash. While this doesn't mean the company will go out of business, it is cause for a closer look.

Another way to assess a company's financial situation is to call the Department of Revenue Services for your state and ask if the business is current with its sales tax payments. (This may not be public information, depending on the state.) If the company is on the delinquency list, that can be a good indication of financial difficulties. One of the first things that business owners let slide when they have cash-flow problems is their sales and use tax payments.

Consider asking the company for the name of its insurance agent, too. Call the agent and ask if the company is current with its insurance pay-

ments. This is another useful indication of cash-flow difficulties because insurance companies may terminate a policy if the insured is even a day late on a payment. Some agents may be reluctant to provide that data for confidentiality reasons, so another way to gauge cash flow is to ask the installer to send you a copy of his or her liability insurance certificate. You won't be able to get a copy of the insurance certificate if the company is even a day late on payments.

Checking a company's track record

Other ways to judge a company's track record include references, word of mouth, and records of complaints. Ask for a list of the owners of systems that the company has installed, with contact information. Contact some of the people on that list, but understand that the installer will have carefully selected the people on the list. Still, by talking with several of them you can often learn a good deal about the company. Ask if they would allow you to visit their home and see the system. If they are proud of the system, they will be glad to show it off.

Talk to friends, neighbors, and relatives who have systems. Find out if they like the system and what they think about the installing contractor. Wait until they have lived with the system and worked with the installing contractor for at least a year. Word-of-mouth information can be invaluable.

Ask your state's consumer protection agency if the company has a history of complaints. Ask if there have been any judgments against that person. Some states may not tell you of the complaints, just the judgments.

Also contact the Better Business Bureau® (BBB) to see if it has any information on the contractors. The BBB issues reports on accredited businesses (members) and nonaccredited businesses. Note: Because members must pay dues, the BBB is less likely to have negative feedback about a member company. If the contractor is not a member, the BBB may not have data on his or her company. Checking with the BBB is still worth the time.

Sizing up the salesperson

You can also take measure of a company by how professional and knowledgeable its sales staff is. Ask the salesperson to lend you a sample of the owner's manual for the system the company proposes to install. A poorly produced owner's manual will include only the product literature on the components used in the installation. A good owner's manual will include a copy of the original quote, the product literature, the warranty statements on the products installed, a

BEFORE A SALESPERSON OR COMPANY REPRESENTATIVE VISITS YOUR HOUSE, be sure your homeowner's insurance policy is current. Also, be sure the company proposing to install the solar system has worker's compensation insurance on the employees visiting your home. If any should fall from the roof, for example, the worker's compensation insurance should cover him or her. If the worker's compensation insurance company claims that for some reason you are liable for an injury, your homeowner's insurance company will defend you.

AN IMPORTANT REASON FOR A SOLAR SALESPERSON OR EXPERIENCED ROOFER to go on your roof is to observe the condition of the shingles. If the shingles are old or even middle aged, you will want to replace the shingles or add a new layer before the solar array is installed. This avoids the added cost of removal and remounting the solar array when the roof is reshingled.

system schematic, and a troubleshooting guide. That guide can be invaluable 5 years to 7 years after system installation, especially if the contractor is no longer in business.

Keep in mind that the salesperson is trying to sell a system and will not necessarily give you an objective assessment of site conditions. If the solar array is to go on the roof of your house, be sure that the salesperson or a technician performs a proper shade analysis on the roof. Older salespersons (even some younger ones) may not want to climb a ladder and get on the roof. But it's nearly impossible to perform this vital analysis while on the ground.

As noted earlier in this book, shade adversely affects the performance of a solar system. An accurate shade analysis is essential. It should indicate the shade condition on the portion of the roof where the collector array is proposed to go.

A salesperson working on commission gets paid only when he or she makes a sale. So you may receive a shade analysis that makes the situation appear better than it really is. For example, if the shade analysis is done only at or near the ridge of the roof, that will, in most cases, be the least shaded area on the roof. Make sure the shade analysis is done at the lower corners of the proposed location for the solar array as well as the upper corners. Finally, be sure to request a copy of the shade analysis.

If the array is to go on the ground, any trees or shrubs that will cast shade on the array should be tagged for removal or trimming. Then ask a tree service company for a quote and add that to your total expected outlay for the system. If a tree blocking full sunlight is on a neighbor's property, you're probably out of luck. In our experience, neighbors rarely are willing to trim or remove trees on their property. But it never hurts to ask.

Ask the salesperson if the installers are company employees or subcontractors. If they're the latter, you may have difficulty getting them to come back for warranty work, particularly if they are from out of state or if there is a dispute over a billing matter and the company has not paid them in full. Ask the company that uses subcontractors to provide some means of ensuring that you can get prompt service when needed. That assurance should be in writing!

Prompt service is key, but so is *proper* service. Ask about the background of the installers too. What is the extent of their training? Do they have licenses? Did they attend a trade school or a technical high school? Have they attended a NABCEP-certified training program? Do they have a certificate to prove that?

Another way to size up a salesperson and the company he or she works for is to ask some questions based on what you've learned in this book. For example, ask what provision is built into a solar hot water or space-heating system to cope with overheating, a reality when the weather is clear for several days and there's no demand for heat or hot water. If the salesperson brushes off the question, look elsewhere.

It might also be helpful to know if the salesperson or any of the principals of the business have solar thermal or solar electric systems on their homes. Many people have jumped into the solar energy business with the sole objective of making a fast buck. That's not a good motive for the long-term prospects for the industry. Owning a system is usually an indication of a deep level of interest in and commitment to the technology.

BUYING DO'S AND DON'TS

At first glance, the following lists of do's and don'ts may seem lengthy. But a solar energy system is a large investment, and it's worth taking the time to understand the process.

Before signing a contract

🏠 **DO** find out if your state has enacted a buyer's right of rescission, a law that typically allows you to cancel and receive a full deposit up to 72 hours after you've signed the contract. In-home sales are usually covered by a buyer's right of rescission, but depending on the state, sales outside the home may not be. In many states, the

Many solar systems qualify for rebates from federal and state programs. A solar domestic water heating system that costs $6,000 installed should qualify for a $1,800 federal tax credit. For a rundown of state programs, go to the Database of State Incentives for Renewables & Efficiency website (www.dsireusa.org).

company selling a product such as a solar system must include a copy of the buyer's right of rescission statement with the proposal to the homeowner.

🏠 DO check whether your town has a property tax exemption for solar energy systems. Without an exemption, a solar system could add hundreds of dollars to your tax bill. (If there is no property tax exclusion, work with your elected representatives to get one enacted.)

🏠 DO check with your town planning and zoning official as well as historical commission to make sure there are no restrictions against solar energy installations. A few states have enacted legislation invalidating restrictions, but most have not. In some instances, a ground-mounted array may circumvent the restriction. You can find information on these states at the DSIRE website (www.dsireusa.org).

🏠 DO be concerned about competent inspection of the work by the local building official. Few building officials are familiar enough with this new technology to perform a competent inspection. Contact the local building official and discuss your concerns. If he or she doesn't know much about solar systems, ask him or her to suggest a qualified inspector. Perhaps the official knows of a qualified inspector in another town who will inspect your system. At least request that the town and the state office that regulate building inspectors offer their inspectors a course in the type of equipment being installed. This may not help you, but it could help others who come after you. If a rebate is part of the incentive that motivates you to buy a system, the rebate-issuing organization may provide a thorough inspection, even if the local code official is unable to do so. Contact the rebate organization to ask if they provide this service.

🏠 DO check to see whether your town or state has enacted solar access legislation, which protects your solar installation from shade cast by buildings constructed nearby. If there is no solar access legislation, work with your state representative or senator to get it enacted. (You can also find out about solar access policies by state on the DSIRE website at www.dsireusa.org.)

🏠 DO check the DSIRE website (www.dsire-usa.org) to find out whether a sales tax exemption or a state income tax credit applies. A sales tax exemption for solar equipment typically covers installation and service.

🏠 DO be aware that there is now a 30 percent federal income tax credit for certain types of solar energy systems. Solar pool heating systems are excluded. The credit allows you to subtract 30 percent of the cost of the system from your federal taxes. Presently, the federal credit is set to expire on December 31, 2016.

🏠 DO determine whether rebates or production credits are available for renewable energy systems. In some states, utilities are required to collect a small fee for each kilowatt hour purchased by the rate payers. The fee goes into a renewable energy investment fund that is usually the source of money for rebates. Typical rebates for solar electric systems are $3 to $5 per watt of d.c. capacity. In some states, rebates are also offered for solar water heating systems used as preheaters to electric water heaters. The amount of the rebate for solar water heating varies. Rebates can be a significant incentive to the installation of either type of solar system.

🏠 DO be aware there may be a lease program or Power Purchase Agreement (PPA) for solar electric systems. Terms vary, but a lease or PPA allows a homeowner to obtain a system with very little cash outlay. Be sure to read the fine print carefully. There can be significant downstream costs at expiration or house sale.

🏠 DO determine whether your utility district offers production credits for the electricity produced by grid-tied renewable energy systems. The production credit pays system owners more money per kilowatt hour than they are charged. The production credit may be two or three times the retail rate for electricity. Where production credits are offered, rebates are less—or not offered at all.

🏠 DO determine whether renewable energy credits (RECs) are available in your area. When offered, these are usually in the form of a contract that you enter into with a company that agrees to pay you some rate, several cents per kilowatt hour, for the solar electricity you generate. That company then resells that electricity in large blocks to utility companies and others.

⌂ DO confirm with your local electric utility or with the state's public utilities department whether net metering is available to rate payers. Net metering means that the portion of the electricity produced by the solar electric system that goes back to the power grid is credited to you at the same rate as that charged by the utility company for the electricity that you purchase. This credit applies up to the point that the energy you supply equals the energy you purchase—that is, up to the net zero point.

⌂ DON'T forget to find out whether a structural analysis of your roof will be required for the installation of a solar array. In some areas of the country where high-wind loads or snow loads are a concern, many building officials will require a written assessment by a licensed structural engineer, which may cost between $500 and $1,500. Further, some structural modifications may be needed to upgrade the roof. Generally, the solar company will require that you pay for the assessment and any needed modifications.

⌂ DON'T ignore other sources of solar funding. At least one state, Connecticut, offers an incentive for the installation of an energy saving improvement, such as a solar energy system, to residences in historic districts.

KNOW YOUR WARRANTY

There are several different types of product warranties, and it pays to know the difference. Under no circumstances should you accept a verbal guarantee.

⌂ Written warranties may be either full or limited. As long as a product is covered by a full warranty, the contractor must repair or replace the item free of charge. The product must be repaired within a reasonable time after you complain. If the product cannot be fixed (or has not been fixed after several attempts), you may choose between a new product or a cash refund. The warranty is good for the specified time, even if you are not the original owner of the product.

⌂ A limited warranty covers only certain parts of a product, covers parts but not labor, or applies to only the original owner, includes a charge for handling, or requires the customer to pay for shipping to and from the factory for the repairs. The customer may be allowed only a prorated refund or credit, depending on the use of the product.

⌂ Lifetime warranties should state whose lifetime, if it covers more than the original purchaser.

⌂ Implied warranties vary from state to state, but generally mean that the seller, merely by offering a product for sale, promises that the product will do what it is sold to do. When a product is described as "irregular," "factory second," or "damaged," express and implied warranties may not apply.

When you review the contract

🏠 DO make sure the building permit is mentioned in the proposal, indicating the approximate amount and who will pay for the permit.

🏠 DON'T skip the fine print. Make sure the system warranty is clearly spelled out. The standard warranty is 1 year on parts and labor, beginning on the date when installation is complete. Manufacturer warranties may be longer, especially on more costly components. Make sure the length of the warranties on major components is spelled out. If a rebate is to be a part of the financing, the rebate-issuing agency may require a longer warranty: 5 years on parts and labor is common. Ask if longer or shorter warranties are available on given components. Usually there will be an extra charge for a longer warranty, but it may be worth the expense.

🏠 DO make sure the contract has a schedule of payments that identifies the amount to be paid and the work to be completed before each incremental payment is made.

🏠 DO ask the salesperson to put any verbal claim made about system performance in writing. You may want to look elsewhere if he or she backs down after having made such a claim.

🏠 DO ask if other contractors will be doing some of the work to complete the installation. If so, that should be spelled out clearly in the proposal. For example, if a wall must be installed before a solar tank is put in, make sure you get to see some sketches and instructions for the contrac-tor who is to do the work. Make sure it's clear who pays for what.

🏠 DO ask for a heat loss analysis, system design schematic, and solar system output analysis when considering a solar space heating system. Although you'll have to pay for it, the system can't be properly designed without it. Few inexperienced installers will be able to do this analysis.

🏠 DO carefully scrutinize the economic analysis presented by the sales company and check any assumptions it makes. For example, does it assume you will pay cash for the system? If so, the economic analysis will look much better than if you pay interest on a loan. Does the analysis rely on solar system output values for your locale? Some companies have used unrealistic West Coast values for projects in the Northeast, or overstated renewable energy credits that may or may not exist.

🏠 DON'T make an emotional buy. Take the time to talk to the owners of systems similar to the one you're considering. On solar tours, get the names of installers who have happy customers and those who do not.

🏠 DON'T assume the lowest price is the best deal or the highest price will result in the best job. Study the proposals carefully.

🏠 DON'T sign the first proposal presented to you without considering others.

🏠 DON'T buy a system from a building contractor or remodeler. They usually look for the solar installer with the lowest price. It will not necessarily be the best system or the best installation. Although a few will make the effort to find the best system, all will mark up the cost between 10 percent and 20 percent. Further, if there are problems after the work has been completed, the builder will have limited incentive to resolve them. In most cases, it is better for you to deal directly with the solar contractor. It's also less costly.

🏠 DON'T finance a system if you can pay cash. Interest on the loan makes the payback period much longer.

🏠 DON'T finance a system sold by a company that requires you to use your home as collateral. If the installer goes out of business or leaves the area and you can't find someone to service your system, you'll be in a bind. If you stop payments, you could lose your house.

🏠 DON'T buy from a contractor who requests a down payment of 50 percent or more. That is a good indication the company is undercapitalized. The contractor is either buying the equipment for your project with the down payment or, worse, paying bills from earlier jobs. The deposit should be no more than 25 percent to 33 percent of the total. Ideally, you should see some major components on site before making a down payment.

🏠 DON'T automatically assume that a licensed heating contractor, plumber, or electrician is qualified to install your solar system. If your state doesn't require a separate solar license, ask to see a certificate showing the contractor has completed relevant coursework from the North American Board of Certified Energy Practitioners (NABCEP).

Training should be from a nationally recognized, independent organization and not a manufacturer for installing a specific brand.

🏠 DON'T do business on a handshake, unless you have known the contractor personally for many years. Even then, a written contract is preferable and could save a friendship.

🏠 DON'T buy a system if you can't get competent service! That includes emergency service.

🏠 DON'T put off buying a system because you are going to move in a few years. According to two separate studies sponsored by the U.S. Department of Housing and Urban Development (HUD) and published in the *Appraisal Journal*, a home's value increases by about $20 for every $1 reduction in annual operating costs from energy savings strategies. This is because historic mortgage rate costs have an after-tax effective interest rate of about 5 percent. If a dollar of reduced operating cost is put toward debt service at 5 percent, it can support an additional $20 for debt. To the borrower, the total monthly cost of ownership is identical.

After signing the contract

🏠 DO ask the installer to have his or her insurance agent send you a copy of the liability insurance certificate with you noted as the loss payee. Don't allow the contractor to start work until you have the certificate.

🏠 DO ask to see a copy of the building permit

GETTING A PERMIT

If the installer tells you that a building permit is not required, he may be right. But he also may be unlicensed and looking for a way to do the work without the local building inspector finding out.

If the installer asks you to get the permit, that's usually a good indication he's not licensed to do the work or at least not licensed in your area. You will have to decide whether you want to do business with an unlicensed installer. Depending on where you are in the United States, there may be no requirement for a license. If that is the case, then your only recourse is to find an installer with a lot of experience and good references. Check with your local building official to confirm the need for a license to do the proposed work.

If the installer says he will get the permit, find out whose name will be on the permit and that person's license number. It's okay if the installer or a principal of the firm has the license and takes out the permit, but some business owners don't have a license and will hire someone to get the permit. If that person is an employee of the company, that's fine.

But it may be that the company simply hires an individual with a license to get the permit, and that is the person's only role in the project. Thus there is no assurance that the people who do the actual installation are trained in the trade.

In many states, hiring someone with a license just to take out the permit is illegal.

before the contractor begins work. Make sure the person who signed the permit is licensed to install the type of system you are buying, and that he or she works for the installer. You can check that with the state licensing board or consumer protection department.

DO check the licenses of the installers who show up to do the work. There should at least be one journeyman on the site and usually an apprentice with an apprentice license. From the point of view of staff training, one apprentice will often be working with one journeyman. Before making this check, contact your state department of consumer protection to determine whether a license is required to

install such a system.

DO make sure the contractor cleans up at the end of each day on the job as well as when the installation is complete.

DO realize you have some leverage over the contractor. Contractors want happy customers. But overplay the card, and the contractor will simply want to complete the project and move on.

DO make sure the installer gives you all of the product literature and warranty statements that came with the product packaging. You may need them if there's a warranty claim. Don't accept a suggestion that you can get the material from the manufacturer's website. Fine print in the warranty shipped with the product may be different. Don't make final payment until you have these documents. Keep them in a safe place.

- **DO** be sure to get a proper owner's manual when the job is finished and don't make the final payment until you get it. The manual should be bound in a durable and professional-looking binder and should contain these items: a description of the system, including the design and operation, a signed copy of the quote or sales order and any literature attached to the quote when it was sent to you, a copy of building permit(s), any rebate documents if applicable, a simple schematic diagram of the system, warranties on all major components, product literature, copies of the owner's manuals for all major components, and a troubleshooting guide.

- **DO** a walk-through of the installation with the contractor at the completion of the work and ask him or her to explain how you can tell whether the system is working properly. Depending on the type of system, there are several simple sound, sight, and touch tests that you can use.

- **DON'T** issue final payment for the project until you've had a walkthrough with the contractor. Point out anything that seems unfinished. Be sure the contractor has cleaned up to your satisfaction. Make sure all of your questions are answered.

When your system needs service

- **DON'T** call a conventional plumbing, heating, or electrical contractor for service and tell him or her you have a solar system; at the present state of industry development, 9 out of 10 will probably not show up.

- **DO** ask for a written estimate before work starts. The estimate should be on company letterhead, legible, and sufficiently detailed so you know exactly what is to be done. It should also state the cost of the work, show the date of the estimate, have the technician's name (which should be legible), and the payment terms. If additional work might be required (such as for a retrofit installation), ask for a separate estimate when the details of that work become clear. If you can't be at home to approve work beyond the original scope of the estimate, arrange for a call from the technician to discuss it, along with the cost. If you won't be available even by phone, set a maximum amount for any extra work. If you can't be there and don't want to approve the extra work over the phone, then expect to pay an extra charge for the service technician to return.

- **DO** expect to pay for a written estimate. Also, expect the contractor to deduct the estimate fee if you decide to have him or her do that work.

- **DON'T** offer an opinion about why service is needed unless you're certain you know. Simply describe the symptom. The technician may determine the problem is elsewhere. If he or she fixes both the real problem and the one you imagined, costs will be higher.

- **DO** ask for an itemized invoice that shows the parts used on the job. Traditional

Make sure your service technician inspects installations regularly (at least once a year) to check for damage due to ice or squirrels.

invoices have included an itemization of the parts used and their prices as well as the hours of labor, labor rate, and job total. This type of invoice is quite acceptable but not necessary. In recent years, most service companies have shifted to flat-rate pricing for plumbing, heating, and electrical work. The flat-rate invoice does include an itemization of the components used, a description of the work done, and the total price for the work. It does not include individual prices for parts, hours, or charge rates for labor. Either type of invoice is acceptable. As a consumer, you do want the detailed list of parts supplied in the event there is

a warranty issue. The individual prices for the parts is not necessary.

🏠 DON'T pay for service until work has been completed. If you pay in full and the work is not complete at the time of payment, you may have difficulty getting the contractor back to complete the work.

🏠 DON'T do business with a service company that doesn't return calls promptly. They may be busy, but at a minimum they should call back within two days to say when they can deal with your service need.

🏠 DO use your home equity line of credit to pay for the repair if you don't have the cash available. Putting the repair on a charge card is very convenient but interest rates are typically very high. Plus, interest paid on a home equity loan is tax deductible.

COMMENTS YOU DON'T WANT TO HEAR

As consumers, most of us look for clues indicating whether the salesperson or installer knows what he or she is talking about. If the salesperson doesn't seem competent, you may want to look elsewhere. If a salesperson makes one of the statements listed here, challenge him or her. Ask for facts and figures that support the claim. A solar system is a big investment, so be a smart, thorough consumer.

⌂ THE SHINGLES ON THE ROOF LOOK FINE. At issue here is the cost of removing and remounting the solar array when the roofing must be replaced, not a minor expense. If the roof is relatively new—3 years to 5 years old—the statement is fair. But if the roof is 15 years to 20 years old, you're better off replacing it before your solar system is installed. If you don't know the age of the roof, pay a couple of roofing contractors to inspect it and assess its life expectancy.

⌂ THIS SYSTEM WILL CUT YOUR ENERGY BILLS IN HALF. Ask for clarification. Which energy bills? All of them? That's unlikely. A solar system to heat a pool could easily cut those heating costs by 50 percent or more, even eliminate them. A solar domestic water heating system could cut your water heating bills by as much as 80 percent, but it will not lower your home heating costs. Make the salesperson qualify claims like this.

⌂ YOU'LL GET YOUR MONEY BACK FROM THIS SYSTEM IN 5 YEARS OR LESS. Once again, details count. Study the salesperson's proposal. A common ploy to make the economics of a solar electric system attractive is to overstate incentives, such as renewable energy credits or predicted output. Ask for an economic analysis to support the claim.

⌂ WE DON'T SERVICE THE SYSTEMS; WE JUST INSTALL THEM. That's a strong clue that you might have trouble getting service on the system.

⌂ OUR SOLAR COLLECTOR IS TWICE AS EFFICIENT AS BRAND XYZ. That is very unlikely. Ask the salesperson for a copy of the test reports from the California Energy Commission (CEC) if it's a solar electric collector or from the Solar Rating and Certification Corporation™ (SRCC) if it's a solar thermal collector.

⌂ OUR EVACUATED-TUBE COLLECTORS WILL PROVIDE THE SAME AMOUNT OF HOT WATER AS A FLAT-PLATE COLLECTOR SYSTEM TWICE THE SIZE. That is simply not true. Perhaps the evacuated-tube system will provide 5 percent to 10 percent more hot water than the flat-plate collector of the same area in locations of heavily overcast skies, but for most of the United States this is not the case. Ask the salesperson to show you test results by a third-party testing organization that supports this claim.

⌂ YOU HAVE TO CHANGE THE FLUID EVERY 2 YEARS. This is a clue that the technician is new to the industry or is trying to build a service business. The fluid he or she is referring to is usually the antifreeze in an indirect-type solar system. While some antifreezes sold in the mid-1970s did require replacing every 5 years to 7 years (sometimes even more often), the fluids available today are much more stable. If they have to be changed once every 15 years that will be often.

🏠 **THOSE SRCC RATINGS AREN'T NECESSARY. OUR COLLECTORS HAVE BEEN TESTED BY A BUNCH OF ENGINEERS AT OUR PLANT. THEY ALL KNOW WHAT THEY ARE DOING.** Don't buy this claim, or product. If their collector is so good, it should be tested by the CEC or SRCC.

🏠 **THE SOLAR SPACE-HEATING SYSTEM THAT WE INSTALL WILL BE INTEGRAL WITH THE CONVENTIONAL HEATING SYSTEM.** In most cases, avoid this type of system. When either side fails, for whatever reason, getting service will be a problem. If you have no heat during the middle of the night, it's unlikely the solar installer will come out to take care of the problem. It's just as unlikely a conventional heating contractor will touch the system once he or she knows it includes a solar component. Tell the salesperson or installer that you want the solar heat distributed by a separate system. If the salesperson doesn't want to do that, find someone else. The issue here is emergency service. In those few instances when the solar system installer is also the conventional heating system contractor, then a solar system that is integral with a conventional system is quite acceptable and usually less expensive to install.

🏠 **IF THE UTILITY COMPANY POWER FAILS, YOU'LL BE ABLE TO OPERATE THE APPLIANCES IN YOUR GRID-TIED SOLAR ELECTRIC HOUSE AT LEAST AS LONG AS THE SUN SHINES.** That's not the case with most basic grid-tied solar electric systems. With most, when the utility company power fails, the output of the solar system is shut off. This is a feature designed into the inverter that protects utility company workers from shock when they are working on the grid. You can purchase a system that does provide electricity to the house when utility company power fails, but a different type of inverter is needed as well as a charge controller, batteries, and an emergency loads panel. That system costs more money than a basic grid-tied system.

🏠 **WE'LL DIVERT THE HEAT FROM YOUR SOLAR WATER HEATING SYSTEM TO YOUR POOL FOR THE SUMMER MONTHS.** This makes sense if you don't use domestic hot water in the house for the summer. But if you must shower or wash your hands, dishes, or clothing, you'll still need domestic hot water. Let the solar water heating system heat the domestic water and install a pool blanket or a separate solar pool heating system. Besides, the two or three collectors used for domestic water heating will not have a noticeable effect on the temperature of your pool and may turn your pool green if the water pH is not carefully maintained.

When deciding which fuel to use for a given application, whether it be domestic water heating, house heating, or pool heating, you should base your decision on the different characteristics of the fuels being considered. The availability of a given fuel, its heat content, the carbon dioxide released when the fuel is burned, the unit cost of the fuel, and the efficiency of the appliance in which the fuel is used must all be considered. This table provides the basic data for making such comparisons.

HEAT CONTENT OF FUEL			
FUEL	Btu/kWh	Btu/gal.	Btu/ccf
Electricity	3,413		
No. 2 fuel oil		138,690	
Natural gas			100,000
Propane		91,333	

POUNDS OF CARBON DIOXIDE PER UNIT OF FUEL			
FUEL	lb./kWh	lb./gal.	lb./ccf*
Electricity	Varies†		
No. 2 fuel oil		22.4	
Natural gas			11.64
Propane		12.68	

UNIT COST OF FUEL**			
FUEL	$/kWh	$/gal.	$/ccf
Electricity	$0.17		
No. 2 fuel oil		$2.30	
Natural gas			$1.90
Propane		$2.65	

COST PER MILLION BTU***		
FUEL	Efficiency of use	$/million btu
Electricity	88%	56.60
No. 2 fuel oil	55%	30.15
Natural gas	55%	34.55
Propane	60%	48.36

*   ccf = therm = 100,000 Btu.
†   When all hydropower or all nuclear power is used, the value is 0 lb./kWh; when no hydropower or no nuclear power is used, then the value is 2.25 lb./kWh.
** Fuel costs vary widely across the United States.
*** For domestic water heating.

These three charts show typical costs of heating domestic water
with fuel oil, natural gas, and electric heaters. Choose the number
of household occupants and the fuel cost that is closest to what you
pay to find your annual cost for heating domestic hot water. Using the
data, you can figure out how much a solar domestic hot water system
can save you in fuel or electricity costs.

(Adapted from F-Chart and other sources by Emaan Ammar)

Cost of Heating Water with Fuel Oil

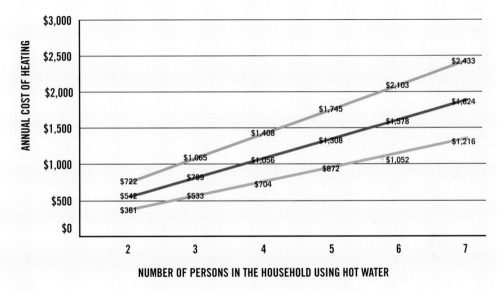

= $2/GAL.

= $3/GAL.

= $4/GAL.

Cost of Heating Water with Natural Gas

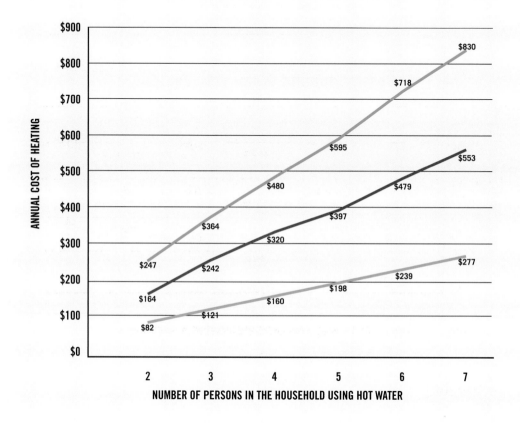

= $0.70/ccf

= $1.40/ccf

= $2.10/ccf

Cost of Heating Water with Electricity

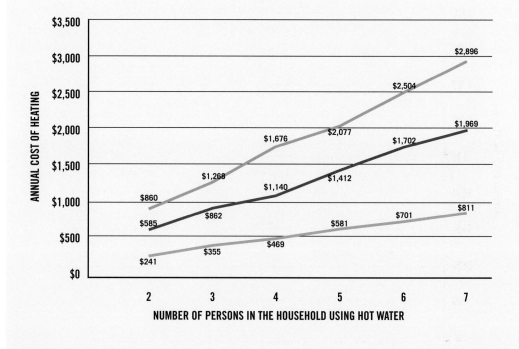

ANNUAL COST OF HEATING

$3,500

$3,000 — $2,896

$2,500 — $2,504

$2,000 — $2,077 — $1,969

$1,676 — $1,702

$1,500 — $1,268 — $1,412

$1,140

$1,000 — $860 — $811

$862 — $701

$585 — $581

$500 — $469

$241 — $355

$0

2   3   4   5   6   7

NUMBER OF PERSONS IN THE HOUSEHOLD USING HOT WATER

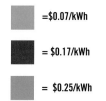

= $0.07/kWh

= $0.17/kWh

= $0.25/kWh

Over a 25-year span, the potential savings of heating a pool with solar collectors rather than conventional means of heating is enormous.

Fuel Cost Escalation Rate = 0% (most conservative scenario)

TYPES OF SWIMMING POOL HEATERS

Year	PROPANE		NATURAL GAS		HEAT PUMP		
	Heater*	Fuel†	Heater‡	Fuel†	Heater§	Fuel**	
1	$3,800.00	$1,500	$3,800.00	$1,000	$5,500.00	$750.00	
2		$1,500		$1,000		$750.00	
3		$1,500		$1,000		$750.00	
4		$1,500		$1,000		$750.00	
5		$1,500		$1,000		$750.00	
6		$1,500		$1,000	$4,500.00	$750.00	
7	$3,000.00	$1,500	$3,000.00	$1,000		$750.00	
8		$1,500		$1,000		$750.00	
9		$1,500		$1,000		$750.00	
10		$1,500		$1,000		$750.00	
11		$1,500		$1,000		$750.00	
12		$1,500		$1,000	$4,500.00	$750.00	
13		$1,500		$1,000		$750.00	
14	$3,000.00	$1,500	$3,000.00	$1,000		$750.00	
15		$1,500		$1,000		$750.00	
16		$1,500		$1,000		$750.00	
17		$1,500		$1,000		$750.00	
18		$1,500		$1,000	$4,500.00	$750.00	
19		$1,500		$1,000		$750.00	
20		$1,500		$1,000		$750.00	
21	$3,000.00	$1,500	$3,000.00	$1,000		$750.00	
22		$1,500		$1,000		$750.00	
23		$1,500		$1,000		$750.00	
24		$1,500		$1,000	$4,500.00	$750.00	
25		$1,500		$1,000		$750.00	
Totals	$12,800.00	$37,500	$12,800.00	$25,000	$23,500.00	$18,750	
Cumulative total	$50,300		$37,800		$42,250.00		

	HEAT PUMP WITH SOLAR ELECTRIC			SOLAR THERMAL	
	Heater§	PV Array††	Fuel‡‡	Heater§§	Fuel***
	$5,500.00	$25,500.00	$0.00	$7,500.00	$0.00
			$0.00		$0.00
			$0.00		$0.00
			$0.00		$0.00
			$0.00		$0.00
	$4,500.00		$0.00		$0.00
			$0.00		$0.00
			$0.00		$0.00
			$0.00		$0.00
			$0.00		$0.00
			$0.00		$0.00
	$4,500.00		$0.00		$0.00
			$0.00		$0.00
			$0.00		$0.00
			$0.00		$0.00
			$0.00		$0.00
			$0.00		$0.00
	$4,500.00		$0.00		$0.00
			$0.00		$0.00
			$0.00		$0.00
			$0.00		$0.00
			$0.00		$0.00
			$0.00		$0.00
	$4,500.00		$0.00		$0.00
			$0.00		$0.00
	$23,500.00	$25,500.00	$0.00	$7,500.00	$0.00
		$49,000.00		$7,500.00	

* Cost of installing a propane-fired pool heater for the first time. Does not include cost of the propane tank or the cost to bury the tank. Subsequent replacements, including labor, are less expensive.

† Assumes June through Labor Day swimming, intermittent use of pool blanket, and pool water kept at 82°F (27.7°C) to 85°F (29.4°C).

‡ Cost of installing a natural gas–fired pool heater for the first time. Assumes natural gas service to house. Subsequent replacements, including labor, are less expensive.

§ Cost of installing an air source heat pump for pool heating, including a 50-amp breaker and buried power supply from the house to the heat pump. Cost for increases to electrical service is extra.

** Assumes June through August swimming, intermittent use of pool blanket, and pool water kept at 80°F (26.6°C) to 82°F (27.7°C).

†† Assumes a 3.0kW d.c. (STC), roof-mounted solar electric array installed at $8.50/W. Cost does not include rebate or tax credit. (Rebate could reduce the cost by approx. 50 percent.) A smaller array could be used at the risk of compromising the pool water temperature. (Note: The tax credit may not be claimed for pool heating; consult an accountant.)

‡‡ Assumes that the output of the solar electric array in kilowatt hours over 12 months is about equal to the requirement of the heat pump over 3 months.

§§ Assumes a 500-sq.-ft. (46.5m²) roof-mounted solar array, installed at $15/sq. ft. of collector. Cost does not include tax credit. (Note: The tax credit may not be claimed for pool heating; consult an accountant.)

*** Because the filter pump must be used to filter the pool water and the same pump forces the circulation through the pool array, assume $0 fuel cost.

FURTHER READING

Books

Beckman, William A. and John A. Duffie. *Solar Engineering of Thermal Processes, 3rd Edition*. Hoboken, NJ: John Wiley & Sons, Inc., 2006.

For engineers and engineering students.

Butti, Ken and John Perlin. *A Golden Thread: 2500 Years of Solar Architecture and Technology*. Cheshire Books, 1980.

For any solar enthusiast.

Chiras, Daniel D. *The Solar House: Passive Heating and Cooling*. White River Junction, VT: Chelsea Green Publishing Co., 2002.

For the layperson, architect, or builder.

Cook, Jeffrey, ed. *Passive Cooling*. Cambridge, MA: The MIT Press, 1989.

For architects or builders.

Ewing, Rex A. and Doug Pratt. *Got Sun? Go Solar, Expanded 2nd Edition*. Masonville, CO: PixyJack Press, 2009.

Introduction to solar electric systems for the layperson.

Florida Solar Energy Center. *Solar Water Heating and Pool Heating Systems: Design and Installation Manual & Repair and Maintenance*. Pub. FSEC-IN-24, January 2006. Cocoa, FL: Florida Solar Energy Center.

Good section on solar basics for the layperson; otherwise, mostly for installers and service technicians.

Halacy, Beth and Dan Halacy. *Cooking with the Sun: How to Build and Use Solar Cookers*. Lafayette, CA: Morning Sun Press, 1992.

Discusses cooker designs and many recipes.

Kryza, Frank T. *The Power of Light: The Epic Story of Man's Quest to Harness the Sun*. New York, NY: McGraw-Hill, 2003.

For any solar enthusiast. Begins with solar technology development, and the people involved, at the start of the industrial revolution. Many parallels can be seen today.

Lane, Tom. *Solar Hot Water Systems: Lessons Learned 1977 to Today*. Gainesville, FL: Energy Conservation Services of North Florida, 2003.

Mostly for installers and service technicians.

Lechner, Norbert. *Heating, Cooling, Lighting: Sustainable Design Methods for Architects, 3rd Edition*. Hoboken, NJ: John Wiley & Sons, Inc., 2009.

Good illustrations, excellent sections on solar geometry, natural lighting, passive solar heating.

For architects, building designers, and architecture students.

Olgyay, Aladar and Victor Olgyay. *Solar Control and Shading Devices*. Princeton, NJ: Princeton University Press, 1957.

For the layperson or architect.

Periodicals

ASHRAE Journal
Heating Ventilating and Air Conditioning industry periodical; mainly of interest to engineers.

FOCUS
Technical solar periodical published by International Solar Energy Society (ISES).

Northeast Sun
Biannual general solar periodical published by Northeast Sustainable Energy Association (NESEA); layperson friendly.

Solar Today
Bimonthly general solar periodical published by American Solar Energy Society (ASES); layperson friendly.

Online Resources

Better Business Bureau: www.bbb.org
Offers consumers and businesses resources for business and charity reviews, complaints, statistics, ratings, and dispute resolution.

DSIREUSA: www.dsireusa.org
Comprehensive listing of information on solar incentives in the United States.

Dun and Bradstreet: www.dnb.com
Provides U.S. (and international) business credit information and credit reports.

F-Chart Software: www.fchart.com
F-Chart Software distributes Engineering Equation Solver and Finite Element Heat Transfer as well as the F-Chart and PVF-Chart solar energy system analysis programs. The F-Chart program for solar thermal systems was used to generate many of the tables in this book. For the technically oriented.

International Electrical and Electronics Engineers (IEEE): www.ieee.org
A leading organization representing electrical and electronics engineers.

International Energy Agency (IEA): www.iea.org
Implements an international energy program of energy cooperation among 24 member countries. Site resources include very comprehensive and extensive statistics and projections concerning energy data for the world.

PVWATTS: http://www.nrel.gov/rredc/pvwatts/version1.html
An easy-to-use, online tool for the calculation of the output of solar electric systems in U.S. cities and many other cities around the world. Try PVWATTS, version 1.

RETScreen International: www.retscreen.net
Free Clean Energy Project Analysis software, includes free solar thermal system analysis and passive solar analysis software. Provided by the Canadian government.

U.S. Energy Information Administration (EIA): www.eia.doe.gov
Very comprehensive and extensive source of energy data for the United States.

Online Resources (manufacturers)

Note that this list does not imply an endorsement of any company, or their products, listed below.

Alternate Energy Technologies
904-781-8305
www.aetsolar.com
U.S. thermal collector manufacturer since 1975 (including grid pattern absorbers).

Apollo Solar
203-790-6400
www.apollosolar.com
U.S. manufacturer of inverters and charge controllers.

Caleffi North America
414-238-2360
www.caleffi.us
Italian-based company specializing in hydronics and valves.

Conbraco Industries
704-841-6000
www.apollovalves.com
U.S. manufacturer of Apollo Valves.

FAFCO, Inc.
800-994-7652
www.fafco.com
U.S. manufacturer of solar pool heating and domestic water collectors since 1969.

Fronius USA LLC
810-220-4414
www.fronius.com
German manufacturer of solar electronics (including inverters).

Heliodyne, Inc.
510-237-9614
www.heliodyne.com
U.S. collector manufacturer since 1976; makes grid pattern absorbers.

Lutron Electronics Co., Inc.
888-588-7661
www.lutron.com
U.S. manufacturer of lighting controls.

MidNite Solar
425-374-9060
www.midnitesolar.com
U.S. manufacturer, assembler of balance of system components for solar electric systems.

Morningstar Corporation
215-321-4457
www.morningstarcorp.com
U.S. manufacturer of inverters and charge controllers.

Parans Solar Lighting AB
+ 46 31 20 15 90
www.parans.com
Swedish manufacturer of daylighting equipment with optical cable.

Pool Cover Specialists (PCS) National, Inc.
800-369-5152
www.poolcovers.com
U.S. manufacturer of solar pool covers.

Radco Products, Inc.
805-928-1881
www.radcosolar.com
U.S. thermal collector manufacturer since 1978, offers grid pattern absorbers.

Schneider Electric United States
847-397-2600
www.schneider-electric.com
U.S. manufacturer of Xantrex inverters.

SMA America, LLC
916-625-0870
www.sma-america.com
German manufacturer of inverters for solar electric systems.

Solar Components Corporation
603-668-8186
www.solar-components.com
U.S. distributor of Kalwall and other solar products.

SunEarth, Inc.
909-434-3100
www.sunearthinc.com
U.S. manufacturer of thermal collectors since 1978, including grid pattern absorbers.

Sun Ovens International, Inc.
630-208-7273
www.sunoven.com
Manufacturer of solar cookers.

Surrette Battery Company Ltd.
800-681-9914
www.rollsbattery.com
Canadian manufacturer of deep-cycle batteries for solar applications since 1959.

VELUX America Inc.
864-941-4700
www.velux.com
Danish company that mainly produces roof windows and daylighting equipment; entered the solar thermal market in 1999.

Viessmann Manufacturing Company Inc.
401-732-0667
www.viessmann.ca
German manufacturer of heating products; makes evacuated-tube and flat-plate collectors.

Wagner & Co
(+49) 06421 / 8007-0
www.wagner-solar.com
European manufacturer of solar domestic hot water systems.

Watts Water Technologies
978-688-1811
www.watts.com
U.S. manufacturer, founded in 1874; makes many types of safety valves.

Wiley Electronics LLC
845-633-2065
www.we-llc.com
U.S. manufacturer of solar site survey tool.

Window Quilt Insulated Shades
802-246-4500
www.windowquilt.com
U.S. manufacturer of moveable insulation for windows.

Organizations

Air-Conditioning, Heating, and Refrigeration Institute (AHRI): www.ahrinet.org
The source of performance-certified heating, ventilation, air-conditioning, and commercial refrigeration equipment and components. Develops the data for Energy Guide stickers for appliances; provides ratings for all types of conventional water heaters (among other appliances).

American Board of Certified Energy Practitioners (NABCEP): www.nabcep.org
National professional certification organization for solar electric and solar thermal installers.

American Society of Heating, Refrigeration and Air-Conditioning Engineers (ASHRAE): www.ashrae.org

An international technical society organized to advance the arts and sciences of heating, ventilating, air-conditioning, and refrigeration. Every few years ASHRAE publishes handbooks that are considered the "bibles" for designers in the aforementioned fields; publishes ASHRAE Journal and has an annual show that includes technical papers and equipment exposition.

American Solar Energy Society (ASES): www.ases.org

The nation's leading association of solar professionals and advocates. Publishes Solar Today and has an annual show that includes technical papers and equipment exposition.

California Energy Commission and the California Public Utilities Commission (CEC): www.gosolarcalifornia.org

The source of performance data on solar electric collectors and inverters.

Florida Solar Energy Center (FSEC): www.fsec.ucf.edu

Provides information on the renewable energy and energy efficiency research, education, training, and certification that they conduct.

International Association of Plumbing and Mechanical Officials (IAPMO): www.iapmo.org

Publishes the standards for practices in plumbing and mechanical systems design and installation.

International Solar Energy Society (ISES): www.ises.org

The largest, oldest, and most comprehensive technical body dealing with the technology and implementation of renewable energy. Publishes FOCUS and has an annual show that includes technical papers and equipment exposition.

National Electrical Code (NEC): www.nfpa.org

The standard for practices in electrical system design and installation. Look for the National Electric Code as one of the products of the National Fire Protection Association.

National Renewable Energy Laboratory (NREL): www.nrel.gov

A facility of the U.S. Department of Energy for renewable energy and energy efficiency research, development, and deployment.

Northeast Sustainable Energy Association (NESEA): www.nesea.org/

Promotes sustainable energy solutions, provides education to those in the building community, and offers a sustainable green pages directory and an annual Building Energy Conference each March.

Solar Energy Industries Association (SEIA): www.seia.org

The U.S. trade association for solar energy and related businesses. Works to expand the use of solar technologies, strengthen research and development, remove market barriers, and improve education and outreach for solar.

Solar Rating and Certification Corporation (SRCC): www.solar-rating.org/

Provides third-party testing of flat-plate and evacuated-tube collectors, and solar domestic water heating systems.

US DOE Energy Efficiency and Renewable Energy (EERE): www.eere.energy.gov

The EERE website provides information on energy efficiency and renewable energy technologies.

Robert Perron

The first question homeowners, architects, engineers, and builders ask about solar energy systems is "well, does it work?" Their next question is "what does it look like?"

Robert Perron is an outstanding professional photographer who has specialized in recording architectural works around the United States, both residential and commercial, for the past 40 years. His work has been published in many books and all the top architectural magazines. Fortunately for the solar industry, Bob has had a keen interest in renewable energy systems, particularly in solar houses, both passive and active. His works, perhaps more than any other photographer, have shown millions, what it looks like.

CREDITS

All photos by Everett M. Barber Jr., except as noted below:

INTRODUCTION

p. 3: Charles Bickford, courtesy *Fine Homebuilding*, © The Taunton Press, Inc.

p. 4: Robert Perron

p. 5: Aspen Community Office of Resource Efficiency

CHAPTER ONE

p. 7: iStockphoto.com/Andreas G. Karelias

p. 9: (left) Wagner & Co.; (right) iStock-photo.com/Diane Diederich

CHAPTER TWO

p. 16: Velux

p. 17: (top) iStockphoto.com/Brian Pamphilon; (bottom) iStockphoto.com/Arpad Benedek

p. 22: Velux

p. 28: Joe Provey

p. 30: Viessmann/Vitosol

p. 31: Viessmann/Vitosol

p. 33: (top) iStockphoto.com/Janine Lamontagne; (bottom) iStockphoto.com/Lena Andersson

p. 34: (left, right) National Renewable Energy Laboratories

p. 36: (left) United Solar Ovonic; (right) National Renewable Energy Laboratories

p. 37: Steven Spencer

p. 39: (top) iStockphoto.com/xyno; (bottom) iStockphoto.com/Alexander Hafemann

p. 40: (top) iStockphoto.com/Jarek Szymanski; (bottom) iStockphoto.com/Richard Schmidt-Zuper

p. 42: (top) Robert Perron; (bottom) Peter Markow

p. 45: (top) Solar Design Associates, Inc.; (bottom) Bill Eager

p. 46: Solar Rating and Certification Corporation

CHAPTER THREE

p. 48: Climax Solar Water Heating ad, 1890s

p. 49: Industrial Solar Technology Corporation

p. 50: iStockphoto.com/Izabela Habur

p. 59: iStockphoto.com/Brian Pamphilon

p. 62: Solar Components Corporation; (left) Viessmann/Vitosol

p. 65: (right) Caleffi

p. 66: Velux

p. 68: Robert Perron

p. 69: Alfa Laval

p. 70: Caleffi

p. 71: Watts

p. 72: Caleffi

CHAPTER FOUR

p. 79: (top) Pool Cover Specialists; (bottom) FAFCO

p. 80: (left) FAFCO; (right) iStockphoto.com/scottbeard

p. 83: Aquatherm Industries

p. 84: Pool Cover Specialists

p. 88: FAFCO

CHAPTER FIVE

p. 100: Charles Mayer

p. 101: Charles Mayer

p. 103: Rob Yagid, courtesy *Fine Homebuilding*, © The Taunton Press, Inc.

p. 104: Robert Perron

p. 105: Weathershield

p. 106: (left) iStockphoto.com/P_Wei; (right) Window Quilt Insulated Shades

p. 108: Sam Garth

p. 109: Robert Perron

p. 111: Solar Components Corporation

p. 114: SunPorch Structures

p. 116: Robert Perron

p. 120: Lutron

p. 122: iStockphoto.com/Terry Healy

p. 123: (top) GreenGrid® roof system by Weston Solutions, Inc.; (bottom) iStockphoto.com/James C. Pruitt and Darren Petrucci

p. 124: Robert Perron

CHAPTER SIX

p. 127: Robert Perron

p. 128: Robert Perron

p. 129: (top) Thomas P. Hopper

p. 131: Roe Osborn, courtesy *Fine Homebuilding*, © The Taunton Press, Inc.

p. 134: EnerWorks, Inc./Natural Resources Canada

p. 137: Robert Perron

p. 140: Robert Perron

p. 141: (top) Robert Perron

p. 145: Robert Perron

p. 149: Robert Perron

CHAPTER SEVEN

p. 154: Maxine and William A. Rhodes, from the collection of Donald E. Osborn

p. 155: Robert Perron

p. 156: (top) National Renewable Energy Laboratories; (bottom) Lutron

p. 161: (top) Pinn Brothers; (middle) Scott Carter; (bottom) groSolar

p. 163: Direct Power & Water Corporation

p. 164: (top left) Astropower; (top right) iStockphoto.com/franckreporter; (bottom) National Renewable Energy Laboratories

p. 165: Fronius

p. 166: Surette Battery Company

p. 167: Apollo Solar

p. 173: Robert Perron

p. 174: iStockphoto.com/Mlenny Photography

p. 179: National Renewable Energy Laboratories

CHAPTER EIGHT

p. 183: Toyota

p. 184: (top) Sun BD Corporation/sunbdcorp.com; (middle, bottom) Sun Ovens

p. 186: Horace McCracken

p. 187: Velux

p. 188: Velux

p. 189: (left) Lutron; (right) Velux

p. 193: (top left, top middle, top right) Parans; (bottom) Joe Provey

p. 194: (top) Toyota; (bottom) Warren Gretz

p. 196: (top left) Earthtech Products, Inc.; (top right, bottom) Gardener's Supply Company

CHAPTER NINE

p. 199: iStock/Gene Chutka

p. 201: Florida Solar Energy Center, Sherri Shields

p. 205: Sam Garth

INDEX